Women Workers and the Trade Union Movement

Women Workers and the Trade Union Movement

SARAH BOSTON

Davis-Poynter
LONDON

First published in 1980 by
Davis-Poynter Limited
20 Garrick Street WC2E 9BJ

ISBN 0 7067 0198 4

Printed in Great Britain by
Bristol Typesetting Co. Ltd
Barton Manor, St Philips, Bristol

In loving memory of Will

Contents

'Knowledge is power. Organization is power. Knowledge and organization mean the right to life, liberty and the pursuit of happiness. Knowledge and organization mean the opening of the cage door.'

Mary Macarthur
The Woman Worker
June 1908

'The goal, accordingly, is not merely the realization of the equal rights of woman with man within present society, as is aimed at by the bourgeois woman emancipationists. It lies beyond, – the removal of all impediments that make man dependent upon man; and, consequently, one sex upon the other. Accordingly, this solution of the Woman Question coincides completely with the solution of the Social Question. It follows that he who aims at the solution of the Woman Question to its full extent, is necessarily bound to go hand in hand with those who have inscribed upon their banner the solution of the Social Question as a question of civilization for the whole human race.'

August Bebel
Woman Under Socialism 1883

Introduction

WHEN I TOLD PEOPLE that I was writing a history of women workers and the trade union movement they invariably replied, 'oh you mean the Match Girls Strike and all that'. By that response it was clear that the Match Girls Strike was the only action taken by women workers which had earned itself a place in history. Even those people who had a good knowledge of labour history failed to offer any elaboration of the history of women workers and trade unions. It was obvious that many of them assumed that there was not much of it worth recording. Almost from the outset of my research I realized that people may be forgiven for their stock response and attitudes, since historians of the trade union movement have largely ignored women. The 1920 edition of *The History of Trades Unionism* by Sidney and Beatrice Webb has less than 20 page references to women in 716 pages of text. Henry Pelling in his *History of British Trades Unionism*, published in 1963, has seven page references to women in a book 260 pages long and historians of individual unions, with a few notable exceptions, usually give little recognition to women. A few books, in particular Barbara Drake's *Women and Trades Unions* (1920) and rather specialized books like J. Ramsay Macdonald's *Women in the Printing Trades* (1904) and G. D. H. Cole's *Trades Unionism and Munitions* (1923), have helped to fill in some of the gaps.

The failure to include women in labour history has had its effect on the development of the trade union movement. It has tended to reinforce the attitude that women workers are not part of the class struggle, an attitude which has perpetuated the sexual division of labour and the sexual divisions within the trade union movement. It has also led to many myths about women workers and organization, myths which do not stand up to historical scrutiny, but which have had a profound influence on attitudes held by trade unionists. Further the lack of recognition of women's struggles and of women working-class leaders has compounded women's sense of their inferiority.

The first object of this book is to offer a beginning in the recording of the history of women workers and trade unions from the early 19th century to the present day. Considerable detail has had to be left out. Since so little has been written on the subject I have had to rely largely on primary material which accounts for much of the imbalance of the book. The period dating roughly from 1900 to 1920 is not only a very rich period in the history of women's organization, but also a well documented period, thanks to Gertrude Tuckwell, who collected a wealth of material concerning all aspects of women's work and bequeathed her collection to the TUC. Unfortunately there is no similar collection for any other period. A large amount of the book is based on the records and journals of the early women's trade union movement, the annual reports, records and publications of the TUC and individual trades unions. Such material has its shortcomings and, where possible, I have supplemented it with other material. Readers may feel that certain important unions have been ignored or given scant attention. Many have been ignored because they ignored women. Since it would be impossible, without writing an extremely long book, to cover every trades union, I have selected unions, either as typical or untypical of the way in which certain unions reacted to women.

Merely to record the development of the organization of women workers is not enough for an understanding of women workers and the trades union movement. It is necessary to look at the broader social, biological and economic factors which have determined women's position in society. The effect of the Industrial Revolution, the types of jobs women did and do in and out of the home, the changing attitudes of society towards women workers, the role of legislation and women's role as child-bearers are all central to an understanding of the complex relationship between men and women workers.

It has usually been assumed that to talk of the trade union movement is to talk of a male movement. Another assumption has been that the history of the trade union movement has been essentially one of a struggle between workers and employers (the latter usually backed by government). Women have shared in the struggle between employers and workers, but in addition they have had to fight for recognition by male trade unionists. They have had to fight to be accepted as members of trade unions and then, as members, they have had to fight for the right to be equal members within the unions.

Despite social and economic changes certain issues concerning women workers and the trade union movement form themes which run throughout the book. Equal pay, or rather the absence of it, has dogged the relationship between men and women workers since the early 19th century. Another issue has been the role of and need for specific legislation for women. Likewise, debates about structures, sexually separate or mixed unions, separate sections, committees or conferences for women have never been far from the surface. On the surface, influencing the whole history, has been the dominant capitalist sexist ideology which trade unionists, with few exceptions, have echoed in their attitudes and policies.

My point of departure for this book was not that of a working historian, but an active woman trade unionist. The policies, attitudes and behaviour of trade unions towards women both puzzled and outraged me. I was puzzled by assertions made about women which I felt were wrong and outraged by the obvious chasm between the principles of trade union and labour movements and their practice in relation to women. More puzzling was that their practice was not only at odds with principle, but with their own self-interest. In the course of writing this book I have, therefore, not looked for historical facts simply as facts in themselves, but as a means to understanding those things which puzzled me. I continue at times to be outraged, but rarely to be puzzled.

In the light of the last paragraph my thanks must go first to my own union, the Association of Cinematograph, Television and Allied Technicians, who, by recruiting me on the first day of my first full-time employment, brought me into the trade union movement. As a member and, latterly, as an executive member I have had considerable first-hand experience of the movement. Secondly, I must thank Reg Davis-Poynter for commissioning an unknown writer with only a trade-union record to write this book. Christine Coates, the librarian of the TUC, has advised, supported and criticized me throughout, as has Sarah Benton, and George and Muriel Jamieson. I should like to give particular thanks to them. My thanks too go to the many other people who have given help in a variety of ways. I apologize for not naming them all. Finally, the period of researching and writing this book coincided with a period of great personal stress. The fact that I kept writing was due largely to the love and support of Ed Buscombe. I thank him.

'Their Proper Sphere
at Home' 1874

BEFORE THE 1870s there is little evidence of any consistent
organization of women workers except in the textile unions. However, the assumption that women outside the textile industry did
not organize at all until the 1870s is false. There is considerable
evidence that women did. It is important, therefore, to record the
early stirrings of militancy amongst women, which one reporter
saw as 'more menacing to established institutions than the education of the lower orders'.[1] It is equally important to look at the
reasons why women did not organize consistently or were not
organized or supported by men. Some of the reasons are the same
for men and women and lie in the nature of early trade unionism.
But many of the reasons relate specifically to women and concern
the type of jobs they did and the wages they received, the attitudes of men to women, the economic relationship in particular
industries and the status, role and position of women in the 19th
century.

From the outset of the Industrial Revolution the one feature
which was common to all women's work was low pay. Records
show that before the Industrial Revolution women earned less as
day labourers than men even for the same work. Where payment
was partially in food, women, likewise, were paid with smaller
food rations regardless of whether they were pregnant or nursing
mothers. The one job done almost exclusively by women, spinning, was poorly paid and a 'spinster', even though she worked
all her working hours, could barely earn a subsistence wage.[2] It
was this tradition of unequal pay, low pay and low evaluation of
'women's' skills which formed the basis of the pay and status of
women workers entering the textile industry in the early 19th
century and other areas of industrial labour subsequently. It was,
in fact, to form the basis of all employment of women in the 19th
century.

The productive role which women had played as part of the

economic unit of a family was largely forgotten in the social and economic changes brought about by the Industrial Revolution. In wealthier families women were relegated to idleness and in poorer families they became low-paid wage labourers. Those women who worked in the home to 'service' their male bread-winners had their recognized role eroded in status to one which was seen as having no economically recognized productive importance. Alice Clark in her book *Working Life of Women in the Seventeenth Century* described this change and its implications for women.

> It has been suggested that the earlier English Commonwealth did actually embrace both men and women in its idea of the 'Whole', because it was composed of self-contained families consisting of men, women and children, all three of which are essential for the continuance of human society; but the mechanical State which replaced it, and whose development has accompanied the extension of Capitalism, has regarded the individual, not the family, as its unit, and in England this State began with the conception that it was concerned only with male individuals.[3]

For all the state's concern with 'male individuals', the Industrial Revolution was based on the labour of child and female 'individuals'. In 1838 only 23% of textile factory workers were adult men.[4] Since women earned on average half what men earned, it was not surprising that they were employed in such large numbers. The level of women's pay was uniform in all branches of textiles throughout the country; there was no such uniformity about the types of jobs that women did. The assumption that the sexual division of labour in industry and its consequent sexual pay structure were based on such things as men's physical strength and their allegedly superior skills is not borne out by evidence. In different branches or geographical areas of textiles women did different jobs. Men quickly gained a dominant position in the cotton industry by controlling the most skilled jobs, those of spinning and weaving, those jobs were almost entirely the province of women in the jute and flax industry in Dundee.[5] From the outset there was clearly little logic in what was regarded as a 'woman's job' or a 'man's job', but equally clearly sexual divisions in labour were quickly established. Once established these divisions became entrenched by a sexual pay structure which paid women about half the male rate. Women working in exclusively 'female' work earned even lower rates. Other industries, which followed textiles in the process of mechanization, adopted a similar pattern of male and female divisions of labour and wage rates. It was against this picture of entrenched divisions between men and women workers, divisions which mirrored the social and legal status of women, that the early trade unions began to organize.

Trade unions in the 19th century developed in a piecemeal way, trying out and settling for a variety of structures, rules, policies and memberships. With the repeal of the Combination Acts in 1824 and the passing of Peel's Act the following year, which gave unions the right to collective bargaining, trade unions were able to widen their scope and recruitment from being merely Friendly Societies or illegal combinations. Despite this freedom trade union organization, for a variety of reasons, remained mainly restricted to skilled or craft workers. It was generally believed until the late 19th century that effective organization of and action by unskilled workers could not be successful. This attitude excluded many men workers and almost all women workers. Since women were excluded from apprenticeships, they were excluded from skilled jobs. The exception to this was the category of 'traditional' women's skilled jobs, such as millinery, mantua making and needlework. Although the craft unions dominated the first three-quarters of the 19th century, other unions with less restrictive membership policies did emerge and there were many more attempts at organization of a variety of semi-skilled workers. Frequently workers took action against intolerable conditions, usually wage cuts, but such spontaneous action by no means necessarily led to permanent organization. Given this piecemeal development of trade unions, it is not surprising that there was no prevailing attitude taken on the question of the organization of women workers. In fact from the beginnings of trade union organization a variety of attitudes emerged towards what was seen as 'the problem of female labour.'

The most advanced and exceptional attitude emerged in a few of the textile unions, who established the first mixed unions for men and women workers. Some men trade unionists, whilst they were not prepared to open up their membership to women, did believe that women should be organized separately and on rare occasions offered support to that end. Not all women were entirely governed by the attitude of men and from the early 19th century some of them took independent militant action, tried to organize and sought support from men. All these attitudes, however, were an exception. The attitude which dominated the policies of the early trade union movement was that expressed by Henry Broadhurst to the TUC in 1875. He maintained that the main aim of a trade union with regard women was to

> bring about a condition . . . where their wives and daughters would be in their proper sphere at home, instead of being dragged into competition for livelihood against the great and strong men of the world.[6]

Since few trade unionists considered the question in terms of the 'rights of women', the attitudes which evolved in relation to the organization of women were adopted in response to women's economic position. The fact that women were paid about half the male rate for the job meant that they, as cheap labour, were seen by men as a potential, or actual, threat to men's jobs. But, with very few exceptions, men did not challenge the wage rate paid for the job; they challenged the women's right to the job. This attitude arose from the unquestioning acceptance by trade unionists of the dominant ideology of Victorian society which saw women as second-class citizens in every sense. However, by accepting the social and economic position of women, trade unionists created a trap for themselves, from which they were only to emerge when they could see women as workers and not as a separate group – women.

This 'trap' was most clearly evident in what seemed the insoluble problem which skilled unions faced, namely 'the problem of female labour'. The problem tended to appear either where mechanization was introduced, causing dilution of the skill and threatening the tight control skilled unions could exercise through apprenticeships, or where employers realized that the jobs, or part of the jobs, could be done by women. The following extract from the records of the Brushmakers Union in 1829 sums up the situation many craft unions faced.

> Now there was another matter the Brushmakers had to put up with. Economic matter known as FEMALE LABOUR.
> This became serious in 1829. Many a man lost his job. The numbers ON THE BOOK were alarming.
> The movement initiated by a few employers was to cheapen labour. Whilst the Society paid £15 to Members willing to emigrate; and 10s a week out-of-work relief to SURPLUS men at home; and Tramping Money to numbers seeking work in all the various towns; certain masters employed women to do men's work at half price.
> So it came to pass that poor women became the enemy of poor men.[7]

The brushmakers recognized that the women were desperate for jobs 'because bread was wanted that day – that hour' and that it was not the women who should be blamed; 'the wickedness was in the hand that withheld the other half'. Again the brushmakers recognized the cause of the trouble, but they could see no solution to the problem other than going 'to reason with the Employers' who 'employed women to do men's work at half price'. Needless to say, they found that 'there is no task more difficult for working men than to go and reason with the employer of cheap labour'. The extracts on that subject ended with this resigned note.

> Be it said, the matter of women being given men's work at half-price was a stubborn fact that had come to stay.[8]

Nowhere did anyone suggest any way around the problem other than trying to control entry, reasoning with the employer and hoping that the practice would somehow go away. So women continued to take jobs at half pay because they needed bread 'that day – that hour' and 'poor women became the enemy of poor men'.

This state of enmity existed in many trades and most unions confronted with it found that they could not resolve it because of this acceptance of women's inequality. Some skilled unions managed to keep the problem under control by rigidly enforcing the exclusion of women, but few could make the policy hold against employers who were determined to employ labour at half price. By not recognizing women, by excluding women from their organizations and by refusing to see women as workers which would have led to a demand for equal pay the craft unions fought a losing struggle. They could merely blindly dream of a day when 'their wives and daughters would be in their proper sphere at home'. This hope was echoed in a statement issued by the Central Committee of the Consolidated Union of Bookbinders, who had found that the employment of women and children on men's work had recently caused them

> a large amount of expenditure in Manchester, and has always been a source of annoyance and disquietude wherever it is allowed, and we trust our members will see their own interest in keeping it within reasonable limits until such time as we can see our way to do away with it altogether.[9]

Whilst unequal pay for the same work was the main cause of enmity between men and women workers, the objective conditions of some industries meant that employment was so structured that men and women workers could have little common interest. In industries like the potteries the skilled potters who were employed for an overall piece-rate, themselves employed women and children as their assistants. Such an employment structure meant that whilst the potters tried to organize in the mid-19th century to protect themselves against their own employers they neither extended union membership nor encouraged union organization of their own employees. This was to have disastrous effects for trade union organization;

> When, in later years, owing to improved methods of manufacture, women were able to compete with men for the same job, they came with a long tradition of low wages behind them and with no experience of union organisation. By their behaviour men had shown that they did not believe that the interests of all workers in the trade, men and women alike, were ultimately identical, and consequently it was not to be expected that women would believe in it either. By their selfish, short-sighted policy, men made of women much more serious and unscrupulous competitors than they otherwise would have been.[10]

For most craft unions a state of warfare between men and women workers seemed the inevitable future until some day when women could be eliminated from the workforce. However, a few proposed another solution – the separate organization of women. Normally this was seen as a way to raise women's wages so that they would present less of a threat to the men's rate, but the more concerned men were also outraged at the appalling exploitation of women workers. Separate action and organization was the obvious expression of a society which was based on evaluating the sexes separately. In the 1830s and 1840s there is considerable evidence of this policy being expressed, and in some instances pursued, either as a conscious policy or as a 'natural' expression of the divided work situation.

Like other craft unions the cotton unions in the early 19th century were concerned about the problems of female labour. Initially their union organization followed typical skilled craft unions in restricting membership and charging high dues and entry fees. However, their strength was constantly undermined, particularly in strikes, by the large numbers of unorganized, mainly women, workers in their industry. Being a little more realistic than most other trade unionists of the time, the cotton workers realized that women were not likely to disappear from their industry; so, in 1830, the Ramsay Congress of Spinners passed a resolution urging women to form their own organizations. During the 1830s and 1840s many women textile workers did take action and organize separately.

In 1833 in Scotland it was reported that 'the women power-loom weavers are driven to form a Union';[11] and in Glasgow that same year women and men spinners and powerloom weavers combined to raise money to fight for equal pay. Evidence to a select committee on manufacture recorded that a man had seen a letter signed by a woman calling upon one house to raise wages equal to the men's.[12] In Leeds 1,500 'Cord Setters in the neighbourhood of Scholes and Hightown, chiefly women, held a meeting . . . at which it was determined not to set any more cards at less than halfpenny a thousand'.[13] Meanwhile the Female Operatives of Todmorden combined to write a letter to the *Examiner* defending their right to work. Without any organizational base and without strike funds, women often needed great courage or desperation to take action. The following account of a strike by six girls in Dundee in 1846 gives a picture of the kind of treatment meted out to those workers who challenged their employers. The six girls demanded an increase of a ½d a day which was refused. The girls in their turn refused to return to work. On the following day the employer, Mr Baxter,

> instead of fining the girls, had them arrested and marched through the streets under police escort to a private office where was seated a magistrate, one of the Baxter family, and the overseer and the manager of the mill. The judicial Baxter there and then sentenced the girls to 10 days' hard labour.[14]

If women were not defeated by 'the law', their lack of strike funds meant that they were unlikely to be able to withstand a prolonged dispute. Being 'hungered back' to work after six weeks, as were women strikers in Glasgow in 1847, was a typical outcome of many disputes of the period.

Women textile workers were by no means the only women workers to take action or to organize separately. Nor were the textile unions the only ones to support a policy of separate organization of women. The Grand National Consolidated Trades Union of Great Britain made a specific point in its charter of laying down guidance for the separate organization of women. Point XX of the charter stated that 'Lodges of Industrious Females shall be instituted in every District where it may be practicable; such Lodges to be considered in every respect, as part of the Grand National Consolidated Trades Union'.[15] Even wives were provided for in the charter, since they could become members of Auxiliary Lodges and thus be included in the GNCTU. Some Lodges of women were formed as part of this grand plan, the most notorious being the Oldham Lodge of Ancient Virgins, who were particularly active in fighting for the ten-hour day. Women lace workers in Nottingham had also established a considerable level of organization in the 1830s. At a meeting held to protest against the transportation of the six Dorchester men (the Tolpuddle martyrs), women unionists turned up in a 'large body' to join the men

> and were greeted with three hearty cheers from their brethren in Union with whom they afterwards walked in procession to the market place where after singing a portion of a hymn the whole assemblage quietly dispersed.[16]

Ten years later, in the 1840s, there was still some organization of women, namely the Nottingham Lace Runners Association, which tried unsuccessfully to organize a 'turn out' of home-workers.[17] However, there are no records of continuing organization of women lace workers. In the 1850s, when men lace workers began to organize themselves on the lines of the New Model Unions, with low subscriptions and an emphasis on mediation, not strike action, women were excluded from membership.

On rare occasions men not only advised a policy of separate organization, for women, but tried to help women to establish them. This kind of co-operation is hinted at in the records of such strikes as the Glasgow 'equal pay strike' of 1833. Such co-operation was even more evident in a series of disputes in the bookbinding trade in London in the 1830s and 1840s. In fact the journeymen bookbinders of London and Westminster in the 1830s decided to act on behalf of the women employed by the British Foreign Bible Society, when the society tried to reduce the wages of both men and women employees. The journeymen petitioned on behalf of about 200 women,

> the whole of whose wages have been reduced in consequence of the late alteration in the prices of these books. Their wages were before very low. Your memorialists respectfully submit that the making it more difficult, and in some cases impossible, for females to earn an honest subsistence, by their labour, is in the same proportion to give potency to the seducers of female virtues.[18]

Whether it was owing to their strength or the moral argument they used, the journeymen did achieve for the women better rates for a ten-hour day. Without organization of the women, rates and conditions worsened to a point at which in 1845 the journeymen decided to protest once again. They petitioned the employers on behalf of the women, claiming that women

> often have not the power to plead their own cause in such matters, and being helpless in many respects where their wages are concerned, they are trodden down until a state of things such as described in the 'Song of the Shirt' appals the mind with the enormity of their injuries, their suffering and their moral condition.[19]

This time, however, the employers did not concede to the journeymen's argument and dismissed a number of women who signed a statement agreeing with the journeymen's claims. The dismissed women were supported by a walkout of about 100 women. The journeymen not only helped the women to formulate a claim, but also contributed to a strike fund for them. Despite that help, the unity of the strikers slowly disintegrated as women either accepted work elsewhere or returned to work at the old terms.

Whilst the journeymen bookbinders of London and Westminster saw clearly the need to fight for improved wages for women as part of a way of protecting their own wage rates, there was no suggestion that they should offer membership to women in their association. In fact the only area in which the idea was considered and acted upon was in certain textile unions. The textile unions were, in the 19th century, the advanced vanguard of the organization of men and women workers.

Despite the hope expressed by the spinners unions that women would organize separately, such organization on any effective scale did not develop. The spinners gradually realized that the lack of organization of all the less-skilled ancillary workers in spinning was seriously hampering and undermining their own organization. The spinners unions, based on craft lines, restricted membership to male spinners who could afford the high entry fees and dues. With such high dues the unions could afford to pay strike pay to their members, but any strike of spinners immediately put out of work large numbers of unorganized workers who had no organization or strike fund. These unorganized workers, who were mainly women, formed a ready group of 'knobsticks', 'blacklegs' and strike breakers. They were often driven to desperate measures to avoid starvation. To try to stop their strikes being broken by other workers, the spinners unions finally accepted the separate organization of piecers and cardroom workers. At first they excluded women, but in 1837 the Bolton Association of Cotton Spinners admitted women to their piecers' section and other unions or sections of unions organizing piecers and cardroom operatives soon followed suit. In an industry in which women predominated, it was ludicrous to form a union from which the majority of workers in that job were excluded. For some time the spinners' sections of unions continued to exclude women from membership, but slowly the rules were changed and women were admitted. The weaving unions followed the same pattern in the cotton industry.

The textile unions became the pioneers of mixed unions. Their pioneering spirit went even further. Not only did they accept men and women into membership, they negotiated rates based on 'the rate for the job' and not on a rate for 'the sex of the worker doing the job'. The fact that the unions organized so widely in the cotton industry enabled them to achieve through collective bargaining fixed wage rates – an achievement that was far in advance of other unions. In 1853 a group of employers conceded collective bargaining and agreed to a list of wage rates in spinning. This historic agreement was known as the 'Blackburn List'. Not only was it a list which fixed rates for each job, but the rates were fixed on the basis of the rate for the job. This precedent was followed by other textile unions, so that in effect, from the outset of collective bargaining and written agreements in the textile industry, there was equal pay. In fact few women earned as much money as men, since the majority of women worked in unskilled and semi-skilled jobs and the men tended to corner the best-paid skilled jobs. However, the policies of the textile unions of having a mixed membership and of negotiating a rate for the job were unique. They led a large and active female membership in the textile unions. No other unions of the period followed their example, but there is no doubt that if they had, the history of women workers in the trade union movement would have been very different.

Whilst women workers did protest, strike, demonstrate and organize, there is little evidence that their action had any real effect in terms of protecting or improving their wages, hours and conditions except in the textile industry. Even there collective bargaining only achieved fixed wage rates. In all industries women workers were appallingly exploited in the 19th century. Bad work conditions, excessively long hours and outrageously low wages were the norm. In addition, they suffered many indignities and humiliations at the hands of foremen and employers. Their already sub-subsistence wages were eroded by excessive disciplinary fines and by deductions made for materials. Those women who were not ground down by years of working seventy-eight hours a week in bad conditions, on a poor diet, with child-bearing the only interruption, might well die from one or other industrial disease. The conditions of working women in the mines, the textile factories, the potteries and many other industries during the first part of the 19th century have been frequently quoted; the exploitation of women was second only to the exploitation of child labour. Outside the textile unions, male trade unionists almost entirely washed their hands of the plight of women workers. It was the government which became the main body concerned with their protection.

The Victorian parliamentarians, confronted with such reports as the Sadler Committee in 1833 on Child Labour, the annual reports of the factory inspectors from 1833 onwards and the many other government reports on individual industries found their consciences stirred. The report of the Children's Employment Commission on Mines and Collieries, with its description of child and female labour, moved parliament so greatly, even some members to tears, that the Mines Act of 1842, which barred women and children from working underground, was hastily passed. This act met with little hostility from the men workers, because in some pits they had tried, sometimes successfully, to ban women from work underground since women prevented 'lads and men from getting their proper wages'.[20] For the government, the passing of the Mines Act was, in the words of B. L. Hutchins and A. Harrison, 'perhaps, the most high-handed interference with industry enacted by the State in the nineteenth century, and it doubtless led the way to the inclusion of women in the much milder Factory Bill of 1844'.[21] Interference by the state with *laissez-faire* capitalism had begun in 1819 with the first legislation restricting the hours of child labour. As legislation increasingly restricted child labour through the 1820s and 1830s, women, the second source of cheap labour, were employed in increasing numbers to work for excessively long hours. Some employers employed married females, whom they found even more exploitable than single women. Lord Ashley, in a speech on the Ten Hours Bill, quoted a letter in which the writer claimed that

> Mr E, a manufacturer informed me that he employs females exclusively at his power-looms; . . . gives a decided preference to married females, especially those who have families at home dependent on them for support; they are attentive, docile, more so than unmarried females, and are compelled to use their utmost exertions to procure the necessities of life.[22]

From the outrage caused by government reports, a movement began to press parliament to legislate for the restriction of hours that women should work in industry. The motives of the men trades unionists who supported the campaign were mixed. In part they hoped that they would gain from 'behind the women's petticoats' a restriction on their own hours. They also hoped for further restrictions on women; the Yorkshire Short Time Committee advocated a restriction on the hours women could work, but wished also to see a restriction on the proportion of women to men employed and a ban on married women working. Women were frightened that a restriction on the hours they could work would mean that they would lose their jobs fearing that the employers would prefer men who could work for any number of hours. The government was swayed, not by trades-union argument, but by a report which brought to light the terrible facts of the long hours, low wages and appalling conditions that were the lot of women textile workers. In 1844 an act was passed restricting the hours of women employed in textile factories to twelve hours a day. The employers quickly found a way of evading the act: they employed women on relay systems, making it virtually impossible for the inspectors to discover the hours actually worked. To try to stop such evasions the 1850 Factory Act was passed. It laid down that the ten-hour legal maximum working hours for women textile workers must be fixed between 6 a.m. and 6 p.m. or 7 a.m. and 7 p.m. As such the Act of 1850

> was an important turning point in the history of English factory legislation, [since] by it a normal working day was for the first time expressly established, or, in other words, the legal working day was made to coincide with the legal period of employment, allowance being made for meal times.[23]

The mid-19th century saw a piecemeal, but ever-growing, body of factory legislation. The textile industry was chosen as the first industry in which the hours of women were restricted, not so much because its hours were longer or their conditions worse than in other industries, but because public attention had been focused on it. As public attention, through government reports was directed to other industries, legislation was passed controlling the hours women could work in a variety of factory-based industries. The potteries, the lace industry, printing, dyeing and bleach works were all included. Through their reports the factory inspectors spearheaded the campaign for the extension of legislation to cover all women factory workers. They even recommended the extension of the factory acts to include private houses and small domestic industries. As more evidence poured in of the pay and conditions of women workers, it was revealed

> that there was nothing special about excessive hours of work, insanitary conditions, overstrain and waste of life and power; that these were not peculiar to any one kind of work or any one form of industry but might be found wherever the workers were cheap and competition unregulated, existing perhaps in their acutest form in the 'cottage homes of England'.[24]

In the 1860s factory legislation was extended tentatively to include certain sanitary provisions as well as regulations about the fencing of machinery. The latter was opposed by the National Association of Factory Occupiers, the Association for the Mangling of Operatives as Dickens called it, an organization of employers whose aims were to oppose further extension of factory legislation.

The 1842 Mines Act and the Act of 1844 restricting the hours of women working in textile factories marked the beginning of the long history of legislation relating to women workers. This state interference into the affairs of employers, which was against the capitalist ethic of *laissez-faire*, was justified by its parliamentary supporters on the ground that women and children were weak, helpless creatures in need of protection. The male textile workers' reasons for supporting the restriction of hours on women were not merely in the interests of their womenfolk. They hoped to gain not only a reduction of their own hours of work, but also a cut-back in the employment of women generally. Other unions would have welcomed the application of the Mines Act to their trades, since it would have solved the problem of women being employed for half pay.

These two acts were not only precedents in state interference with employers 'rights', they were also precedents in state interference with free collective bargaining. From these acts right through the extensions of the factory acts to the Trades Boards Acts (Wages Councils), the Equal Pay Act and the Sex Discrimination Act, the trades unions have accepted, in relation to women, statutory interference in the basic spheres of collective bargaining – hours and pay. From the outset of protective legislation the trade union movement has looked to parliament rather than organization to deal with some of the most critical problems relating to women workers. The history of women workers' struggle for better wages, hours, conditions and opportunities is closely linked with legislation.

Whilst the organization of women workers was, before the 1870s, mostly confined to the textile unions, the roots of that organization had been strongly laid. The roots, too, of divisions and attitudes which were to influence the varied developments of the organization of women workers had been firmly laid. Unequal pay and the acceptance of cheap female labour; the attitude that a woman's proper sphere was the home; the change to the individual male as the basic unit in the capitalist labour market and the attendant non-recognition of women's productive role as bearer of children and homekeeper : all these were entrenched in the early 19th century and gave rise to a heritage of tensions, misunderstanding and lack of clear socialist thinking which hindered the development of the trades union movement. The social and economic position which women were forced into by the Industrial Revolution created the conditions which made it difficult to organize women, even though the behaviour of the textile unions showed that it was by no means impossible.

Working-class women were not only economically oppressed. Their social and legal inferiority inhibited their self-assertion. The fact that Victorian middle-class men deified the mother and wife at home and denied middle-class women the right to work or to study meant that, within the world of work, women had nothing to aspire to. They could merely aspire to marrying a man who would earn enough to support them. To become that very rare phenomenon, a forewoman in a factory, was perhaps the highest peak they could reach. A poor girl working in a milliner's shop might dream of becoming the proprietress, but she was much more likely to have to turn to prostitution in times of slack trade to keep herself alive. In the 1850s and 1860s a few middle-class women had begun to open up other horizons than the lonely, ill-paid job as governess. Miss Buss and Miss Beale pioneered serious education for girls and other women fought for the rights of women to enter the professions, particularly medicine.[25] But in Victorian society women, Queen Victoria apart, took no leadership roles. They looked to men for leadership.

In talking of the oppression of women in the 19th century women's role as child-bearers cannot be omitted, since much of the oppression of women by men was justified by reference to it. Child-bearing took a great toll on women's health and lives. In 1845 the average number of live births born to married women was 5.71. The numbers of miscarriages and still births are unrecorded. Poor diet, unsanitary housing conditions and poverty and ignorance led to appalling suffering and high death rates in women through pregnancy and childbirth. The infant mortality rate was high, but contrary to the popular belief of the time it was not higher among children of working women than among children of non-working women. The highest mortality rate was found in mining communities, where the women traditionally did not work. Poverty, ignorance and dirt were, and still are, the main causes of infant mortality, not the assumed neglect by working mothers of their children. The life of a woman worker in the 19th century was hard; economic necessity was the only reason why married working-class women worked. Teenage girls, if all their wages did not go to support their families, could enjoy a brief few years of independence, money to spend and a little free time. They had little to look forward to. They faced a future of relentless child-bearing and rearing, hard toil and a short life-expectancy, for only one third of the girls who reached the age of 15 could in 1845 expect to survive until the age of 65.

1 Quoted in Wanda Fraiken NEFF *Victorian Working Women* George Allen & Unwin 1928 p.32

2 Alice CLARK *Working Life of Women in the Seventeenth Century* Frank Cass & Co Ltd 1968   p.106f

3 Ibid   p.307

4 E. J. HOBSBAWN *Industry and Empire* Penguin Books 1969   p.68

5 See *Report by Miss Collett on Changes in the Employment of Women and Girls in Industrial Centres. Part 1 Flax and Jute Centres.* HMSO Cmnd 8794 1898

6 Quoted in H. A. TURNER *Trade Union Growth, Structure and Policy. A Comparative Study of the Cotton Unions* George Allen & Unwin Ltd 1962 p.185

7 William KIDDIER *The Old Trade Unions from Unprinted Records of the Brushmakers* George Allen & Unwin 1930   p.99

8 Ibid   p.108

9 Quoted in Clement J. BUNDOCK *The Story of the National Union of Printing, Bookbinding and Paper Workers* Oxford University Press 1959 p.35

10 W. H. WARBURTON *History of Trade Union Organisation in the Potteries* George Allen & Unwin Ltd 1931   p.37

11 Thomas JOHNSTON *A History of the Working Classes in Scotland* Forward Publishing Co Ltd 1920 p.306

12 Quoted in *Women in the Trade Union Movement* TUC 1955   p.36

13 NEFF op.cit. p.32

14 JOHNSTON op.cit. p.310

15 Sidney and Beatrice WEBB *History of Trade Unionism* Longmans, Green & Co 1920   p.727

16 Quoted in Jo O'BRIEN *A Case Study from Nottingham* Spokesman Pamphlet No 24   The Bertrand Russell Peace Foundation   p.8

17 Norman H. CUTHBERT *The Lace Makers Society* The Amalgamated Society of Operative Lace Makers and Auxiliary Workers 1960   p.24

18 Quoted in J. Ramsay MACDONALD *Women in the Printing Trades* P. S. King & Son 1904   p.32f.

19 Ibid p.33

20 Ivy PINCHBECK *Women Workers and the Industrial Revolution* Frank Cass & Co Ltd 1969 p.265

21 B. L. HUTCHINS & A. HARRISON *History of Factory Legislation* P. S. King & Son 1911   p.82

22 Quoted in PINCHBECK op.cit.   p.194

23 B. L. HUTCHINS & A. HARRISON   op.cit.   p.107

24 B. L. HUTCHINS & A. HARRISON   op.cit.   p.165

25 See Ray STRACHEY *The Cause. A Short History of the Women's Movement in Great Britain* G. Bell & Sons Ltd 1928

2

'... and Women' 1874-1906

THE 1870s brought the second main development in the organization of women workers after the organization of women textile workers. In 1874 Emma Paterson, née Ann Smith, founded the Women's Protective and Provident League. Although of middle-class background, daughter of a headmaster, she had had in her brief working life before 1874 considerable contact with both feminist ideas and the working class. As a girl she was an apprentice bookbinder. She then worked for five years as the secretary of the Working Men's Club and Institute Union, finally resigning to become the secretary of the Women's Suffrage Association. But it was in the United States, where in 1873 she went with her husband, Thomas Paterson, that her plans for starting trade union organization amongst women in Britain were really formulated. In New York she attended a meeting of the Female Umbrella Maker's Union and became convinced of the need for similar organizations in Britain. Soon after her return to London she put her ideas into action and formed the Women's Protective and Provident League, which she dominated until her death in 1886.

The aims of the league were essentially those of a Friendly Society with trade union overtones. The expressed main aims of the league was to foster a protective and benefit union in every trade in which women were engaged. The functions of each union were to be

(1) To protect the trade interests of the members by endeavouring, where necessary, to prevent the undue depression of wages, and to equalise the hours of work.

(2) To provide a fund from which members may obtain allowance weekly in sickness or when out of employment.

(3) To arrange for registration of employment notices, so that trouble in searching for work may be avoided, and to collect useful trade information.

(4) To promote arbitration in cases of dispute between Employers and Employed.[1]

The league was set up as a central body to help with the establishment of individual unions. This help extended to financial assistance, advertising, convening meetings, and generally giving advice as to how a union should be organized and administered. The league hoped that, having given this initial help, it would be able to withdraw, leaving each union as a self-reliant, self-supporting organization which could, if necessary, appeal to the league for help when in difficulty. The league itself was financed mainly by subscriptions and donations from middle-class sympathizers and by fund-raising campaigns. At the end of the first year it had a bank balance of £80 13s. During its first years of existence it helped to establish unions for women employed in bookbinding, millinery, mantlemaking and other skilled sewing trades. They were small, mainly London based organizations, in areas of work which were traditionally regarded as skilled or semi-skilled women's work.

The early years of the league were marked by a strange mixture of feminism, trade unionism and middle-class attitudes. This mixture derived partly from the character and ideas of Emma Paterson and partly from the dominant ideas of the trade union movement of the period. So whilst the aims laid down for each union reflected the aims of many craft unions of the period, the difference was the league's belief that such unions should be for women. This was not just a response to the fact that women were excluded from most men's unions; it was also a point of feminist principle. Emma Paterson believed that women would gain confidence in their ability to take action on behalf of themselves only through developing their own self-reliance and their own leaders. This feminism and the middle-classness of the league seeps through the pages of the *Women's Union Journal*, the organ of the league, which was published monthly and sold at the high cost of 1s. a copy – a cost which would have been prohibitive to the majority of the working women whom the league was trying to organize. The journal printed articles on remarkable women, poems by women and thrilling serial stories like 'The Dumb Maiden of Cremona'. It also encouraged more practical things, such as opening a 'half-penny bank' for working women and a home in Southend where they could take holidays. In 1878 a Women's Union Swimming Club was set up to promote a knowledge of swimming among women. The benefits of swimming for women were so highly regarded by the league that it offered prizes of 5s. and 7s. to women who learned to swim one and two lengths. For some women such a prize was the equivalent to a week's wages.

The most controversial policy of the league in its early years was its policy of opposing any factory legislation which restricted the hours women could work or the jobs which women could do. Their opposition was based on two main principles: first, that women should have, like men, the right to do any job and to work the hours they wished, and second, that the way to restrict hours was by organization and not legislation. The first principle arose from their experience as middle-class women. Largely deprived of the right to work, let alone the right to choose any job, to them any further restriction on the right to work seemed an outrage. The 1877 Annual Conference of the league was dominated by their feelings with regard to a bill, then passing through parliament, which proposed further extension of legislation restricting the hours of women factory workers. Mrs Mark Pattison put the league position clearly in her speech.

> Women of full age under the Bill are subject to the same regulations as boys under eighteen. Should they wish to work at other hours than those permitted by this Bill, it is illegal for them to do so ... Now I do not intend to discuss whether it is or is not desirable for women to work on Sundays, or at hours not specified in this Bill, or during meal times; all that I wish to maintain is that these points are best left to the discretion of the women themselves, to be decided by their convenience, and that of the trades in which they are engaged, and by the action of the Unions by which their interests should be protected.[2]

Miss H. P. Downing, addressing a meeting in Nottingham, argued that it was 'a monstrous thing, that a woman not being an idiot or a lunatic should be interfered with where an adult man's labour was not interfered with'.[3] What these women failed to realize, in their eagerness to fight for the right for women to work, was that working women could not decide upon the hours they worked to suit their convenience. Their wages were so low that the only possible way they could earn even the barest minimum was to work excessively long hours. Since most women were not organized, they had no control over either their hours or their wages.

The league's belief that hours should be controlled by organization not legislation was not so 'middle-class' as its critics made out. Experience has shown that trade union organization has gained better protection for women workers than statutory protection. However, given the low level of organization of women in the 1870s, parliament continued to offer women workers the only protection most of them had. The argument over organization or legislation dominated the early battles between the league and the TUC. The women, quite justifiably, were suspicious of the wholehearted support which most men's unions gave to those sections of the factory acts which restricted the hours women could work. Emma Paterson wrote in 1874 an article on the need for separate women's unions in which she sharply criticized men trade unionists for their support of such legislation and their lack of support for organization.

> It is true that working men, who are joining in these well-meant but mistaken endeavours to improve the position of working women, might offer the same kind of protection which they themselves adopt. They might invite women to join their trade unions, or assist them to form similar societies. But they do not seem inclined to do this. At three successive annual congresses of leaders and delegates of trades unions, the need of women's unions has been brought before them, and each time some one present has asserted that women *cannot* form unions. The only ground for this assertion appears to be that women *have not* yet formed unions.[4]

This attitude towards legislation affected the way in which the women were received and treated in their first years as delegates to the TUC. Gaining the right for women delegates to attend the TUC was one of the great advances made by the league, for women, in its early years. In 1875 the first two women, Mrs Paterson representing the Society of Bookbinders, and Miss Simcox representing the Society of Shirt and Collar Makers, were admitted as delegates to the 8th TUC congress. At that congress a motion was carried unanimously : 'That the members regard with much satisfaction the development of the self relying trades union movement among women employed in the various industries and pledge themselves to assist in promoting it in their various localities'.[5] Having gained for women the right to attend the TUC conference, Emma Paterson then used it as a platform to campaign against the proposed extension of legislation which restricted women's hours of work. The women's campaign met with little sympathy from the men, who saw a restriction on the hours women could work as a way of controlling unfair competition from low paid women. Despite the league's protests the Factory and Workshop Act was passed in 1878 without having been amended on the lines they demanded.

In that same year Emma Paterson found herself in the somewhat contradictory position, which some men were only too quick to point out, of proposing the appointment of women factory inspectors to enforce a piece of legislation sections of which she had opposed. Regardless of criticism, she successfully moved at the TUC conference an amendment to add the words 'and women' to a resolution instructing 'the Parliamentary Committee to take immediate action to secure the appointment of a number of respectable working men (and women) as assistant inspectors'.[6] Thus began a long battle. Each year the men would propose a similar resolution and each year the women successfully moved an amendment to add the words, 'and women' to the resolution. Men delegates made moral objections to the amendment, claiming that it would be 'highly objectionable for a young lady to go as an inspector into a workshop where men as well as women were employed'.[7] But the moral objections were merely a disguise for their real objection, which was the fear that if they passed the motion as amended 'it would be to postpone indefinitely the reform sought'. The men's fears proved unjustified; in 1881 the women could comment that 'it is gratifying to find that these forebodings have not been justified and that within six months of the Dublin Congress a working class representative has been appointed'.[8] The women continued annually to demand women factory inspectors and after twelve years of perseverance they triumphed.

By the time, 1893, that the first women factory inspectors were appointed, the league had changed its policies towards legislation. The active campaign against the extension of legislation died after the passing of the Factory and Workshop Act in 1878, but the league's public policy did not change until after Emma Paterson's death in 1886. In the early 1890s the league, not untouched by the wide changing mood of trade unionism, changed its financial base and its policies. It also changed its name to the Women's Trade Union League. To put that change on a firm financial basis, rooted in the trade union movement and not in middle-class donations and subscriptions, Lady Dilke, who emerged as the effective leader of the league following the death of Emma Paterson, devised a scheme whereby any *bona fide* trade union which admitted women to membership could affiliate to the league for the small fee of ½d. per year per female member. By the 1890s some sixty unions had affiliated, including thirty local associations of cotton operatives. In return for affiliation the league would help to organize women. Speakers and organizers were sent by the league all around the country and help was also given in raising money for strike funds.

This latter function marked another change in policy. The new policy was one of supporting strikers and seeing strikes as a fertile ground for recruiting and forming trades unions.

The organizers of the league were on certain occasions, in dramatic demand, as this request to the League shows: 'Please send an organizer at once, for our Amalgamated Society has decided that if the women of this town cannot be organized, they must be exterminated.'[9] The scheme of affiliation gave the league both a sound financial basis and a recognized status in the trade union movement.

A strike was often the first contact women workers had with the ideas of trade union organization. A typical example of the league's utilizing a strike to help organize women came in 1888, when 300 'dandy loom' weavers in Leeds struck against a reduction of wages. The Women's Trade Union League lent its help to local unions in an attempt to organize the striking women. One of the league's organizers went to Leeds to help the Leeds Trades Council and the West Riding Power Loom Weavers organize meetings. A reporter commented on one meeting that the women's questions 'showed a singular ignorance hitherto of the meaning and purpose of a union, and the need of business training which the Union gives was perceptible but no less perceptible was the *esprit de corps* which would make it a disgrace for one to go in without the rest.'[10] A year later a similar joint effort between the Leeds Trades Council and the Women's Trade Union League resulted in the formation of a union of women tailors. Again, it was a strike which was used to establish a union.

The league naturally became the mouthpiece for women workers, particularly with regard to legislation. This role marked the other main change in the league's policies. Far from campaigning against legislation restricting the hours women could work, the re-structured league found that it spent an increasing amount of its time at the turn of the century in campaigning for extensions to existing legislation. Although the organizational side of the league expanded and its involvement with women workers grew, the head office of the league looked more to parliament than to organization for redress of the problems of women workers. During these years the league campaigned not only for restrictions on the hours of women workers in almost all types of employment, but also for much stricter legislation on sanitary facilities and safety conditions.

Their campaign for more extensive factory legislation was given a great stimulus by the appointment in 1893 of the first two women factory inspectors. In 1895 three more were appointed and a separate women's section of the factory inspectorate was set up under Adelaide Anderson. The women trade unionists had good allies in those first few women factory inspectors. They were outspoken women of courage who gave untiring devotion to their work. They were not content merely to perform their work, but continually investigated areas which they thought ought to be controlled by legislation or made suggestions as to how existing acts might be extended. The annual reports of the women factory inspectors provided authoritative evidence which was a powerful weapon in the campaign for greater protection of women workers.

The appointment of women to the factory inspectorate marked a great advance for women. For the first time the government had given women highly responsible jobs. Their appointment was remarkable, since their work involved travelling extensively around the British Isles, not just to factories, but to back-street workshops and places like the wilds of Donegal. They were required to have an intimate knowledge of the law regarding factory legislation and the Truck Acts and, what was more, they had to be able to argue their case in court thirty years before women were officially admitted to the bar.

Adelaide Anderson, in her book *Women in The Factory*, listed what she, as a factory inspector, found to be the five main characteristics of women workers in the 1890s.

(1) mute sense of industrial inferiority . . . .
(2) an absence in the great majority of factories of any women in a position of authority
(3) in spite of protective laws, a working day and week in which the standard hours worked by women frequently exceeded those for which men, in certain trades, had by means of trade unions secured recognition from employers
(4) a frequent lack of suitable or even decent and sufficient sanitary accommodation, of cleanliness of a domestic nature, and of other hygienic requirements sometimes injuriously affecting conduct and morals
(5) not only low average and individual wages, but on the part of pieceworkers an intolerable uncertainty as to what their rates really were; and for all, a liability to arbitrary deductions for fines and alleged damages to work, which often brought earnings below subsistence level.[11]

Although the women factory inspectors were by no means an arm of the trade union movement in the early years there was obviously a close overlap between their work and that of the trade unions. They managed to get restrictions imposed on the hours that women could work in a greater number of jobs including laundries. They also won strict controls on women working with two dangerous chemicals, lead and phosphorus. (The former led to a high rate of still-births and miscarriages and the latter caused phosphorous necrosis, or phossy jaw.) Whilst the women's factory inspectorate did make an important contribution, their numbers were far too small to make much impact on the widespread evasions of the laws. And many working women who were used to seeing those in authority as enemies were reticent to seek, even anonymously, protection from the law through the inspectorate.

In the late 19th century the Women's Trade Union League,

operated in a limited way, as a Women's TUC. The majority of organized women who were affiliated to it were in the textile unions. Textile unions formed at least 75% of all organized women at the turn of the century. In the cotton industry the latter part of the 19th century brought an extension of mixed unions. One or two spinners unions tried to persist in excluding women, but the majority of cotton unions gave women full rights of membership. The leadership of the unions remained almost all male, although women sat on local committees and a woman president of a union was not unknown.

In contrast to the cotton unions, the unions formed in the heavy woollen section of the textile industry – mainly in Yorkshire – were, as often as not, started or effectively run by women. Although attempts had been made in the mid-19th century to organize workers in the heavy woollen industry, they did not result in the forming of permanent organizations until the 1870s and 1880s. In this development women played an important role. In the 1870s it was a group of Dewsbury women who formed what was to be the first branch of the General Union of Textile Workers. Ben Turner, in his *Short History of the General Textile Workers*, records that, although there had been unions in the heavy woollen trade based in the Dewsbury district, it was as a result of the 1875 strike, led by a committee of women, that a union was permanently established. The Dewsbury dispute in 1875 arose out of a co-ordinated attempt by the employers of the area, involving 'upwards of fifty firms of manufacturers, two or three finishers and twelve dyers' to cut wages. Three women. Hannah Wood, Ann Ellis and Kate Conran, formed the Heavy Woollen Weaver's Strike and Lock-out Committee, which led a strike against the wage cuts. They established a strike fund which between 12 February and 27 March raised £1,200. The women were not inhibited from speaking in public: one meeting at which they spoke was attended by 9,000 people. Throughout the strike the women appealed for unity between men and women workers, and in one speech Ann Ellis attacked men who had been heard to remark that her husband must earn a lot of money 'or she could not make the appearance she did'. In fact, she said, her husband was often on short time, earning only 12s. a week, and they had three children and had 'buried a child the week before Christmas'.[12] The dispute lasted several weeks until a settlement was reached. At a large meeting, held in April 1875, a public statement was issued by the three women of the strike committee thanking the workers for their solidarity and support through the strike and announcing the new union.

The formation of the union was as important a result of the strike as the settlement. The public statement said of the union that 'There will be nothing novel in its constitution; one code of rules will regulate the entire body of the trade, so that there will be every probability of harmony of proceeding and a beneficial result to its endeavours'.[13] The minutes of one of the early meetings recorded that the entrance fee would be 6s. per member and that contributions were to be 2d. a week for full benefits and 1d. a week for half benefits. There is no mention of different union rates for women and men but, as was so often the case where there were two rates, women tended to pay the lower rate. A photograph of the Dewsbury Heavy Woollen Union Committee shows an all-woman committee of thirteen members. Ann Ellis moved to become an active trade union organizer in Yorkshire, but Hannah Wood continued as president of the union, which developed into the Dewsbury, Batley and Surrounding District Heavy Woollen Weavers Association. In the early 1880s the employers reduced wages again, but this time the workers failed to resist the reductions successfully. During that strike as part of the propaganda, the union published a poem which showed how much women were in the forefront of the struggle.

> Be true, be true, you weavers all,
> And do not flinch one pick;
> And all be well united,
> Like female Briton's stick,
>
> And never mind poor Ossey's talk,
> About brooches and fine dress;
> Work by the statement you have got,
> Take not a farthing less.[14]

The poem went on to appeal to 'every weaver, woman and man' to help one another.

It was not only in Dewsbury that women played an important role in the formation of the separate unions that were later to amalgamate into the General Union of Textile Workers. A photo of the strike committee in Bradford, which led a strike against a reduction in wages, shows that there were more women on the committee than men; and in Halifax the records show that women were on the union committee. In Huddersfield, although men led the big strike in 1883 which consolidated the Huddersfield and District Power Loom Weavers and Woollen Operatives Association, their statements were directed to 'men and women' and the union recruited both sexes, although there were different subscription rates for each.

In the textile unions women were as active as men, even if men dominated most unions. It is often hard to gauge the relative militancy of men and women workers in a union, but whilst women have been less prominent in leading unions, there is little evidence to show that they were less militant. A government report on strikes and lock-outs published in 1898[15] confirms this picture that is if the number of strikers can be used as a yardstick. According to the report, there were fewer disputes in 1898 than in the preceding five years: 99 disputes involving directly or indirectly 24,978 workers. The report for 1898 analysed these figures into the percentages of men, women and young persons involved in strikes and lockouts in the textile industry. They found that, although men formed 32%, women 42% and young persons 26% of the work force, proportionate to their numbers in the workforce more women than men were involved.

Women employed in the jute and flax industry, like their fellow workers in cotton and wool, faced attempts by their employers to reduce wages in the late 19th century. In 1884 employers in Aberdeen announced a reduction of wages for jute mill workers and the women, followed by a few men, walked out. A meeting between the employers, the women and an arbitrator was set up by the local trades council. It resulted in a partial victory for the women. Only weavers, and not all workers, suffered a reduction in wages and the reduction was only 5% and not the 10% proposed by the employers. A year later women jute workers in Dundee struck against similar wage reductions and finally returned to work accepting a 5% reduction; but to enable themselves to fight more effectively against further reductions in wages the jute workers formed the Dundee Mill and Factory Operatives Union. The rules of the union stated that it was open to all men and women over ten years old; the entry fee was 3d. for adults (1½d. for half-timers); there was a 1d. subscription a week and all members were to receive the same benefits. This union, with its low subscriptions, its strike and lock-out fund and admittance of all men and women in the industry, was a forerunner of the new type of union that was to emerge in the late 1880s and 1890s. Those women taking action, with no union, like the women in Aberdeen in 1884 and again during another strike there in 1888, often had to rely on the help of their local trades council to organize, support and negotiate for them. Local trades councils helped women in a large number of disputes throughout Great Britain. Men who were reluctant to organize women were often willing to help women who were involved in disputes.

The principle established by the early cotton unions of negotiating the rate for the job was followed by most of the textile unions. Equal pay thus became the norm in the textile industry. However equality of opportunity was far from the norm and the sexual divisions of labour were as evident in textiles as in any other industry. These divisions were subject to considerable regional variations. The Amalgamated Association of Beamers, Twisters and Drawers tried to prohibit women from practising those trades. However, in some areas where women had traditionally worked as twisters and drawers-in they were organized in those grades by the local branches. Conflict between men and women arose in areas where organization was weakest and where employers tried to take advantage of that weakness by employing women to do 'men's' jobs for less money. New machinery was usually the occasion for the employers to try such a ploy. A dispute erupted over just such an issue in Kidderminster in 1884. The employers introduced new looms and hired women to work them, claiming that the lightness of the machines made them suitable for women to work; but it was the lightness of the wages bill, not of the work, which led the employers to introduce female labour. The men weavers struck against the employment of women and a reporter just returned from Kidderminster wrote that 'the town is in uproar with the men on strike who were perambulating the streets with bands and boards on which were drawn men turning mangles and men washing and then came a procession of perambulators wheeled by men, containing infants'.[16] The strike lasted for seven weeks and the men's weavers' association ended up by agreeing to a certain degree of female labour.

Such a conflict between men and women over the introduction of women to work on new machinery for less pay was more typical of other industries than textiles. In the well organized areas of textiles, where the principle of the rate for the job had been established, conflict occurred between workers and employers over wages, not the sex of the workers. In all other industries rates were fixed according to sex and in the late 19th century this led to considerable conflict between men and women workers. Many craft unions found that they were fighting a losing battle against the employment of women, particularly where mechanization meant that jobs needed less skill. Developments in manufacturing processes in such industries as the potteries, lace making, boot and shoe making, printing and food usually led to erosions of the skilled men's jobs and the introduction of cheap women's labour into semi-skilled and unskilled jobs. Mechanization which increased the divisions of labour very frequently led to an increase in the employment of female labour. The response to these changes varied, but most unions were forced to realize that it was a problem which they had to face and not one which they could ignore until it went away. Unfortunately unions were given little guidance as to how to resolve the problem. The policy of the TUC, that of encouraging the separate organizations of women, although it may have helped women in areas of 'women's' work, created divisions in industries where both sexes worked. In most industries the policy of separate organization meant no organization of women, and by the turn of the century many craft unions were re-considering their policies of excluding women from membership. By refusing to face 'the problem' of cheap female labour as the textile unions did, other unions found themselves having to work out a variety of other solutions, all of which perpetuated the sexual divisions of labour and wage rates and consequently undermined the potential for sexual unity within the trade union movement.

Male trade unionists often offered moral objections to the employment of men and women in one place of work. The Amalgamated Society of Tailors took a high moral tone to justify their policy of trying to prevent the employment of women. At their annual conference in Dublin in 1879 they resolved

> That this Conference having a thorough knowledge of the evil effects of women working in the same workshops as men and boys in our branch of industry, we deem it our duty, in the interests of morality and in the interests of those both male and female, engaged in the occupation, to call public attention to this grow- ing evil, in order that the youth of the present and future may be protected from the evil effects of close interworking of the sexes that has been adopted in certain classes of establishments in all large towns in Great Britain and Ireland.[17]

The men nail and chain makers used morality as part of their argument in the 1880s to get women barred from certain jobs in their trade. They tried, through pressure by the parliamentary committee of the TUC, to have a Bill introduced into parliament to prohibit girls under the age of sixteen from making nails, rivets and chains and to restrict the type of work adult females could do in those trades. The employers, who wished to perpetu- ate the employment of women, staunchly defended the morals of the women they employed. The local newspapers, too, rushed to the defence of the women's moral reputation, arguing that the claim made by those supporting the demand for legislation that 'our female chain and nail makers were brutal and unchaste' was false, as was the claim that women 'work amongst men in a semi-nude state'.[18] The crux of the conflict was that women, especially girls under the age of sixteen, were paid half or less the amount paid to men. Men, short of work and unable to earn enough to support their families, thought that by excluding or at least restricting women they could both get more work and protect their rate from being lowered. The men did not achieve their aim of legislation, nor were they organized strongly enough to impose their demands on employers. Women continued to be employed in large numbers for very low pay.

The print unions tried to exclude women from certain grades, but they were not always successful. In Scotland the employers tried to break the strength and policy of the men's union by employing women. In 1872, the men members of the Scottish Typographical Association went on strike for a 51-hour working week. The employers used female labour to break the strike and to foil the policy of the Typographical Association, which refused to allow women to work as compositors. One employer had had some girls trained as compositors (or as 'stickit teachers' as the men called them) and the strike afforded the ideal opportunity for the employers to introduce them. The men's strike was broken and women compositors became employed at several Edinburgh printing firms. In other towns in Scotland women were also introduced into men's grades, but always they were paid at half the wage to do the same job. 'The women put in a bill at the end of each week', wrote the secretary of the Perth Typographical Society 'worked out on the men's scale of rates, and the cashier then divides the total by two and pays the women accordingly.'[19] In 1886 the International Conference of Typographical Societies passed a resolution stating that 'while strongly of opinion that women are not physically capable of performing the duties of a compositor, this Conference recommends their admission to membership of the various Typographical unions upon the same conditions as journeymen, provided always females are paid strictly in accordance with the scale'.[20] A remarkable resolution which, if carried out, would have meant equal pay and the organization of women with men. There is no evidence, however, that the unions tried to put the resolution into practice. Women were not admitted to any of the print unions in any grade until thirty years later and equal pay was not introduced into the print industry for another ninety years.

The bookbinder's union was still struggling with the problem of cheap female labour. Since they had failed 'to do away with it altogether' they had opted for a policy of keeping 'a strict watch over the encroachment of female labour'. In a speech of 1891 the chief secretary of the bookbinder's union both pinpointed the problem of female labour and posited a solution.

> How is it, when some kinds of labour pass from men to women, that the value falls nearly 50%? Is it a just thing that women should be paid 10/- or 12/- for doing work that is worth 20/- when done by men? That is simply a matter of might and right;

and its obvious explanation is the fact that women are not organised, and therefore unable to defend or uphold their rights.[21]

What was so clear to the chief secretary of the bookbinder's union was not clear to most trade unionists of the period. Although a few men did suggest organizing women, the union, outside the textile unions, which first took the step of changing its rules and accepting women into membership was the National Union of Boot and Shoe Workers. The Union started in 1874, organizing men in the most skilled grades, the rivetters and finishers; they soon decided, as more grades became factory-based, that it was necessary to organize all the men's grades in order to build up industrial strength. Although women had always worked in the trade, much of their work had been done at home. But as processes became more mechanized they were increasingly employed in the factories and by the 1880s considerable numbers of women were working as fitters and machinists and in the closing processes. In response to this situation the union in 1885 officially opened its doors to women. The initial female membership was the 136 women who were organized in the Leicester women's branch. Whilst women were recruited into the union from the outset, the union tried to establish and maintain strict demarcation between 'men's' and 'women's' jobs, thus avoiding the problem of women doing men's jobs for half pay. In the 1890s and at the turn of the century one or two more craft unions followed the example of the National Union of Boot and Shoe Workers and decided to admit women into their unions in certain grades.

The introduction of women as cheap labour was not confined to industry. It occurred in other areas of employment, including government employment. In 1870 the telegraph system passed into government control. In taking over the private companies the controller of the post office was obliged to take over and employ the women who had been employed as telegraph operators in the private companies. The post office thus became the first department of the civil service to employ women. Far from trying to ease out the women, the post office quickly saw the advantages of extending the employment of women. Mr Scudamore, a post office official, drew up a case for the further employment of women which was to be the basis on which women were employed in the civil service.

Mr Scudamore argued that women were more desirable than men for clerical work since they were quick and accurate and accepted sedentary occupations more readily. Female operators, at the wages offered them, would come from a better class than the male operators. The benefits of employing a superior class were that women would write better and spell more correctly and that 'where the staff is mixed, the female clerks will raise the tone of the staff'. Besides the advantages of class, tone and correctness, Mr Scudamore saw even more positive advantages in the employment of women

> They are also less disposed than men to combine for the purpose of extorting higher wages, and this is by no means an unimportant matter. On one other ground it is especially desirable that we should extend the employment of women. Permanently established civil servants invariably expect their remuneration to increase with their years of service, and they look for this increased remuneration even in cases, necessarily very numerous, in which from the very nature of their employment they can be of no more use or value in the twentieth than in the fifth years of their service. . . . Women, however, will solve these difficulties for the Department by retiring for the purpose of getting married as soon as they get the chance. On the whole, it may be stated without fear of contradiction that, if we place an equal number of females and males on the same ascending scale of pay, the aggregate pay to the females will always be less than the aggregate pay to the males; . . . and further, that there will aways be fewer females than males on the pension list.[22]

Whilst Mr Scudamore did not lay down a marriage bar as such, it was clear that he assumed women would retire on marriage. (The marriage bar was imposed later and ensured the government a continuous supply of cheap female labour.) It was not surprising that the post office decided to employ women in increasing numbers. For middle-class women the civil service opened up a new field of work. Restricted as they had been to being either governesses or teachers, many of them no doubt felt it was a privilege to be allowed to work. It was some time before they realized how the privilege was to be exploited.

The introduction of women into other clerical areas of the

civil service soon followed, there were objections from various quarters. Many objections were the familiar moral ones about men and women working together. When, in 1875, forty young ladies were introduced to the savings bank, the gentlemen in the office thought it would cause 'grievious dangers, moral and official' and threatened to hold an 'indignation meeting' to protest against the employment of women.[23] Another gentleman protested against the employment of women : as clerks they might be able to do the light type of work, but they would have difficulty in writing cross-entry acknowledgments, which had to be written 'with heavy pressure by means of very hard pens and carbonic paper'.[24] But the economic advantages in employing women were stronger than the male protests and so women became a significant sector of government employees.

The introduction of women to the civil service and other areas of clerical work and the basis on which they were hired had little immediate relevance to the development of the trade union organization of women, even though the advanced National Union of Clerks admitted women members from 1890. However, it marked the beginning of what was to be one of the major areas of 'women's' work and as such was to be closely related to the whole question of the development of trade union organization amongst women. Of much more immediate relevance and importance to the whole trade union movement was the development of trade unions for unskilled workers. The Match Girls who struck in 1888 can claim to have been the match that lit the explosion of 'new unionism'. The centre of the explosion was the London Dock Strike of 1889. In that strike unskilled and poorly paid workers continued what the Match Girls had shown the year before, that unskilled workers could take organized action effectively. Their action was followed by a surge of organization of unskilled workers in the newly formed general labour unions. These 'new' unions were based on low subscription rates. Often they offered only strike benefit. The general unions opened up to women workers a whole new dimension of possible organization. Craft unions, with their restrictive policies, apprenticeship demands, high entry fees and subscriptions, directly or indirectly excluded women. In the late 19th century craft unionism offered women very little. The new general unions offered unskilled women at least minimal trade union protection.

The radical development in the organization of workers previously regarded as unorganizable was started by a group of women workers who were traditionally seen as having no industrial muscle. The majority of trade unionists at the time, even those struggling to organize unskilled men workers did not consider extending organization to the grossly exploited, unskilled women factory workers. The more radical women in the Women's Trade Union League, women like Clementina Black, had begun to call for such organization and action, but they were criticized. Even Annie Besant, who 'led' the Match Girls strike, in an article written shortly before the strike, criticized the Women's Trade Union League for espousing unworkable ideas.

> Trades Unionism may teach them (women) comradeship and stir up social feeling, and improve their business faculty, and brighten their lives in many ways; but raise their wages – no. How could a trades union be formed among the girls of Bryant and May's spoken of in another column? Let us suppose it formed, and the girls strike. The foremen notify the neighbourhood that they want so many hands at the old wages, and their doors will be besieged by applicants eager to work 10½ hours a day for 8d.[25]

It was those very girls spoken about by Annie Besant in that other column of *Link* who were to disprove her. It was, indeed, that other column which started off the dispute which led to the Match Girls Strike. In that column, headed 'White Slavery in London', Annie Besant described the hours, pay and conditions of the women employed by Bryant and May. The women worked between a 10-hour to 11½-hour day for wages that ranged from 4s. a week to 9s. a week. Those low wages were further subject to innumerable fines and deductions : 'if the feet are dirty, or the ground under the bench is left untidy, a fine of 3d. is inflicted; for putting "burnts" – matches that have caught fire during work – on the bench 1s. has been forefeited'. A girl who was late for work was shut out all morning and had 5d. deducted from her day's pay of 8d.

> One girl was fined 1s. for letting the web twist round a machine in the endeavour to save her fingers from being cut, and was sharply told to care for the machine and 'never mind your

fingers'. Another, who carried out the instructions and lost a
finger thereby, was left unsupported while she was helpless.[26]

One shilling was also deducted as a compulsory 'contribution' to
a statue of Gladstone erected by Mr Bryant. The girls lost a
further day's pay when they were forced to take a day's holiday
for the unveiling of the statue. Annie Besant, having described
such wages and conditions, pointed out in her article that
Bryant and May paid their shareholders a dividend of 20%.

Messrs Bryant and May threatened to sue Annie Besant for
libel and made their intentions known through the press. Annie
Besant made it equally clear publicly that she would stand by the
statements she had made in her article. In an effort to intimidate
their employees Bryant and May dismissed three women who
were known to have talked to Annie Besant. The manner of
their sacking was typical of Messrs Bryant and May 'they did
not dismiss them at once, but kept them on for a week making
their work very slack and finally discharged one of them with
2s. 8d. for her week's wages, promising a second 3s. 6d. and a
third 1s. 8d. The *Link* commented that 'It is hard to understand what kind of non-human beings they can be who can put
into a woman child's hand 1s. 8d. as the price of her week's
labour, and then bid her go forth into the cruel streets'.[27] In
the press Bryant and May denied that the girls had been sacked
for talking to Annie Besant. Annie Besant publicly stood by her
claims and made an appeal, in a letter to the *Pall Mall Gazette,*
for donations to support the dismissed girls. In that letter she also
announced that a meeting was shortly to be called to protest
against the action of Bryant and May. Throughout this dispute,
carried on mainly in the pages of the press, Annie Besant advocated the boycotting of matches made by Bryant and May.

The dispute came to a head when the management asked some
girls to sign a statement saying that Annie Besant's claims were
false. They refused to sign and one girl regarded as the ring-
leader of the revolt was sacked. The women working in her
department walked out with her and before long all 1,400
women employed at Bryant and May had also walked out. A
deputation of them flooded into Annie Besant's office, determined
that they would not go back to work 'without their pennies'.[28]
Annie Besant, despite her opposition to strikes by unskilled

workers, launched herself into helping to organize a strike. A strike fund was established. It received widespread support from both middle-class liberals and from the labour movement. Public meetings and demonstrations were held. A deputation was sent to the home secretary to ask him to enforce the law against Bryant and May on the grounds that they imposed illegal fines and deductions. Bryant and May continued to assert that Annie Besant's article was a 'tissue of lies', though they did not proceed with their libel case. They also tried to break the strike by threatening to move the factory to Norway or to import black-legs from Glasgow. Supported by some of the press, they claimed that the strike was being led by socialist agitators who had intimidated the majority of the strikers into staying out.

A deputation of match girls went to the London Trades Council to seek its support. The council responded positively, donating £20 to the strike fund and offering to act as mediators between the girls and employers. They helped the strikers to draw up a list of grievances and arranged a meeting with members from the trades council, the women's strike committee and the directors of Bryant and May. At that meeting Bryant and May conceded almost all of the women's demands. It was agreed that all fines and most deductions were to be abolished, that the 'pennies' (a deduction made for the employment of girls to carry material for the box-filling women which had continued long after the practice had died out) were to be restored, that 3d. was to be restored to the packers and that there would be no victimization and the firm would recognize a union formed by the women. Later that day the terms of the agreement were put to the strikers, who unanimously accepted them and agreed to return to work.

On 27 July 1888 the inaugural meeting of the Union of Women Matchmakers was held. Clementina Black from the Women's Trade Union League gave advice on rules, subscriptions and elections. Annie Besant was elected the first secretary. With money left over from the strike fund, plus some raised from a benefit held at the Princess Theatre, enough money was raised to enable the union to acquire permanent premises. By October 666 members had been enrolled (their numbers having swelled by the return of women from hop picking). Yet despite its solid funding, the union was soon faced with difficulties. The management clearly victimized women who were committee members of the new union and the women, though they challenged the management on the issue, only gained promises for an investigation. By the end of the year the union changed its rules and name. It became the Matchmakers Union, open to men and women. Although the Matchmakers Union continued to exist only until 1903, the action taken by the Match Girls in 1888 had both immediate and long-term reverberations in the trade union movement.

From the outset the 'new unions' did not exclude women from membership on the grounds of their sex, but since they tended to organize mainly in areas of transport and labouring, few women came into their areas of recruitment. However, the spirit of new unionism led some members to adopt a new attitude towards women workers. It led to curious liaisons, even where the men and women workers were not members of the same union. The struggle of the Sanders girls (confectionery workers) and the dockers in Bristol against their respective employers was one of the most remarkable examples.

The dramatic sequence of events and struggles began in 1892, when women employed at the confectionery factory of Messrs Sanders struck against the imposition of an extra hour's work a day, excessive fines and being locked in during the lunch hour. A small group of socialist women who had been active in Bristol during the late 1880s saw their opportunity. With the help of one of them, Enid Stacy, the Sanders women formed a branch of the Gas Workers and General Labourers Union. They then negotiated a favourable settlement to their dispute; but a fortnight after their return to work one of the girls who had been active in the strike was dismissed. This was followed by the dismissal of a further thirty to forty employees who had a similar record of militant action. On 5 October 1892 the rest of the women workers walked out, determined not to work until their comrades had been reinstated and their right to belong to a trade union recognized. The union took the case to a committee of arbitration. but they found the arbitrators' terms unacceptable and began organizing for what was to be a prolonged dispute.

The strike committee devised a variety of tactics to persuade the employers to capitulate. They tried moral tactics. On each Sunday they organized a parade to Highbury Chapel, the church Mr Sanders attended, and joined in the service. After two weeks of attendance at the church by the women's strike committee, the minister argued in his sermon that it was unfair of the women to attack a member of his congregation. The women strikers were unmoved. In November they persuaded the local trades council to join in the Sunday protest. The trades council declared that

> In their opinion so righteous was the girls' case, that they decided to establish a precedent on their behalf by participating in a Sunday parade for the first time in their history.[29]

So on Sunday, 6 November, a procession headed by the president of Bristol Trades Council solemnly marched to where Mr Sanders worshipped, accompanied by a brass band and waving banners stating 'God Save the People' and 'Where Justice Prevails, Charity is not required'. The women's strike committee was denied entry to the church, while the deputation from the trades council were allowed into the church only in groups of five who were dispersed throughout the congregation. Two weeks later the dockers, who had just been locked out, joined the girl confectionery workers in their Sunday protest march to Highbury Chapel. They found the main gates to the church closed and several constables on the pavement barring their entrance.

This parade marked the beginning of a period of remarkable unity between the locked-out dockers and the Sanders girls. Throughout December joint protests and demonstrations were organized and a mass demonstration was planned for 23 December. Both strike committees agreed that they should have a torchlight march through Bristol to collect money from Christmas shoppers and that the march should end in a mass meeting at Horsefair. As the day approached, the Bristol authorities became increasingly edgy about the demonstration and, although the strike committee liaised with the police, on the eve of the demonstration both strike committees were given a list of regulations by the police containing instructions for the march. These laid down the route for the marchers, warned them that police would line the route and that the carrying of torches, lanterns or any other article that could be deemed dangerous would be

illegal. Tom McCarthy replied in a letter to the police on behalf
of the dockers' committee that the strikers would agree to abide
by the regulations with regard to the carrying of torches but that
they would not agree to the route and would 'only give way
when a stronger force than our own is pitted against us, and
then only with strong protest'.[30] Unknown to Tom McCarthy
and the other strikers, a stronger force was being brought into
Bristol by train that same evening – a squadron of 20th Hussars
and the 4th Dragoon Guards.

The march through Bristol was a violent one. The Sanders
girls followed the police route to Horsefair, but the dockers determined to follow their own route past the docks, which were being
manned by blackleg labour. They arrived at Horsefair, but
only after some of them had sustained injuries from police batons.
At Horsefair about 20,000 people were congregated. The Sanders
girls held a meeting at one end and the dockers at the other.
Both used upturned wagons with lanterns on each shaft to make
a lighted platform for their speakers. Whether because of these
few lanterns or a scuffle between a group of strikers and the
police, the go-ahead was given to the military to clear Horsefair. Many of the civilians, both men and women, at the meeting
received head injuries. The men leaders were arrested, the
speakers charged with 'inciting riot' and the others with breaking
the peace. That day went down in Bristol's history as Black
Friday.

The Sanders girls and the dockers were not cowed. In January
1893 they held more mass demonstrations. Ben Tillett addressed
one meeting and was charged for his part in it, though when his
case was heard in the Central Criminal Court he was found 'not
guilty'. After twenty-six weeks of struggle the strike of the Sanders
girls was brought to a close. They failed to achieve their main
aim, recognition of their union, the Gas Worker and General
Labourers union. But they improved their wages and, like the
Match Girls, left their mark on the wider labour movement, as
one contemporary commented.

> The vigorous way in which the strike was carried on was also a
> primary means of arousing the great attention in this part of the
> country to the Labour Question now so prominent; not the least
> successful result of which is the great increase of membership

to the Trade Unions. Moreover, it was the means of raising the standard of wages, with improved conditions to the workers now engaged in both this and other factories.[31]

The spirit of co-operation between the Dockers Union and women workers continued in the 1890s. In 1896 the dockers union helped to organize a group of women workers at a vinegar and pickle factory who struck against a reduction in their wages. Their action was being undermined by blackleg men and boys. Tom McCarthy described his reaction to the situation when, as a representative of the dockers union he moved in to help the women.

> For what was the position of the strikers? They were without funds, and worst of all, without a Trades Union; held together, however, by a few resolute and plucky girls whose grit lasted right through the fight, and whose efforts were rewarded by a pronounced though limited success.
> I seldom give way to anger when I hear of 'blacklegs' where only men workers are concerned, the feeling is usually that of pity. But in this case there was cause for anger and shame. The men (I call them so for want of a fitting name) deserted and went back to work, and the places of women and girls were partly filled with boys. I suppose these so-called men would class themselves as being much superior to mere women, and would claim their places as 'Lords and Masters', such a claim, however, carries with it a responsibility to protect women and children, and it can only be assumed that these nondescripts were too thick headed to recognise the justice of sexual equality and too cowardly to perform duties of chivalry.[32]

The women's pluck, a strike fund launched by the dockers union which managed to give the women strike pay of 4s. a week and Tom McCarthy's help enabled a compromise settlement to be negotiated. Although wage cuts were made, they were reduced to 5% and 10% instead of the 10% and 25% which the employers had proposed. Recognition was gained for the new union and the boys who had been employed on the women's jobs during the strike were dismissed. The final clause in the settlement stated that 'should any future claim be made by employers, or any other difficulty arise, it shall be first discussed with the secretary of the Docker's Union and the Women's Committee'.[33]

In the 1890s ideas and attitudes towards the trade union

organization of women, mixed or separate unions, legislation, the rights of women, particularly married women, to work and the rights of equal pay were all being debated. There had been splits within the Women's Trade Union League on many of these questions, but after the league's re-structuring in the late 1880s, it helped to organize women in any way, be it in separate organizations, craft unions or the new general unions. The new policy bore fruit. During the 1890s the number of women unionists affiliated to the league grew from 2,000 to more than 70,000. If there were splits in the league on policy relating to these questions, the membership of the league was at least united in its recognition of the need and the ability of women to organize effectively. This basic belief was not shared by many men trade unionists. In a series of articles published in the 1890s by the *Women's Trade Union Review* a variety of trades unionists were invited to write on their attitude to the trade union organization of women.

The first of the series was by Ben Tillett,[34] who delivered an outspoken attack on the 'lady Bountifuls' who treated their sisters as children, taking up disputes with the masters and leaving the women merely to curtsey and say thank you and hope 'the Lady' will return to help them next time they were in trouble. 'We want a woman's Trade Union that shall be in all executive and administrative matters a self-reliant body. The income should be derived from the workers, the spending powers relegated to the properly constituted authority.' Tillett advocated separate women's organizations and stated that men resented 'the interference of "petticoats" in their organizing work'. His virulent attack on the 'goody-goody, preachy, patronising reformers' was undoubtedly directed at many of the middle-class women who ran the league, but it was only partially justified, since the policy of the league had from the first been to encourage women to form self-reliant, self-supporting organizations. John Hendry, organizer of the Brechin branch of the Scottish Mill and Factory Workers Federal Union, was even more critical of women.

> Women, as we in Scotland say, are 'kittle cattle', and if anyone has lingering doubts on that point which he desires to dispel, let him spend a few weeks, in organising work amongst women, and

his cure will be complete. Women, broadly speaking, from a Trade Unionist standpoint are bad subjects. This is due not a little to the dependent and subordinate position the woman has been so long taught to look upon as her proper place. She is difficult to get, and being got is difficult to keep.[35]

Whilst warning trade unionists against trying to organize women, John Hendry did not advocate any other way of dealing with the problems women workers faced. Will Thorne equally recognized the problems, but saw their answer in legislation, not organization. He came to this conclusion after less than a decade of trying to organize women into the National Union of Gasworkers and General Labourers. Despite stalwart help in the task from Eleanor Marx-Aveling, he concluded that the double workload of women, home and work, left them with little time or energy for organization. Legislation, he thought, 'is the strongest weapon that can be used for the benefit of all women workers. Give them the franchise and they will help to solve the problem for themselves because I don't think that they would vote for people who would keep their nose to the grindstone, although many men do.'[36]

Despite his doubts about the effectiveness of organization, Will Thorne continued to uphold the basic principle of a general union with both women and men members. A. Keegan, president of the Birmingham pen workers, saw mixed unions as the only way forward for women. Unless women's organizations 'without losing their individuality, be affiliated with existing men's trade societies, there is little hope of their being successful'. He added that 'women, as a class, appear to have little faith in themselves, either as individuals or, collectively as Trades Unionists'. This latter comment revealed a sympathetic understanding of the problems women in the pen making trade who wished to become trade unionists faced. They not only faced, like all workers, the hostility of the employers. They also faced trouble at home.

The father, if he be a non-unionist, is not in favour of the union; if he be a unionist, he does not like his daughter to join, telling her that she must be looking out for something better than pen-making. The mother urges that there was no such thing in her young days, and that she has reared a family without such help. Then there is the sweetheart who tells her that when they are married pen-making will, for her, be a thing of the past. Although they see around them such a great number of married women who have returned, after a few months of wedded life, to the press, the girls refuse to believe that a like fate awaits them. Then there is always the insurmountable objection to women-folk being out at meetings.[37]

Although Keegan was speaking of the pen trade, his remarks could well have applied to the vast number of employed young women at the turn of the century.

Almost all the contributors to the *Review* realized that the main problem facing women was their low level of wages. One positive approach to improving women's wages had become TUC policy in 1888. Clementina Black, delegate to the TUC, moved the historic resolution which was carried thus committing the TUC to the opinion that 'it is desirable, in the interests of both men and women, that in trades where women do the same work as men, they shall receive equal payment'.[38] Although the motion was carried, outside the textile unions it did not influence any negotiations and it is doubtful whether most trade unionists were convinced of the desirability of equal pay for equal work. Equal pay was not, for most women workers in the late 19th century, the central issue. Low pay was. Whilst it was generally agreed in the trade union movement that women's wages were disgracefully low, few men or women in the movement believed that women had the right or the need to earn a living wage. This attitude arose from the assumption that women's wages were 'secondary wages', despite the fact that for one reason or another a woman's wage was the primary wage in many households.

Sidney Webb, who investigated and wrote about the question of men's and women's wages, did not believe in a rate for a job. He believed that most wage rates based on sex were justifiable. In an article of 1891 on the 'Difference in Wages Paid to Men and Women', he wrote that women's average earnings were 41% of the average male earnings but he claimed that 'Where the inferiority of earnings exist, it is almost always coexistent with an inferiority of work.' He allowed that the 'genteel vocations' were an exception. In them 'women receive habitually less than men; and (in the case of clerks and teachers) for work of quality and quantity equal to men's'.[39] Webb claimed that women were paid less, not only because they produced less and because their work had a lower market value, but also because women have a 'lower standard of life, both in physical needs and mental demands'.[40] That Fabian writers like Webb put forward the employers' and men's case for the exploitation of women indicates how little support women had in their struggle for basic rights. The denial of women's physical needs frequently led to the malnutrition of pregnant and nursing mothers and babies; the most nutritious food was reserved for men. Since most education was denied to women, few had access to any field which could make mental demands on them. Webb's assertion that women should be paid less because they needed less was not merely an individual attitude.

At the beginning of the 20th century women faced a long hard struggle to win even the right to earn a living wage. They began it, however, having laid down firm roots in the 19th century trade union movement.

1 The Women's Union Journal   Jan 1877
2 The Women's Union Journal   July 1877
3 The Women's Union Journal   July 1877
4 Annual Report of the Women's Protective and Provident League   1875
5 Annual Report of the Women's Protective and Provident League   1876
6 The Women's Union Journal   Oct 1878
7 The Women's Union Journal   Oct 1879
8 The Women's Union Journal   May 1881
9 Quoted in Barbara DRAKE   *Women in Trade Unions*   Labour Research Dept   1920   p.31
10 The Link   29th Sept 1888
11 Dame Adelaide ANDERSON   *Women in the Factory*   John Murray   1922 p.24f
12 Ben TURNER   *Short History of the General Textile Workers*   1920   p.89
13 Ibid   p.91
14 Ben TURNER   *The Rise and Progress of the Heavy Woollen District Branch of the General Union of Textile Workers.*   General Union of Textile Workers   1917   p.51f.
15 *Report by the Chief Labour Correspondent on the Strikes and Lock-Outs of 1898*   HMSO   Cmnd 9427   1899   p.xxxviii
16 The Women's Union Journal   March 1884
17 The Women's Union Journal   Nov 1879

18 Wednesbury Borough News   22 Sept 1883
19 Quoted in DRAKE   op.cit.   p.33
20 Quoted in DRAKE   op.cit. p.32
21 Clement J. BUNDOCK   *The Story of the National Union of Printing,*
Bookbinding and Paper Workers Oxford University Press 1959 p.67
22 Quoted in Hilda MARTINDALE   *Women Servants of the State 1870–1938*
George Allen & Unwin   1938   p.17f
23 Ibid   p.25
24 Ibid   p.26
25 The Link   23 June 1888
26 Ibid
27 The Link   7 July 1888
28 The Link   14 July 1888
29 Quoted in Samson BRYHER   *An Account of the Labour and Socialist*
Movement in Bristol British Labour Weekly 1929 p.35
30 Ibid   p.39
31 Ibid   p.49
32 The Women's Trade Union Review   April 1896
33 Ibid
34 Woman's Trade Union Review   Oct 1896
35 Women's Trade Union Review Jan 1900
36 Ibid
37 Ibid
38 Annual Report of Women's Trade Union Provident League   1889
39 The Women's Trade Union Review   Oct 1891
40 Ibid

3

'The Wage that Never Rises' 1906-1914

Don't think of the Empire on which the sun never sets, think of the wage that never rises. *Mary Macarthur.*

IN 1906 Mary Macarthur formed the National Federation of Women Workers which, during its short existence from 1906 to 1920, when it merged with the General Workers Union, organized more women, fought more strikes and did more to establish women trade unionists than any other organization. Much of its achievement was due to the clear-sighted and determined leadership of Mary Macarthur. In 1903 Mary Macarthur came to London to become secretary of the Women's Trade Union League. Unlike most of her predecessors in the league she came to her job, although only 23 years old, with experience of trade unionism and the labour movement. Her father ran a successful draper's store in Ayr and Mary worked for her father as a bookkeeper and also did a little 'freelance' journalism. Her first direct contact with trade unionism occurred when she went to a meeting of the shop assistants union to cover it for a Conservative local Scottish newspaper. That meeting was a turning point in her life. 'I went to a meeting in Ayr to write a skit on the proceedings, going to scoff, I remained to pray. I became impressed with the truth and meaning of the Labour movement.'[1] She not only remained in the labour movement, but until her early death in 1921 continued to make a remarkable contribution. Following that meeting in Ayr she joined the shop assistants union and in 1902 became the only lady president of a branch in Scotland and was elected president of the Scottish National District Council. At that period, too, she became involved with the Independent Labour Party. At the annual conference of the union in 1902 Mary Macarthur met Margaret Bondfield, who had also been active in the south as an organizer for the shop assistants union. This contact gave Mary the encouragement to move to London, where she took the job of secretary of the Women's Trade Union League. As secretary she immediately threw her energy into getting the league properly organized and its finances set straight.

During this period Mary Macarthur became increasingly convinced that a union was needed for women who were working in unorganized trades or who were not accepted into membership of the relevant male unions. The National Federation of Women Workers was modelled on the type of general labour union which had been first formed in the early 1890s, with low subscriptions, a strike fund and membership open to unskilled workers in any industry. Mary Macarthur believed that women workers, some of whom had started small organizations in different industries around the country, needed the strength of one united body. She regarded the formation of a separate women's union as a necessity of the time, not as a matter of feminist principle. Since many unions for male workers either excluded women or did not attempt to organize women, particularly in areas of predominantly 'women's work', a separate women's union was the only organization to which many women could belong.

Close contact was maintained between the older body, the league, and the newly formed National Federation of Women Workers. Three members of the league were elected to serve as advisory members of the executive committee of the Federation. Mary Macarthur was the first president of the federation, but in 1908 she changed her position to become general secretary and Gertrude Tuckwell, who had been honorary secretary of the league became president. Despite the involvement of leaders in both organizations, the federation was a very different body from the league. The league continued to function as a TUC for unions with women members. Its aims at this period were organization, legislation and social work – including the arrangement of 'entertainments and weekly club nights and social evenings for members and their friends'.[2] 1906 also marked the death of Lady Dilke whose personality had dominated the League since the death of Emma Paterson. In recognition of the contribution she had made to the trades union movement a memorial fund was launched to which over 130 unions donated money.

The federation, on the other hand, was a union rooted in the ideas and militancy of the early general labour unions. In its

struggle to improve wages and conditions, it usually found that
the strike was the only weapon at its disposal. Its record between
1906 and 1914 was largely one of strikes. In 1920, shortly before
the federation merged with the General Workers Union, J. J.
Mallon wrote his memories of the federation and his early
memories were 'memories of strikes'.

> The Federation, in its early years, was weak and poor enough to
> be audacious with a light heart. It had other reasons for
> audacity. One reason was the employers would not take it
> seriously. A Trade Union of men moved them to anger. A Trade
> Union of women moved them only to mirth. The Organisers of
> the Federation were laughed at as often as rebuffed. A strike was
> often the only demonstration that the Federation could give of
> its power and resolution.[3]

'The Federation,' Mallon remarked 'kept strikes in being for
weeks and months entirely at public expense'.[4] The weakness
and poverty of the league did not, as Mallon pointed out, inhibit
the federation from using the one strength they had – the with-
drawal of their members' labour.

The federation had as its driving force the leadership of Mary
Macarthur who had a clear understanding of the problems facing
the organization of women workers and a firm belief in women's
trade unionism. Her analysis of the problems of organizing
women, perhaps more than any other, touched the central core
of the problem.

> There is no inherent sex incapacity to recognise the necessity for
> corporate action. The probability of marriage is not the insur-
> mountable obstacle we are often led to believe it is. One recog-
> nises, of course, that lack of permanence in women's employments
> militates against organisation, because it discourages technical
> instruction and lowers the standard of work. The lack of perman-
> ence, however, from other causes affects men in the same ways.
> The real difficulties may be classified in two ways : first, the
> low standard of living may be stated to be at once the cause
> and consequence of women's lack of organisation. This sounds
> paradoxical, but it is nevertheless true that while women are
> badly paid because of their unorganised condition they may be
> unorganised mainly because they are badly paid. . . .
> This brings me to my second difficulty which is found chiefly

among higher grades. It is a narrow class prejudice which causes
the semi-professional class of workers to look askance upon anything in the nature of trade unionism.[5]

In the years immediately following 1906 Mary Macarthur and
the federation fought a battle on two fronts. They fought to get
women organized and to encourage membership in the federation, but they also fought to get legislation passed fixing minimum
wages for women working in the worst sweated trades. A report
on the sweating system published in 1890 by a select committee
of the House of Lords provided the initial stimulus for the campaign. The select committee, whilst evading a precise definition
of sweating, listed its evils and stressed that 'these evils can
hardly be exaggerated'. They found that sweated work was
characterized by earnings so low that they were 'barely sufficient
to sustain existence', hours of labour so long they made 'the lives
of the workers periods of almost ceaseless toil' and sanitary conditions at the workplaces so bad they were 'not only injurious to
the health of the persons employed but are dangerous to the
public'. They recognized that these conditions did not just
apply in so called 'sweat shops' and amongst homeworkers, but
also 'in the main, to unskilled or only partially skilled workers'.
Since almost all women workers were in those categories the
characteristics of sweating applied to almost all women workers.
They also commented on the particular exploitation of married
women homeworkers who, 'working at unskilled labour in their
homes, in the intervals of attendance on their domestic duties and
not wholly supporting themselves, can afford to work at what
would be starvation wages to unmarried women'.[6] The select
committee, like so many before and after them, accepted the
idea that married women workers could 'afford' to work at
sweated rates. They failed to realize that married women with
dependent children had to take the work they could get. Their
work far from being something done 'in the intervals of attendance on their domestic duties', dominated their life.

We have heard of the one room dedicated to all purposes of life –
workshop, sleeping room, kitchen, children's nursery, hospital,
and, as the Factory Inspectors tell us, often mortuary as well. In
this one room all the members of the family work – the children
on their return from school working through meal hours, 'play-

hours' and the hours which should be given to sleeping; the sick and the old, the idiot and the unfit, all pressed into the service to earn the means for bare subsistence, on work, paid, perhaps, at the rate of $1\frac{1}{2}$d. an hour.'[7]

One can only estimate the amount of homework done by married women. At the beginning of this century the numbers of married women going out to work was very small, about 13% of all adult women (compared to 25% in 1851); the number of married working-class women who took in work at home was probably quite considerable. Besides the kind of sweated home-work described in the select committee report – chain-making lace-making, box-making, carding – many married women took in laundry, sewing, mending, babies, and children.

Although sweated conditions applied to most unskilled workers including many girl shop assistants and clerks, the homeworkers were the most exploited and the most in need of the protection of trade union organization. But their isolation, their low wages (which kept them deprived, oppressed and almost continually at work) and their fear that any action would lose them their small earnings all militated against organization. It is not surprising that trade unionists looked to the government to legislate for the fixing of minimum wages for workers in sweated trades as the means of affording them at least minimal protection. In the early years of the 20th century the campaign for fixing minimum wages in sweated trades gathered momentum. Women like Mary Macarthur and Gertrude Tuckwell campaigned tirelessly and gained considerable liberal support. An Anti-Sweating League was formed. In 1906 the *Daily News* mounted a 'Sweated Industries Exhibition' at the Queens Hall with exhibits of the products of sweated labour and of sweated workers working. Each stall listed the rates of pay, the hours of work, the overheads to the worker and the sale price of the article. In 1908 Edward Cadbury and George Shann published a study called 'Sweating',[8] the Women's Industrial Council published a pamphlet on 'Home Industries of Women in London'[9] and the liberal press gave the campaign sympathetic coverage. An element of liberalism even entered the magistrates courts. A woman charged with attempted suicide was 'sympathetically discharged' from a Westminster police court in 1909 by a magistrate who, having heard evidence of her long hours of work and low pay, remarked that, 'it was obvious it meant starvation'.[10]

The campaign bore fruit. In 1909 the Liberal government passed the Trade Boards Act. It was modelled on a piece of legislation passed in Victoria, Australia, in the 1890s, which had established trade boards to fix minimum wages in certain trades. The first four trades to be scheduled under the British act were chain-making, box-making, lace-making and finishing, and the making of ready-made clothing. The boards formed for each of these industries were to consist of representatives from employers, employees and the government. In 1910 the first board was established to fix the rates in the chain-making trade, of which the select committee had commented that nowhere was 'so much poverty found combined with such severe work and so many hardships'.[11] The board agreed on a minimum wage of $2\frac{1}{2}$d. an hour. Low as this was, for most women it meant a 100% rise. Their wages had been 4s.–6s. for a 50–58 hour week. The new rates would give them an average of at least 10s.–11s. a week for a 55-hour week. The federation and the workers' representatives on the board agreed to accept this figure as a basis on which they could improve. This list of rates became known as the White List.

Some employers agreed to pay the new rates immediately, but many took refuge in a clause which allowed them six months before they were legally compelled to pay them. The representatives of the workers were concerned that employers might use the six months' period at the old rate to stockpile goods made at the old rates, thus leaving women with a period of little or no work when the new rates were enforced. Some of the employers had persuaded their employees to sign a document agreeing to the old rates for six months. Many women obviously did not understand what they were signing and some signed with a cross.

It was into this confused situation that Mary Macarthur, who was a representative on the workers' side of the board, moved in to demand the immediate implementation of the White List rates. A mass meeting was called in August 1910, at which the women resolved not to accept work except at the new rates. Women who had signed agreements to work at the old rate tore them up and the 'strike' of chain-makers in Cradley Heath began. To organize the women and maintain solidarity in their resolution was a mammoth job, since the women were isolated, spread over a relatively large area and, some of them, illiterate. At the outset of the strike only about one-quarter of the women were organized in the Chain-Makers Association. Despite the odds Mary Macarthur and the federation were determined that the strike should be won for the women. It was a crucial test case on which the future of trade boards and their effectiveness to fix minimum wages rested.

The Chain-Makers Association and the federation agreed that all women who could not get work at the new rates of pay, whether they were members of the union or not, would receive strike pay of 4s. a week. This and the militancy of the women was the cornerstone of the success of the strike. The association took on the job of organizing the women in Cradley Heath. Besides distributing the strike pay, it organized marches, demonstrations and deputations to seek support from other unions and trades councils. Not surprisingly chains became the symbol of the strike. Mary Macarthur and Gertrude Tuckwell threw their energies into raising funds for the strikers. They not only got substantial support from the Anti-Sweating League and the Women's Trade Union League, but, by launching a publicity campaign in the national and local press, raised donations from a wide variety of sources in and out of the labour movement. Support for the women even came in the form of prayers, backed by appeals for donations to the strike fund. The plight of the women chain-makers moved the *Christian Commonwealth Paper* to pray for solidarity and victory for women.

> Give them grace to cherish under the new surroundings the old sweetness and gentleness of womanhood, and in the rough mingling of life to keep the purity of their hearts and lives untarnished. Save them from the terrors of utter want. Teach them to stand by their sisters loyally, that by united action they may better their common lot.[12]

At the beginning of September, with 700 women refusing to take work at the old rate, a meeting was convened, under the auspices of the board of trade, between the Chain Manufacturers Association and the workers' leaders. In the meeting the unions agreed with the Chain Manufacturers Association that employers who were members of the association would pay the new White List rates from the day of the agreement and that the unions would black non-associated employers who continued to offer only the old rates. The union also promised its members 'that all the chain-makers whether members of the union or not shall be paid the minimum sum of 4s. per week whilst out of employment owing to their inability to obtain work except at less than the minimum rate'.[13] This agreement was put to a mass meeting of the women and accepted, leaving at least 500 women on strike unable to get work at the new rates.

By mid-September about 60% of the employers had agreed to the White List. The blacking of non-associated employees remained solid. A delegation of women went to the TUC conference carrying their chains and they pleaded with the delegates 'to help us get two-pence-halfpenny an hour for making these. We mean to fight for it. We shall succeed if you help us.' The congress apparently heartily shouted 'We will'.[14] The chairman ruled that it would be 'undignified' to take a collection for the chain-makers there and then, but a collection was taken before the congress adjourned. The strike continued until mid-October, ten weeks in all. By that time virtually all the employers had been forced to sign the White List. The Chain-Makers Association with the help of the federation, had managed to pay all those members and non-members who had not been able to get work at the new rates. Figures for the final total of the strike fund vary, but a sum close to £4,000 was recorded as collected. The Chain-Makers Association swelled in membership to 1,700 and although after the strike many members fell off, continued for a period to remain a strong union. Two years later it managed to increase the minimum rate from $2\frac{1}{2}$d. an hour to $2\frac{3}{4}$d. an hour.

Other workers in Cradley Heath were encouraged by the success of the chain-makers. The Cradley Heath hollow-ware workers, men and women, both struck in 1912. The men demanded a 10% increase.

> Twelve of the forty-five firms conceded their terms at once, leaving 600 men on strike. As a result, many women workers were asked to do men's work and there seemed a likelihood that the employers would try to use women's labour to defeat men.

> We [the Federation] decided therefore, that we should call the
> women out to demand the 10s. minimum for a 54hr. week, and
> at the same time support the men in their demands. All the
> women called out received strike benefit.[15]

The women formed a branch of the federation. They successfully gained their demand of a minimum wage of 10s. a week
and the men's strike was not broken by women blacklegs.

As the leaders of the federation believed, the victory at
Cradley Heath influenced the fixing of minimum wages in the
other three scheduled trades without recourse to strike action.
In lace-making the average weekly earnings of the women
workers was raised from 7s.–8s. to 11s. 11d.; in paper-box-
making from 8s. 5d. to 13s.; and in wholesale and bespoke
tailoring from 8s. to 14s. 1d. The new rates were still all below
the 15s. a week regarded as a minimum subsistence wage, but
they were a great improvement.

In the decade before World War I, prices rose faster than
wages, so that most workers suffered an appreciable reduction in
their standard of living. Strike action as a way of arresting this
decline was used successfully by many trade unions and many
women workers saw it as a way to improving their wages. Mary
Macarthur believed that industrial unrest among women workers
should be utilized and given direction. 'A strike of unorganized
workers', she wrote, 'should always be utilised to form a trade
union amongst them. In such cases one is frequently able to
point out that had an organisation existed the strike in all
probability would not have occurred, because the employer
would not so confidently have ventured to assail the rights of
trade union workers.'[16] The history of the federation between
1909 and 1914 was not one only of strikes, but also of growing
membership. Between 1906 and 1914 the membership of the
federation grew from 2,000 members at the end of its first year
to 20,000 members in 1914.

A typical example of the federation's capitalizing on a strike
to organize women occurred at the Corruganza works in London
in 1908. The women struck in protest against wage cuts. Once
on strike, they found themselves floundering from their lack of
trade union organization, strike pay and experience of negotiations. Mary Macarthur held a mass meeting to hear the griev-

ances of the strikers and to form a strike committee. J. J. Mallon attended the meeting and later described the militancy and solidarity of the women.

> One of the most effective was a strong dark-browned girl whom the employer had slightenly dubbed 'the Battersea Bruiser' and who is reputed to be an expert at fisticuffs. 'Perhaps', she said after several breakdowns, 'Perhaps I AM a bruiser. There may be some in the crowd as could give me a hidin' though,' rolling a critical eye over the assembly, 'I don't think there is. But don't 'e employ me because I'm a bit big?' Ow could I 'andle 'is bloomin' machine if I weren't a bruiser? 'As any other woman ever 'andled it?' 'No Lizzie' cried the Chorus.

Another speaker got up.

> I'm an orphan . . . But I've kept strite, and, please Gawd, I'll keep strite till I die'. 'Never mind Bessie' said a chum consolingly ' 'ell ev a bad time sum day'. 'Gawd's slow but sure' was the comment of another striker.[17]

The strike was successful except for the dismissal of a woman forewoman whose re-instatement the union failed to negotiate.

The wave of industrial unrest which swept across the country in 1910 and 1911 affected women in all parts of the country, but particularly those in the East End and South of London. Like a chain reaction, in the hot summer of 1911 women in London, jam and pickle workers, rag-pickers, biscuit-makers, bottle-washers, tin-box makers, cocoa-makers, distillery workers – all sweated-factory workers earning between 5s. and 10s. a week – came out on strike for wage increases. Mostly they were success- ful in getting rises of between 1s. and 4s.; in many places branches of the federation were formed and union recognition gained. In all the strikes the league sent an organizer to help the federation. Enrolling members to the federation, forming strike committees, launching a strike fund, negotiating with the em- ployers and trying to gain recognition for the union were the main tasks. The federation also worked with other trade unions. The Millwall strike during that summer was an example of co-operation between men and women workers and between the federation, the National Union of Gasworkers and the General Labourers' Union. About fifty women struck against the intro- duction of young girls at low rates to operate machines usually operated by adult women. 1,200 women, men, girls and boys came out in support of their claim. All the workers put up a united front and the women not only won their demand, but a general wage increase of between 10% and 25% was also won. About 960 women were enrolled by the federation.

Solidarity between men and women workers was not always achieved. In a strike at the Idris factory in St Pancras in 1911, although the women strikers received support from some men, male blacklegs broke the strike. The trouble had started the previous year when the women, organized by the federation, resisted two threatened wage cuts. The management then tried to make deductions from some of the women's wages to pay for the improved sanitary facilities which the union had made the management install. The federation managed to get the deductions refunded, but the management, still determined to break the union, dismissed a woman named Mrs Lowin who was the leader of the union at the factory. The women walked out, claiming that it was a case of victimization. The management claimed that Mrs Lowin had been three minutes late for work, which they thought just cause for dismissing a widow with two children to support who had worked for them for more than fourteen years. A strike fund was set up and the girls immediately set about picketing the building, organizing demonstrations and chanting, 'only nine bob for a most unpleasant job'.[18] The employees of the printing works next to the Idris factory agreed to pay a levy of 6d. a week into the strike fund and some of the car men at the Idris factory agreed to a levy of 3d. a week. But not all men displayed such solidarity. The management brought in men and boys to do the women's jobs and claimed that they were much more efficient. Those blacklegs broke the strike. Mrs Lowin was not reinstated and many other women found that they had to find work elsewhere. This strike was not only a case of division between some men and women workers; it showed how determined management was to break the newly formed women's union.

Reading accounts and records of these and other strikes of the period, one gets the feeling of a sudden welling-up of confidence among women workers. They marched in their Sunday-best, picketed, organized and raised funds with gusto. Women like

Mary Macarthur, Gertrude Tuckwell and Susan Lawrence gave many women their first experience of leadership and organization. It was an important experience. The strike at Murrays Confectionery factory by 300 women in 1911 was a strike in which the confidence and exuberance of the women was reflected in many press reports. It was quickly dubbed the strike of Murrays White Mice, since the women were often covered with a fine white dust when they walked home from work. The women demanded the abolition of fines and a tea break. A mass meeting on Clerkenwell Green was addressed by Mary Macarthur. A union was formed and a strike fund started. The federation helped to formulate a claim which not only set out the initial demand of the strikers, but demanded a wage increase. Two weeks later the management moved from rejecting the claim completely to agreeing to arbitration. With that agreement the women voted to return to work.

In the course of the strike women organized meals for the strikers; an anonymous crate of fish was sent to help feed them. The Peel Male Choir and Band gave a concert on Clerkenwell Green to raise money. On one glorious day, the pickets managed to capture a convoy of food which was being taken to some women blacklegs. Having captured it, the strikers promptly ate it and then immortalized their victory in a strike song.

> Murrays White Mice, See How they fight,
> They collared the fish, the cheese and the bread,
> 'Twas meant for the blacklegs, they ate it instead,
> And the boss was so wild he stood on his head.[19]

* * *

In 1906 the female membership of all trade unions was 166,803; by 1914 it had risen to 357,956. The textile unions in 1914 accounted for over two-thirds of all organized women. The clothing, general, distributive and clerical unions accounted for almost all of the remainder of organized women. This growth in membership was particularly stimulated by the 1911 Insurance Act. The act was an important piece of legislation for workers in many ways. Most important, it introduced health and unemployment insurance schemes for a large proportion of workers. To implement the system, Lloyd George declared that Friendly

Societies and trade unions should be allowed to be 'approved societies' for the operation of the state insurance system. Undoubtedly this was one of the major causes of the increase in trade union membership between 1911 and 1913. In 1911 there were 1,661,000 trade union members affiliated to the TUC, an increase of 10% since 1901. In 1913 membership had jumped to 2,682,000 an increase of about 60%. Along with other unions the federation took infinite pains to explain the state insurance system to women and to encourage them to join the federation or an appropriate union if only, in the first instance, to be covered by sickness and unemployment insurance.

During this period 1906-1914, besides the federation, and a few other separate unions for women workers, the organization of women fell into four main groups. First came the textile unions and the National Union of Boot and Shoe Operatives, which had organized substantial numbers of women for decades and were, in many senses, a stage in advance of the other unions. Although they continued to recruit, questions concerning the under-representation of women in the textile unions and the neglect of the interests of women in the National Union of Boot and Shoe Operatives were the main concerns. The second group, the clothing, distributive and general unions, was concerned with the basic problem of recruitment and organization. In this group the tensions between men and women workers were considerably less than in the craft unions, but their organizational problems were very great, particularly in the distributive trades and domestic service. The latter, after industrial employment, was the largest employer of female labour before 1914. The emergent white collar unions formed the third group, they took a variety of attitudes towards the recruitment of women and the claims of women workers. Since many women white collar workers were of middle-class background, class attitudes were a great hindrance to organization. Finally, there were the craft unions, which continued to debate the problem of 'female labour'. Those who wished to see women eliminated from the trades were still active, along with those who thought women ought to be organized separately, but some began to argue for changing their rule books to admit women.

The textile unions accounted for the most dramatic increase in women members and catered overall for the vast majority of organized women workers. Their agreements continued to be based on 'the rate for the job' regardless of sex, thus eliminating the central cause of tension and fear in other industries. Although equal pay technically existed, the better-paid jobs were male preserves and jealously guarded, whilst women, numerically the greatest proportion of the workforce, remained in the lower paid less skilled jobs. The fact that the workforce was so predominantly female and that the textile industry slipped from its dominant position in the economy contributed to the erosion both of the comparative standard of living of textile workers and of their union strength. 19th-century sectionalism between the various textile unions continued despite amalgamations in some areas and was another contributory factor to the weakening of the textile unions. Although women formed by far the largest section of the textile unions, they took little part in their management. In the older cotton unions women had never been leaders, and as their membership increased the unions continued to be administered almost entirely by men. The Northern Counties Weavers' Amalgamation, although its membership was at least two-thirds women, had no women at the executive level. It was the same in most other cotton unions. Men made the familiar complaint that women were not interested in union affairs, even though women had a considerable history of shop floor militancy. On the other hand, there was hostility from men to the intrusion of potentially active women into their union 'club' meetings. In 1903 the all-women Salford Power Loom Weavers Association tried to join the larger Northern Counties Weavers Association. They were turned down on the grounds that their subscriptions were a mere 2d. a week, whereas the Northern Counties Weavers Association had a minimum of 3d. a week and for that mere 2d. a week paid 'sick pay', a benefit most unions did not have. By 1908 the women's union had grown to a membership of 1,200; this time the Northern Counties Weavers' Association approached the women. The women had the confidence of their strength and demanded not only local autonomy for their members, but also the right to appoint a woman secretary and a woman representative to the executive of the Northern Counties Executive Committee. Far from conceding the women's demands, the Association decided to organize women themselves in the Salford area, poaching some women members from the Salford Power Loom Weavers Association. They succeeded in causing a serious reduction both in the number of women weavers organized in that area and also in the number of women in leadership positions.

In the woollen section of the textile industry, where women had in some cases been founder members of unions, the early 20th century saw a decrease of women in executive positions in unions. By 1918, in the General Union of Textile Workers, there were three women on the executive committee and two women organizers. For the time that was fairly remarkable, but, given the proportion of women members and their role in the founding of the different branches of the union, it represented a marked decline, although women continued to be well represented at branch level.

In contrast to the cotton and woollen unions, the Dundee Jute and Flax Workers Union, which after several false starts was finally established in 1906, had a constitution in which representation on the executive by men and women was in direct proportion to the number of men and women members. The Dundee and District Mill and Factory Operatives were the only mixed trade union of the period which had 50% or more women on their executives. The textile unions generally were open to male and female members, did not differentiate between the two for purposes of subscriptions and benefits and did not have separate female sections, rules or rates. Most had a sliding scale of subscriptions. Members contributed according to earnings, which meant their women contributed the lower rates.

The problems of the National Union of Boot and Shoe Operatives, which, after the textile unions, had the longest history of organizing women in a mixed union, were related directly to the under-representation of women and its consequence – the failure to act in their interests. Almost twenty years after women had been admitted to the union, they began to agitate. Women members were getting much less for their subscriptions than men. By 1904 the union had negotiated fixed minimum rates for men, but not women. That same year the first two women delegates, representing the Leicester Women's Branch, attended the union's annual conference, and in response to their presence the president stated that 'as women are now becoming well organised there ought to be some minimum wage for adult women as well as adult men. . . . At the present time the wages women receive is a scandal, and something ought certainly to be done to improve their conditions. We ought to try to establish a minimum wage of 20s. a week for all adult females.'[20] By 1908 the union had still not negotiated minimum rates for women and the women were getting restless. The Women's Leicester Branch had grown to a membership of 1,213 and since 1906 had been officered by women; Lizzie Wilson was elected secretary.

In 1908 this issue of fixing minimum rates for women was discussed at the annual conference. A resolution was passed that women members be recognized on the board of arbitration – a recognition which in the preceding year they had failed to gain because the employers had refused to recognize that the union acted for women. Despite the resolution no progress was made in getting recognition or in fixing rates. The women were angry and were further incensed when the union raised its subscription by 1d. They objected that it was unfair for them to pay the same fee as the men since they did not get the same service. Finally, in 1910, a meeting was held between the union and the board of arbitration at which the union settled for shop statements instead of a uniform agreement to cover all rates. This outraged Lizzie Wilson. On the union's council (of which she was the first woman member) she attacked the president 'the now venerable Freak in terms so unrestrained as to shock all but her followers.' Fox, the historian of the National Union of Boot and Shoe Operatives, had little sympathy with Lizzie Wilson. Whilst conceding that the women had a justifiable claim, he thought that she was tainted with the fanatical ideas of the suffragettes, that she had secured her place on the council 'by what was almost certainly a manipulated vote on the part of her Branch' and that she made the issue a sex war and not a union war.[21]

When the union failed to secure a uniform agreement for women, Lizzie Wilson by-passed the arbitrator and called in Margaret Bondfield to negotiate on behalf of the women, claiming that 'a man is not fit to arbitrate on a woman's cause'. She also stated that the council of the union was totally incapable 'of dealing with the needs of members of the present day, especially women'.[22] Whilst this dispute between men and women members of the union was continuing, a dispute occurred in a firm in Wigston, Leicestershire. The employers changed the system in the closing room to the disadvantage of the women. Lizzie Wilson instructed the women to restrict their output, which caused the men to go on short time. The men did nothing to support the women, but merely claimed dispute pay from the union to compensate for their loss of earnings. Things came to a head when the firm made a claim on the guarantee fund, asserting that women members had violated the terms of settlement between the employers and the union. Their claim was successful and the union was fined £200. Since the women had gained nothing out of the terms of settlement, they asked Margaret Bondfield to negotiate an agreement for them and threatened to form a breakaway union. The threat was made in a letter published by the *Leicester Daily Post,* signed by 'Portia' (Lizzie Wilson). She urged that 'considering the very unfair manner in which the women have been treated, there is only one honourable course for them to pursue, and that is to sever their connection with the Union . . . and immediately form the British National Union of Women Shoe Operatives'.[23] The union replied by suspending her. Undaunted, she formed a separate union, the Independent National Union of Women Boot and Shoe Workers. She also continued to attack the National Union of Boot and Shoe Operatives through the pages of the Leicester press.

> 'Might I suggest', Portia wrote, after complaining that if the same set of conditions had occurred in a men's branch of the union the council would not have dared to suspend any members, 'that the real reason underlying all this was that Miss Wilson was not wanted on the Council and therefore must be got rid of. She is too energetic to suit the old reactionary members who compose the Council (should I say Cabinet?)'.[24]

The majority, about 600, of the members of the Leicester Women's Branch, defected to the independent union. Even Fox remarked that 'the extent of the defections indicates that resentment among the women was widespread and was not confined to a few fanatics'.[25] The Independent successfully negotiated rates for its members. It also gave better terms to women members, including benefits until the age of fifty, instead of forty as previously. It survived until the mid-1930s, although the National Union of Boot and Shoe Operatives tried hard to bring the defectors back into the fold. Soon after the breakaway, Mary Bell, who had remained in the Leicester Women's Branch, set about rebuilding it. She had the support of such women as Mary Macarthur, who wrote to the secessionists saying that to form a separate union was to be 'deprecated'. More important the National Union of Boot and Shoe Operatives, to forestall the loss of more women members, began to negotiate and fix minimum rates for them. This they first achieved in certain areas; then in 1914 the National Union negotiated a national agreement, at that time an almost revolutionary achievement. This agreement included women, whose minimum rate was raised, on average, by 3s. The women's breakaway union had also the effect of pressurizing the national union into proposing the appointment of a woman organizer at the 1914 conference. Mary Bell opposed the suggestion, on the ground that 'a permanent woman organiser would be inadvisable, but that the work ought to be taken up by women in the branches'.[26]

The report of the conference in the *Daily Citizen* commented that

> later, it was discovered that according to the rules of the Union no difference could be made in elections between men and women members, and if four women were nominated for the new posts of organisers and secured a majority over the men candidates, the women would be elected. Conference took no steps to deal with the problem, the delegates appearing to view with amused unconcern the avenue provided for women.[27]

This 'amused unconcern' of the male members of the national union had allowed the union to be weakened by forcing a breakaway; it was later to allow its union to be weakened further by allowing the employers to use the sexual division of labour which the union upheld, to divide the male and female workers. In the 1920s, Mary Bell found that she had to fight the union over many of the same issues Lizzie Wilson had fought for fifteen years earlier. The battles between men and women members in the National Union of Boot and Shoe Operatives are typical of those fought in many other unions. Lizzie Wilson and Mary Bell were pioneers of the rights of women as trade union members; through them the issues were clearly articulated.

From the outset the general labour unions were open to members of either sex, but in the pre-war period their recruitment of women was relatively small. At the turn of the century several other unions either established themselves with a mixed membership or decided to admit women. These unions, however, accounted for an even smaller number of organized women. Although they accepted women members, they seldom concerned themselves with their problems. They took the view that women could be better controlled in the union than out. Most of them had no women on their executives, no women organizers and only a few at district or branch level. Like all other mixed unions of that period, with a few notable exceptions, they restricted women from holding certain grades and jobs. There were some exceptions. The National Union of Shop Assistants, through their secretary, Margaret Bondfield, pursued a much more positive policy towards the recruitment of women and encouraged their active involvement. Shop assistants, particularly women in the low grades, could certainly claim to be in the sweated category. They worked excessively long hours, often had to 'live in' in overcrowded and insanitary conditions and earned wages which, as Margaret Bondfield remarked, 'were generally despised by the industrial workers who used to say that "counter-jumpers are paid by the year because their wages are too small to divide by the week" '.[28] The union's public campaign to abolish the 'living-in' system was not successful, although it kept the pressure up until 1914. However, it did successfully promote the Shop Hours Act of 1910, by which shop assistants gained one half-day holiday a week and stated meal times.

The nature of their work made shop assistants hard to organize. Domestic servants proved even harder and most attempts to organize them, men and women, met with failure. Another sector that was rapidly growing, clerks and secretaries, was also hard to organize. Like shop assistants and domestic servants they too often worked in small, isolated units in direct relationship to their employers. However, attempts were made to organize women clerks and secretaries, particularly those employed in the government sector – cheap, docile, middle-class labour. The largest group of women government clerks were those employed by the Post Office. In 1902 the Women's Trade Union League organized some of the women (they later joined the Postal, Telegraph Clerks Association) and in 1909, Mary Macarthur took issue with the government over women's right to a living wage, not the 'pocket money' wage which the government paid. The government claimed that women were supported mainly by their families, not their earnings. But in 1911 there were in Great Britain 1,327,000 more women than men, so that there was a large number of single adult women dependent on their earnings to support themselves. There were also women whose husbands or families for one reason or another could not support them. In 1909 the government announced increases for Post Office workers, but the new scale of wages gave no increases to women. Mary Macarthur attacked the new rates, which fixed women's pay at 2¾d. an hour and labelled it the 'Government Hall-Mark of Sweating'. The government justified the rates on the grounds that they prevented 'the exploitation of female labour' and saved contractors from 'the temptation of employing sweated labour'.[29] It went even further and claimed that, since girls were not 'breadwinners in the ordinary sense of the term', many of them would be happy to earn less a week than the 13s. 6d. established by the new rates. In such cases, the government argued, 'to compel a girl to earn 13s. 6d. savours of benevolent despotism'.[30] 'Surely,' Mary Macarthur remarked 'this is the last word in Official futility.'

Another union which recruited women clerical workers in the pre-war period was the National Union of Clerks. It stood out against the attitudes of almost every other union towards women workers. Formed in the early 1890s, it found itself faced with the same problem as other unions – that of women being employed at lower rates for the same work to undercut men. The private employers, like the government, justified the practice on the grounds that female clerical workers only earned a secondary wage, just as they used the fact that some girls were not wholly dependent on their wages to justify the generally low pay to all women workers. The National Union of Clerks became increasingly concerned about the low rates of pay to women and their eroding effect on the men's rates. Its approach to the problem was radical. In 1909 an organizer of the union wrote to the *Evening News*: 'We are not against female labour, we recognise their "right to labour" but we are against sweating and cheap labour. . . . We stand for equal pay for equal work. We want women to join our ranks and demand our minimum wage . . . 35s. a week for all competent clerks and 27s. 6d. in the rural districts.'[31] The union elaborated its attitude in 1911, when the secretary, Mr Elvin, speaking on the problem of low paid female clerks said that

> the suggestion has been made to us that we should treat the girl clerk as an absolute enemy – in other words should try to drive her out of the market – but in view of the necessity which many women are under of earning their own livelihood this attitude would be unjust. The union has adopted the saner attitude of insisting upon equal recognition of men and women without sex distinction and demanding payment should be according to capacity.[32]

No other mixed union of the period had such a sound and clear policy towards women. By recognizing women's 'right to work', the need for women to work and the right of women to complete equality, they avoided the pitfalls which most men trade unionists continually created for themselves. Besides fighting for the principle of equal pay for equal work and for a general improvement of wages, the National Union of Clerks also conducted a campaign against the appalling conditions in which many clerical workers had to work. Basement offices in the city of London were typical. They were sometimes infested with rats. They were badly lit, airless in summer, cold in winter, and often overcrowded. In 1913 the union organized a series of marches in London to bring the bad conditions to public attention. It hoped to force the government to include offices under the Factory and Workshop Act. Women clerical workers in the demonstration wore masks, whether to avoid identification and victimization or for dramatic effect is not recorded.

Another area of growing employment for middle-class women was the teaching profession. The Forster Education Act of 1870 empowered local authorities to set up school boards to ensure that education was available for all, whether in private or state schools. Women were heavily employed to staff the growing number of state elementary schools. In the 1890s the National Union of Teachers accepted both men and women elementary teachers into membership; however, Miss Lane, an active member, found out that women members received lower benefits than men, even though they paid the same subscriptions. She campaigned against this and in 1903 won for women equal benefits for equal subscriptions. Another member, Mr Tate, impressed by this campaign moved a motion for the annual conference at his local branch calling for equal pay. The motion was passed unanimously, but it was dropped from the minutes. When Tate pressed the secretary on the matter, he was told that the secretary had thought it 'only a clever bit of bunkum to get women to join the Association'.[33] Mr Tate did not rest with that reply. Despite hostility and derision, he formed an Equal Pay League in 1904. Though it added to its title 'and the National Federation of Women Teachers', the league operated merely as a pressure group within the NUT, not as a separate union. Besides calling for equal pay, it demanded equal government grants per head to girls' and infants' schools and greater representation of women in the NUT, especially on the executive.

Largely because of the reception it received from the men members of the union, the Equal Pay League broke away to become a separate organisation called simply the National Union of Women Teachers. A description by Miss Lane of a meeting in 1907, at which Miss Phipps tried to move a motion for equal pay indicates the hostility which the women's claim met.

Miss Lightman was howled down, and for some time neither she nor I, who attempted to second from the body of the Hall, could be heard. Whistles were blown, feet stamped, comic songs were sung by organised opposition, and finally the meeting had to be adjourned, and broke up in disorder. This conduct was repeated at subsequent meetings, at one of which Mr Mark Wilks (who in later years suffered a term of imprisonment for a technical breach of the law owing to his support of women's freedom), attempting to speak in favour of the motion, was attacked and pulled off the platform.[34]

Other tactics, less violent but equally hostile, were used to ensure that equal-pay motions were not discussed. Frequently they were placed at the end of the list of motions and frequently the meeting never had time to discuss them.

In 1910, the Federation of Women Teachers held its first annual conference, quite separately from the NUT. In 1911, with the resignation of Mr Tate, who for some ten years had campaigned tirelessly for women, the honorary secretaryship of the federation (at his suggestion) went to a woman. The federation thus became an all-women organization. For a period it continued to support the mixed NUT, but the hostility which the women received, when they tried to table motions demanding women's suffrage, was even greater and more determined than that which the men had mustered against equal pay. At one meeting, when a male delegate tried to move a motion calling for adult suffrage,

> hundreds of men, massed at the back of the hall, prevented Mr Croft from obtaining a hearing. They stamped, howled, hurled insults at the speaker and at suffragists, and utterly refused to allow Mr Croft's speech to proceed. This continued without intermission for thirty minutes at the end of which Mr Croft had to resume his seat. The Motion was lost by 40,653 votes to 12,276.[35]

By 1914 the National Federation of Women Teachers had 58 branches and in the following year they established themselves on their own premises.

The craft unions continued to have no clear policy towards women. The various print unions provide a good example of the tensions between men and women workers. In the printing trades, as in most other skilled trades, women's wages were entirely unregulated and the women unorganized. In 1904 women were admitted to the National Union of Printing and Paper Workers, chiefly because the men saw in the organization of women a way to maintain the sexual division of labour in their industry. But women were not admitted to the National Union of Bookbinding until 1918 after several decades of debate.

The debates on the issue of admitting women brings to light both male attitudes towards women and the way in which employers used women workers to undercut and challenge the skilled men's rates. The National Union of Bookbinders and Machine Rulers convened a special conference in 1901 to consider 'unfair labour', that is women doing men's jobs at rates below the union's rates. At that conference a motion was put forward that 'a vote of the Union be taken to empower the Central Executive to form a Female Section of the Union, and in the event of this resolution being carried the Central Executive shall, at the earliest opportunity ask for suggestions from the branches, from which they shall draft a code of rules and submit (it) to the membership'.[36] The reaction to the motion as well as the voting was almost evenly divided – 11 for and 10 against. One delegate from London complained that 'the women of today are of pushful manners, and displace men in every walk and profession', and another, Mr Dempster from Glasgow, maintained that 'all attempts to organize women would be a miserable failure, and if organized they would be a stumbling block in the long run'. Mr Balsillie from Edinburgh saw the issue much more clearly: 'We are between two alternatives – that we get the girls in our power, or leave them disregarded for employers to use them against us.'[37]

The general membership of the union reversed, again by a very narrow margin, the decision of the executive and women remained excluded. Female labour continued to present a problem to the union. In 1906, it tried to get a national agreement with the employers about the areas in which women should be allowed to be employed. These talks floundered, since the employers claimed that, out of fifty-six jobs, forty-six could be done by women, which was unacceptable to the men of the union. At the 1911 annual conference two more motions were submitted calling for the admission of female members to the union. The second stated 'that in view of the growing menace to our trade in the competition of unorganized female labour, this Council is of the opinion that the time is opportune for the admission of skilled women to our Union'. Both motions were heavily defeated. Dempster, who once again led the opposition, stated that 'female labour is competitive and where female organization exists it will be competitive. The women will fight male labour wherever it is possible.' Another delegate made the classic remark that 'if we organize females we shall recognize their work as legitimate'.[38] Once again, in 1914, a similar motion was brought up at annual conference calling for the organization of women; but this time a new element had entered the debate. Another union, the Cutters Union, had begun to move in and organize women in the bookbinding trade. Mr Milton of Birmingham warned: 'The female workers are being organized, whether we like it or not. The question is settled – they are going to be organized. The Cutters Union have organized the girls and have laid their plans very carefully.' Milton admitted that 'he had been an opponent of the organization of female workers, but they had seen one of the greatest statesmen in Birmingham change his coat and it seemed the best thing for the Bookbinders to do'. Despite Dempster's continued opposition, the conference voted 25 to 10 for a sub-committee 'to consider the advisability of drawing up details of a scheme for the establishment of a women's branch of the National Union'.[39] This process took some time. It was not until 1918 that the rules were finally amended to read: 'For the organizing of all qualified men and women engaged in the trade.'[40] The amendment was carried with only one dissentient.

Denied entrance to the National Union of Bookbinders and Machine Rulers, some women had decided to organize themselves. There was an attempt in the 1880s encouraged and helped by the Women's Trade Union League, to organize women sewers and folders in Manchester, but they failed to establish any permanent organization. A more successful attempt was made in 1896 by Isabel Forsyth, who started the Manchester and Salford Society of Women Employed in Bookbinding and Printing Trades. She herself had started work in a printer's at the age of thirteen earning 3s. 6d. a week. By eighteen she had become a relatively highly paid woman, earning 12s. a week; however, many girls earned only 9s. for a 52½-hour week. The need for organization was obvious. In the first year 135 members were enrolled and, although subscriptions were only 2d. a week, by the end of the year the union had taken in £42 and had a balance of £30. Isabel Forsyth continued working full-time and acting as secretary in her spare time. In 1918 she became the union's first full-time secretary. In the early years the union managed to secure advances in wages of 2s. to 3s. a week for its members. In 1901 Isabel Forsyth appealed to the bookbinders union to advertise in their journal the existence of the womens' union. This the union agreed to do, but couched the appeal in the self-interested phrase, 'in order to safeguard our trade'. In 1908 the union was registered under the Trades Union Act and became affiliated to the Printing and Kindred Trades Federation. It also expanded over the years to organize in other areas, causing 'Manchester and Salford' to be dropped from the name. The Society of Women Employed in the Bookbinding and Printing Trades survived until 1942, when, on the retirement of Isabel Forsyth, the union amalgamated with the National Union of Printing, Bookbinding and Paper Workers. After £1,500 had been put aside for Isabel Forsyth's retirement, the union had funds of £11,677, despite the fact that in support of the General Strike, it had spent £2,394.[41]

In London, bookbinders were mainly organized by the London Society of Machine Rulers. Their solution to the problem of female labour was to exclude women from certain jobs. This policy arose from a committee which had been appointed in the 1890s to inquire into the problem of female labour 'as it was an evil which would sooner or later have to be met'.[42] A report of an executive meeting of the society when a Mr Race was asked to explain why he had accepted the job of foreman at a firm where a female ruler was employed, shows how women were sometimes dealt with. Mr Race defended himself by saying that he had 'accepted the situation "with the determination of displacing the female in question, and he had succeeded in his object the first week he was there". He had given her a job to do "allowing her to do it in her own way, not caring to interfere with her". She had, as he had expected spoilt the job and was given notice to leave. The Chairman commended Race for his diplomacy and discretion in the matter.'[43] When the Machine rulers stopped women from working in certain grades in London, employers merely looked elsewhere for cheap labour. Since the machine rulers were organized only in London they had no control over the sexual division of labour in the provinces, where the National Union of Bookbinders had not yet organized women. London employers had, therefore, merely to send work out of London to have it done more cheaply by women. The

London Society of Machine Rulers learned little from this and continued to oppose organization of women, seeking instead to find 'the best and most effective way of abolishing female labour, or of discouraging it'.[44]

The National Society of Amalgamated Brassworkers and Metal Mechanics provides an example of the extreme lengths to which a craft union would go to defend men against women. The issue of female labour came to the fore at the 1908 conference, when a resolution was passed calling for legislation to prevent the employment of women in metal polishing, turning and screwing. Mary Macarthur, who was present at the conference, opposed the resolution on the grounds that it was 'antediluvian' and 'brazen-faced' and that the way to prevent women from undercutting men's wages was to pay women the same rate for the job. Her suggestion was violently attacked. The *Sunday Chronicle* said of her that she 'apparently believes that what man can do women ought to be able to do. She flouts sex, defies nature and practically returns to the savage theory that woman is admirably fitted for a beast of burden.' The main reason, however, for the attack on the women brassworkers had nothing to do with real concern for them. The reason was that 'there are hundreds of male workers walking the streets unable to find work. A man is paid 32s. to 34s. a week, whereas a woman only receives 10s. to £1 a week piecework and many of them are glad to come away with 8s. a week'.[45]

Mr Davis, secretary of the society, in reporting the conference, also attacked Mary Macarthur and the women workers for being willing to work for 8s. a week. 'I am surprised and disgusted', he said, 'that there should be any women in this country defending the practice of allowing working at a trade that unfitted them as sweethearts and mothers. It is not that employers want to find women work, but because they will work at 8/- per week instead of 38/- which a man would receive.' His speech was greeted 'with peals of laughter and cheers of applause'.[46] At that conference the executive promised to continue to try to get women banned from certain jobs by legislation. As part of the campaign, handbills were printed and distributed around Coventry.

> At *reduced* wages females are doing dirty unhealthy cycle polishing at one of the leading Cycle Manufactories in Coventry.

Parents and friends of females should persuade them not to do this dirty and unhealthy work, as they sacrifice their health, their lives will be shortened and they will receive no more than they would obtain in a cleaner healthier trade.

FEMALES

If you agree with Miss McArthur that females SHOULD do men's work chimney sweeping etc.

DO IT

but not without you have the same price for your labour as men.[47]

Clearly the National Society of Amalgamated Brassworkers and Metal Mechanics did not consider that the bad conditions which harmed women's health would also harm men. The call for equal pay for equal work for chimney sweeping was no doubt added to make the whole claim for equality appear ludicrous. At no other time did the society consider equal pay for equal work; its policy was one of excluding women from any men's jobs.

This policy was clearly outlined to Miss Smyth, who in that same year had begun to organize women brassworkers in Birmingham. She wrote to the National Society, asking for their support and co-operation. Mr Davis, as general secretary, replied that he wished her every success in organizing women who did 'women's work' and agreed that they should receive more money and better treatment. His executive, however, could not sanction women doing men's work. 'I feel quite sure that Miss Tuckwell, and the lady organizers, do not share the views of Miss Macarthur but as she is in your movement it makes it extremely difficult for the members of this Society to assist an organisation when one of the chief representatives advocates that which no man who knows the nature of the employment she advocates can agree to.'[48]

Between 1908 and 1910 Mr Davis campaigned hard to get legislation forbidding the hiring of women for various jobs in the brass trade. He gave evidence to a government committee which was considering the extension of the Factory and Workshop Act to control certain dangerous and unhealthy trades, but failed to get them to recommend the extension of the act to cover women working in the brass trade. He then threw in his weight behind the campaign against sweating in the Birmingham metal trades and tried to get women brassworkers included in an extension of the Trade Boards Act, hoping that the fixing of minimum wages would drive cheap female labour off the market. He continually argued that employers did not want to employ women but that they were forced into doing so because their competitors did. By 1910 his stand modified slightly. Although he continued to press for an amendment to the Factory Act to get women banned from metal polishing, turning and screwing, he accepted an amendment moved by Mary Macarthur, calling for the same rate as men for the same job, with the proviso that a government inquiry should be asked to look into the whole matter. Following this the employers and the brassworkers society came to an agreement that workers in the trade should be graded according to qualifications and capacity. This scheme was put to the members at a mass meeting, who were told by Davis that 'they had received a little encouragement from the employers. One of them who employed about sixty women, confessed he should like to see female labour abolished (Hear Hear). As soon as the present scheme was through they intended to ask the Government to interfere and by Home Office Regulation prevent the disgraceful employment of women in such a black and unhealthy trade as brass polishing.'[49]

The scheme for a graded wage structure was accepted, but the problems of female labour remained unsolved. Not surprisingly, the employers did not abolish female labour; neither did the government ban women from certain jobs on health grounds.

Down to 1914 the trade union movement was divided in its attitude to women workers and divided within itself. The piecemeal development of trade unions in the 19th century had led to a vast number of unions, pursuing their own craft or sectional interests, sometimes within the same industry. There were the general labour unions, open to men and women workers in any industry. They were based on low entry rates, low subscriptions and few benefits except strike pay. There were the separate women's unions, mostly for semi-skilled women workers, and the National Federation of Women Workers, modelled on the general labour unions. In contrast, the craft unions usually had high entry fees, high subscription rates and were restricted to skilled men workers. These unions leant heavily on restrictive practices and arbitration, not confrontation, as a means to protect their members' jobs and rates. Some unions were organized on an industry basis, like the National Union of Boot and Shoe Operatives; although they recruited both men and women they insisted on preserving clear demarcations between skilled, semi-skilled and unskilled workers, men and women. There were the emergent unions for clerical workers, the first trade union organization of the middle or lower middle class. Rarely affiliated to the TUC, they were often more professional associations than trades unions.

Before 1914, however, some trade unionists, especially the syndicatists, had begun to agitate for greater unity and the amalgamation of separate unions into single organizations. The most important step towards such unity was taken in 1914, when the National Union of Railwaymen, the Transport Workers' Federation and the Miners' Federation formed the Triple Alliance. Their aim was to arrange concerted strike effort. The Triple Alliance was not just a sign of the new unionism which opposed the craft union sectionalism; it also represented a shift of power within the TUC, a shift related to changes in the distribution of labour. At the beginning of the 19th century, agriculture and textiles were the main employers of labour; by the beginning of the 20th century, the transport and mining industries had grown enormously. Many industries – the potteries, the food and drink industry, the clothing trade – had grown from small domestic industries to large factory-based ones, dependent on coal and transport. The shift from the domination by the textile and craft unions in the mid-19th century to the Triple Alliance unions in the early 20th century reflected those changes.

Techniques of production were also changing. The streamlining of production led to the increasing division of labour; this process normally eroded the position of the skilled man and created more unskilled and semi-skilled jobs. In some industries, one worker was no longer required to follow through the production of an article from the raw material to the completed product. Tensions between the craft unions and unskilled labour, particularly female labour, arose from the increasing division of labour and the erosion of craft skills. Management was also introducing new techniques – the so-called 'scientific management' which led, inevitably, to tension between employer and employed. The stop-watch was introduced and 'speed up', the bane of all workers on a production line, became one of the new managements' goals. A short article in the *Women's Trades Union Review* in July 1901 showed the more extreme results of 'speed up' on employees. A girl committed suicide after being discharged from a factory. At the inquest the coroner questioned the foreman on the girl's earnings.

'She earned 22s. per week?'

'Yes.'

'How much ought she to have earned?'

'24s.'

'You had an interest in this girl's earnings?'

'Yes. I was paid a commission on her earnings.'

'For slave driving!'[50]

The coroner returned a verdict of suicide, but said that the foreman was morally, if not legally, responsible for the girl's death.

Besides backing demands by women workers for a decent wage, women trade unionists were involved in the wider struggles of the labour movement. Many of the women trade union leaders were closely involved in the Labour Party and the Independent Labour Party. The ability of trade unions to support Labour MPs and the labour party had ended in 1908, when it was ruled in the Osborne Case that trade unions could not use their money for any other purpose than the 'regulating of relations between workmen and masters'. This meant that unions could not use their funds for educational purposes, benefits or for political purposes. It was a major set-back to the trade union movement and the Labour Party. It was only with the passing of the 1913 Trade Union Act that trade unions were allowed to use funds for political purposes. The years 1906–1914 were also a period when the women's fight for the vote, for legal rights and for opportunities to enter the professions was being waged – sometimes violently. The women in the trade union movement supported the socialist campaign for adult suffrage for men and women, as opposed to the Women's Social and Political Union's demand for 'votes for women'. Their journals printed many articles on the demand for adult suffrage.

One journal was *The Woman Worker*, founded in 1908 by Mary Macarthur. It had a newspaper format and sold for 1d. It gave unequivocal support to the Labour Party. In the first editorial Mary Macarthur explained the aims of the journal.

> Knowledge is power, Organisation is power. Knowledge and Organisation mean the right to life, liberty and the pursuit of happiness. Knowledge and organisation mean the opening of the cage door.'[51]

The National Federation of Women Workers was Mary Macarthur's organizational arm and through *The Woman Worker* she hoped to give working women knowledge. She herself resigned from editing the paper after a short period, having decided that her energies were best spent agitating not editing, though she returned to edit it again in 1916. *The Woman Worker* covered many issues. It had a series of articles on full adult suffrage, the Labour Party and socialism. All issues relating to the liberation of women were discussed. Equal pay had become a well entrenched demand; maternity benefit was an important issue; so were the clothes women wore, not from a fashion point of view, but as a way of liberating their bodies and enabling them to work in comfort. There were articles on women workers abroad, one of them an interview with Alexandra Kollontai about the role of women in Russia in 1905–6. Conditions and safety at work, the victimization of girls who did not comply with the sexual advances of foremen, infant mortality, hygiene and nutrition were all covered by the journal. It was designed to inform working class women in a way that the journal of the league had never attempted.

Anyone concerned or involved with women could not but be appalled by the high maternal and infant mortality rates, particularly in the working class. Poverty was one of the main causes. Many working people could not afford to pay the doctor's fees for delivering a baby. The factory act of 1891 had stated that women must not knowingly be employed for four weeks after giving birth. The act fell down in practice on two grounds. It rested on the word 'knowingly' and it was very easy for an employer not to know; more important, it made no financial provision for women during those four weeks. Most women's incomes were too low to allow them to save and those who were either deserted or unmarried mothers had to work in order to support themselves and their child.

A small step forward was taken in the 1911 National Insurance Act, which included a maternity benefit of 39s. for insured workers. A system of local and national government maternity welfare health visitors was also established. Many women felt that the provisions of the 1911 Act did not go nearly far enough. It was, even so, a step forward. The campaign for its extension was led by the Women's Co-operative Guild, supported by other women's groups, in particular the women's trade unions. The guild wanted maternity and pregnancy sickness benefit available to all women under the income-tax limit. They also wanted it to be increased and made payable for three weeks before birth and four weeks after. They demanded more and better women health officers, more women doctors at municipal centres, maternity and infant centres for expectant and nursing mothers, an increase in maternity hospitals, milk depots ensuring safe milk and household helps. They went further and stated that more working women ought to be on local maternity committees and that a Ministry of Health for Maternity and Infant Life, staffed by women, should be established.

The Women's Co-operative Guild was well placed to know the needs of women. It had groups all over the country which held meetings on basic hygiene, nutrition and care for mother and child. It was not just infant mortality that concerned the Guild; it was also the terrible suffering which many women endured in the course of childbirth and pregnancy. To support the campaign the Guild published a small booklet called *Maternity, Letters from Working Women*, a collection of letters written by women on their experiences of childbirth. The picture that emerges of poverty, ignorance and suffering can be captured only by reading the letters. Certain general themes recur. Most complained that they were totally ignorant about sex, conception and childbirth when they were married. They had learnt through bitter experience. A few had husbands who did heavy work around the house, but many husbands were either unhelpful or, after working 10 to 12 hours a day had little time or energy to help. Most of the letters came from women whose husbands earned between £1–£2 a week; nearly all of them had been through very hard times when their husbands were either sick, laid off work, on seasonal work, on strike or unemployed. Most of the women had worked when they were young but, since having children, had had to supplement the family income by taking in lodgers, sewing, laundry and other forms of home work. Poverty led to malnutrition in the pregnant woman; ignorance and subservience meant that she usually gave the most nutritious food to her husband. Descriptions of physical suffering, miscarriages, still births and complicated births with little or no medical attention, reveal the dreadful mental and physical oppression women suffered through their function as child-bearers.

Extracts from the letter of a woman mill weaver capture the burden of oppression on working mothers.

> I myself had some very hard times, as I had to go out to work in the mill. I was a weaver, and we had a lot of lifting to do. My first baby was born before its time, from me lifting my piece off the loom on to my shoulders. . . . If I had been able to take care of myself I should not have had to suffer as I did for seven weeks before that baby was born and for three months after; and there was the baby suffering as well. . . . But I could not do so as my husband was so short of work; when I had my second baby I had to work all through again, as my husband was short of work and ill at the time . . . I had to go out to work again at the month end and put the baby out to nurse. I had to get up by four in the morning, and get my baby out of bed, wash and dress it and leave home by five as I had half an hour walk to my mother's and then go to my work and stand all day till half past five at night and then walk home again with my baby. I had to do this with three of them.[52]

Many women expressed a deep bitterness that their lot had been one of work, poverty and pregnancies. One woman described the effect of the endless strain of poverty and pregnancies.

> The utter monotony of life, the lack of tone and culture, the drudgery and the gradual lowering of the standard of living consequent upon the rising cost of living and increased responsibilities, was converting me into a soulless drudge and nagging

scold. I felt the comradeship between myself and husband was breaking up.

Her solution to the nightmare was dramatic. 'Preventatives are largely used. Race suicide, if you will, is the policy of the mother of the future. Who shall blame us . . . ?'[53]

1 Mary Agnes HAMILTON *Mary Macarthur* Leonard Parsons 1925 p.7
2 Annual Report of the Women's Trade Union League 1910
3 The Woman Worker 1920
4 Ibid
5 *Women in Industry from Seven Points of View* Duckworth and Co 1908 p.73–75
6 House of Lords Select Committee on the Sweating System HMSO 1890 p.xliif.
7 *Women in Industry from Seven Points of View* op.cit. p.8
8 Edward CADBURY and George SHANN *Sweating* Headley Brother 1908
9 *Home Industries of Women in London* The Women's Industrial Council p.46
10 The Woman Worker 12 March 1909
11 House of Lords Select Committee on the Sweating System op.cit. p.xxv 1908
12 The Christian Commonwealth 31 August 1910
13 The Birmingham Mail 3 Sept 1910
14 The Birmingham Post 14 Sept 1910
15 Annual Report of the Women's Trade Union League 1913
16 Barbara DRAKE *Women in Trade Unions* Labour Research Dept 1920
17 The Woman Worker 21 Aug 1908
18 Evening Times 13 April 1911
19 Weekly Times and Echo 27 Aug 1911
20 Quoted in Alan Fox *A History of the National Union of Boot and Shoe Operatives 1874–1957* Basil Blackwell 1958 p.308
21 Ibid p.309
22 Ibid p.311
23 Ibid p.311
24 The Leicester Mercury 5 Sept 1911
25 Fox op.cit. p.312
26 The Daily Citizen 5 June 1914
27 Ibid
28 Margaret BONDFIELD *A Life's Work* Hutchinson and Co Ltd 1949 p.62
29 The Woman Worker 24 Feb 1909
30 Ibid
31 The Evening News 23 April 1909
32 The Daily Dispatch 14 Dec 1911
33 Quoted in A. M. PIEROTTI *The Story of the National Union of Women Teachers* National Union of Women Teachers 1963 p.1
34 Ibid p.3
35 Ibid p.5

36 Clement J. Bundock *The Story of the National Union of Printing, Bookbinding and Paper Workers* Oxford University Press 1959 p.68
37 Ibid   p.69
38 Ibid   p.86
39 Ibid   p.107
40 Ibid   p.108
41 Ibid   p.471
42 Ibid   p.297
43 Ibid   p.297
44 Ibid   p.306
45 The Sunday Chronicle 20 Sept 1908
46 Report on the Conference from the National Society of Amalgamated Brassworkers and Metal Mechanics. Issued by the Society   18 Sept 1908
47 Handbill   The National Society of Amalgamated Brassworkers and Metal Mechanics.
48 Letter to Miss Smyth from W. J. Davis, General Secretary, National Society of the Amalgamated Brassworkers and Metal Mechanics   17 Sept 1908
49 The Birmingham Daily Post   21 Oct 1910
50 Women's Trade Union Review   July 1901
51 The Woman Worker   June 1908
52 The Women's Co-operative Guild   *Maternity: Letters from Working Women* G. Bell and Sons Ltd   p.107f.
53 Ibid   p.46f.

4

'Don't Blackleg Your Man
in Flanders' 1914-1918

THE DECLARATION OF WAR had an immediate effect on women workers. Almost instantly it caused thousands to be thrown out of work. In September 1914, one month after the declaration of war, men's employment had contracted by 8.4% and women's by 14%. The immediate contraction, affecting women workers in particular, was caused chiefly by a wave of patriotism. People stopped buying luxury goods and turned their minds and pockets to the serious business of war. The cotton industry, which had already undergone a certain contraction, was badly hit; so were other areas of high female unemployment like millinery, dressmaking, confectionery shops and other luxury industries. Sylvia Pankhurst, in her book *The Home Front*, gives a vivid picture of the sufferings of East End women trying desperately, with little success, to find any kind of employment.

As a gesture towards those suffering from the immediate effects of the war a National Relief Fund was established. The government also set up a Central Committee on Women's Employment, whose job it was 'to consider and from time to time report upon schemes for the provision of work for women and girls unemployed on account of the war'.[1] A scheme was devised to provide work for women. It was patronized by Queen Mary and became known as 'The Queen's Work for Women Fund'. It had started as Queen Mary's Needlework Guild, which was to 'organise a collection of garments for war sufferers. Women trade union leaders immediately protested against the scheme, which brought in unpaid, volunteer ladies to make, mend or re-design garments when women, particularly dressmakers, had been thrown out of work. The scheme was rapidly changed and its aim became the provision of limited employment for unemployed working-women. The protest from women trade unionists gained them places on the Central Committee on Women's Employment. Mary Macarthur was honorary secretary and Susan Lawrence, Margaret Bondfield, Dr Marion Philips and Mrs Gasson, were committee members. They balanced the upper-class and titled ladies who formed the rest of the committee. The committee had two main functions : first, to assist in the distribution of work for women in industry and to re-deploy skilled workers put out of work by the war; secondly to help local representative committees established by the National Relief Fund provide relief work for the unemployed.

In 1915 the committee published an interim report showing that it had had a limited success in creating employment for women. It persuaded hesitant firms to take army clothing contracts. It gave firms advice about production and loans from the relief fund to install new machinery or change production lines to meet war production needs. The Committee reported it had placed orders with firms for 20,000 cut-out army grey shirts and 2,000,000 pairs of army grey socks. The wages paid to women in the army clothing factories for this period are not recorded, but they were probably similar to the low wages paid generally to women in clothing factories. The wages paid to women employed by the local relief committees – 3d. an hour for a maximum 40-hour week – were laid down by the central committee and drew outspoken and justifiable criticism from Sylvia Pankhurst. The committee justified the figure by stating that it had chosen a middle road between wages so high as to compete with or attract women from other employment and so low that women could not subsist on them. By the time of reporting in 1915 the maximum, owing to the rise in the cost of living, had been raised from 10s. to 11s. 6d. per week. Many of the workrooms did not pay the full rate or provide a full 40-hour working week. It is hard to understand why a committee dominated by women who knew the problems of women workers with wages of 10s. a week and less and who had so often decried such wages should have given official sanction to 'sweated' rates of pay. Sylvia Pankhurst attacked them at the time and later in *The Home Front*.

> 'Queen Mary's Sweat-shops!' was the slogan I coined to attack their parsimonious standard, the influence of which was to depress

D

even the existing most beggarly economic status of the woman wage earner . . . How unnecessarily low was the standard fixed for the unemployed woman war worker by those who affected to be the unique custodians of her interests, may be gathered from the fact that 3d. per hour was below the minimum rate fixed by the Clothing Trade Board.'[2]

She went on to describe the more serious long-term effect this had on wages for women war workers.

From their inauguration until February 1915, when war work had largely liquidated unemployment and relief work came to an end, only some 9,000 women passed through the Queen's workrooms. Yet they had set the common standard for women's war relief wages organised under other auspices, and they undoubtedly contributed towards riveting sweated wages on women who were flocking into all branches of industry to replace men. This was the desire and intention of the employing interests, which blindly regarded cheap labour as the greatest of industrial boons.[3]

There were other criticisms of the committee and the workrooms. Not only did they fail in that early period to promote new openings for women, but they provided little real training. The main employment provided was sewing in one form or another, and sewing which did not even train women for factory work. Only in London were some training courses established in LCC Institutes; but these were mainly in dressmaking, design, embroidery, tailoring and millinery – hardly useful at a time when all these trades had suffered acute contraction. The City of London instituted a scheme to train clerical workers, which was probably the most useful training scheme offered to women. In Cradley Heath, where the women chain-makers were suffering acute unemployment, the local relief committee, along with representatives from the Chain Makers Association, set up a workroom. Women were taught sewing, cooking and hygiene · and 'it was proposed in addition to teach cradle making. But difficulty in procuring banana crates has prevented the Committee from carrying out this part of the scheme'.[4] None of these schemes provided anything substantial to satisfy the needs of women for training, work or a living wage. The committee had one other solution to offer to unemployed women, the age-old one of emigration. It reported that the Australian government had offered a very favourable emigration scheme for women workers.

Events took over the work of the committee. Great Britain soon faced the problem of finding enough labour to keep the ever-growing war machine in action, while releasing enough men from work to serve in the army. Although the large-scale use of women as war workers did not begin until the spring of 1915, as early as the autumn of 1914 some employers had begun to introduce women into areas regarded as men's work. The tensions which arose from this initial introduction were indicative of the problems over substitution and dilution which were to concern trade unions throughout the war.

Although practically all industries at some point in the war had to confront the problem of women doing men's jobs the engineering industry and allied trades, since they were most heavily involved in munitions work, were the most concerned. Skilled engineers had already had some experience of dilution and the erosion of skilled status and rates of pay and, not surprisingly, they were concerned when after the outbreak of war employers attempted to introduce further dilution with the introduction of women workers. The first important dispute occurred at the Vickers works at Crayford, where the skilled men organized by the Engineers and Toolmakers Societies objected to 'setting up' work on machines which were to be operated by women. The dispute led to a conference on 26 November 1914 in London, attended by the Engineering Employers Federation and the two unions concerned. The main points of the agreement reached were that the work of skilled men was not to be given to women, that all machines requiring adjustment of tools either before or during an operation were to be operated by male labour and that 'female labour shall be restricted to purely automatic machines used for the production of repetition work.'[5] This agreement basically maintained the pre-war sexual division of labour.

By December the Engineering Employers Federation was demanding that restrictive trade union customs which prevented the employer from utilizing all grades of workers as he thought best be abrogated for the duration of the war. The employers argued that they needed at least 15,000 additional workers and proposed that 'in consequence of the Union's inability to supply the requisite amount of labour, they agree to remove certain trade restrictions without prejudice during the continuance of the war'.[6] The engineering unions brought forth counter-proposals which they hoped would meet the shortage of labour without entailing a significant loss to them of control over the relationship between skilled and unskilled workers or wage rates. Some of the proposals were totally unrealistic. Not one suggested the training of unskilled men or women to do skilled jobs. Rather, they proposed to import skilled workers from Australia, Canada and South Africa, on the assumption that they could be exported again at the end of the war. The employers and the unions failed to reach agreement and in January 1915 a letter was sent from the war office to both employers and the Amalgamated Society of Engineers (ASE) requesting that both sides work out some way of dealing with the labour shortage.

In February, with still no agreement reached between the employers and the unions, the board of trade set up a committee to investigate the best way to increase production in the engineering and shipbuilding trades. This became known as the Committee on Production; its findings were to form the basis of the Munitions of War Act. It was the first step towards comprehensive state control of the war industries. March 1915 was in many ways the decisive month for setting the pattern on which all further dilution and substitution schemes were to be based. Early in the month the Defence of the Realm (Consolidation) Act was passed. It gave the government power to take possession of factories required for munitions work and to issue orders to workers employed in them. It also gave the government power to 'direct the work done or the engagement or employment of workmen'. These powers in the government's hands threatened the unions' control of custom and practices and spurred them into coming to an agreement with the employers and the government over the question of dilution.

The first agreement signed between the ASE and the engineering employers was known as the Shells and Fuses agreement. This set out in detail the conditions under which the ASE would accept dilution in the making of shells and fuses.[7] Women who took over men's jobs were to get the rate for the job, but the agreement was to last only for the period of the war. Women would be the first to be discharged when the labour shortage was over.

At the same time as the ASE were negotiating this agreement with the employers, the government was negotiating an agreement with all the major trade unions which were, or would be, involved in government-controlled industries. The agreement, known as the First Treasury Agreement, was signed on 19 March by all the major unions except for the miners, who had withdrawn after the first day of the conference, and the ASE, who demanded further safeguards. The trade unions agreed that, for the duration of the war, there would be no stoppages on any war work and disputes would be referred to a court of arbitration. The ground of the agreement had been laid at the outset of war. On 24 August 1914, the Labour party and the General Federation of Trades Unions resolved that 'an immediate effort be made to terminate all existing trade disputes, whether strikes or lock-outs, and whenever new points of difficulty arise during the war period a serious attempt should be made by all concerned to reach an amicable settlement before resorting to a strike or lock-outs'.[8] The trade unions also agreed to relax trade practices to enable substitution to take place in all munitions factories. The government made various promises, the most important of which were that at the end of the war there would be a return to all trade union customs relaxed during the war and that ex-servicemen and workmen in employment at the beginning of the war would be given priority of re-employment. The promise in the agreement which was to give rise to a continual battle between women trade unionists and the government was the promise that 'the relaxation of existing demarcation restrictions or admission of semi-skilled or female labour shall not affect adversely the rates customarily paid for the job. In cases where men who ordinarily do the work are adversely affected thereby, the necessary readjustment shall be made so that they can maintain their previous earnings.'[9]

Without the signature of the ASE this agreement was of little value and a week later, after some hard bargaining, between the government and the ASE, a Supplementary Treasury Agreement, acceptable to the ASE, was drawn up. The additional clauses stated that trade practices were to be released only on 'work done for war purposes during the war period' and that 'in the case of the introduction of new inventions which were not in existence in the pre-war period the class of workmen to be employed on this work after the War shall be determined according to the practice prevailing before the War in the case of the class of work most nearly analogous'.[10]

At the conference which drew up the treasury agreement, no representative of women workers was present. Presumably none was invited because neither the government nor the trade unions believed it to be necessary to consult women on an agreement which would largely concern women workers. Since the ASE did not admit women members it was not surprising that women were not party to the supplementary agreement. Sylvia Pankhurst was quick to note the ambiguity in the clauses of the agreement which related to the wages of women dilutees. She wrote to Lloyd George asking for an official interpretation of the clauses and received the following reply, on 26 March 1916.

Dear Miss Pankhurst,
The words which you quote would guarantee that women undertaking the work of men would get the same rates as men were receiving before the date of this agreement. That of course means that if the women turn out the same quantity of work as men employed on the same job they will receive exactly the same pay.

Yours sincerely
D. Lloyd George.[11]

Sylvia Pankhurst was not satisfied. She wrote again asking if women would also receive equal war bonuses (an increase of wages given because of the rise of the cost of living during the war) and whether the same time rates would apply to women as to men. The government continued to stand by Lloyd George's interpretation that the equality of pay would apply only to piece rates. Needless to say the employers did not dispute that and tried to justify the inequality of time rates by claiming that women had a lower productivity rate. They also argued that the lower wages paid to women helped to offset the capital costs of new machinery. Both arguments held little weight, since once women were trained in most jobs their productivity rates were on a par with men and the large profits most employers made during the war made their argument about capital investment invalid. In fact, the low wages paid to women contributed substantially to their profits.

In the early months of the war, the Women's Trade Union League and the National Federation of Women Workers had been primarily concerned with unemployment, and it would appear that the First Treasury Agreement was signed before they were fully aware of its implications. They certainly had not made their voices loud enough to ensure their inclusion in the discussions which led up to the agreement. Thus the clauses which stated that women would be paid the same piece-work rates as men were included with the sole intention of protecting the male rate during the war. Considerations of the rate of women's wages or the justice of equal pay for equal work did not enter the discussions. Sylvia Pankhurst's letter to Lloyd George on the question of equal rates was the first public demand that women dilutees should receive equal rates for equal work.

Besides the signing of the First Treasury Agreement in March 1915 the government made another radical decision in its efforts to recruit women to war work. It announced a scheme of War Service for Women, in which it asked women who were available for work, whether trained or untrained, to register at their local labour exchanges. It invited 'all women who are prepared, if needed, to take paid employment of any kind – industrial, agricultural, clerical etc to enter themselves upon the Register of Women for War Service which is being prepared by the Board of Trade Labour Exchanges'. The object of the scheme was 'to find out what reserve force of women's labour, trained or untrained, can be made available if required'. The document ended with a patriotic rallying call to women : 'Any women who by working helps to release a man or to equip a man for fighting does national war service.'[12] The press immediately took up the government call. There was a great flurry of articles which told of the way women could serve their country by doing war service and for the first week or two after the first day of registration, 19 March, the newspapers kept up a running list of the number of women who registered. In London 700 women registered on the first day. Most of these, the press thought, were middle-class women who had now become the great reserve of untapped labour in the country. There was also a flurry of articles by women on the role they could play in the service of their country. Lady Aberconway, writing in the *Daily Chronicle*, claimed that women were perfectly capable of doing a wide variety of jobs but that 'all the higher branches of employment have been reserved for men, and women have been relegated to lower grades or kept out altogether by trade union rules'.[13] Mrs Pankhurst took an anti-German line in her article, 'Why Women should be Mobilized. Germany Denies Women the Right to Speak, Or Even Think As Independent Human Beings'.[14] German women were regarded solely as bearers of children and that was why women should answer the call to work for their country to help beat the Germans.

Sylvia Pankhurst, on the other hand who had opposed the war from the beginning wrote a letter calling for a conference of women workers to formulate the basis on which women should accept war work. Mary Macarthur had already expressed concern that the government had issued the registration forms without consulting men or women workers or their representatives. Before endorsing the scheme, women needed guarantees about the wages they would be paid and the conditions under which they would work. The *New Witness*, too, drew attention to the dilemma women workers faced. It was one of the few articles written throughout the war which perceived the long-term problem of women dilutees.

> What guarantee is to be given to men that, when they return to civil life, their situations will be open for them, and that the standard of conditions in their trades will remain unimpaired? And if the men receive satisfactory guarantees, what is to happen to the women who have taken their places when they return, if in the meantime the women have become self-dependent? There is no getting away from the difficulty. On the one hand, the women who have liberated shop-assistants and the like, and enabled them to serve their country at the front, will be sent packing, to starve or go on the streets. On the other, as seems more probable, Tommy will return to find that a woman has got his job and that he must begin life over again, and the position he won by years of hard work is to go to a woman new to the trade.[15]

A conference convened by the Women's War Workers Committee was held at Caxton Hall, London, on 16 April 1915. It was attended by delegates representing about 5 million women workers. Mary Macarthur presided. In her opening speech she expressed surprise at the government's call for women to register for war work, since there were still 40,000 women registered as unemployed at the labour exchanges. She was suspicious of the government's overt reason for the register, arguing that it was one thing for women to fill the jobs of men who had voluntarily enlisted, but 'quite another thing for them to allow themselves to be used as instruments to force economic conscription on men. . . . no woman should be used as an instrument to force men to go to the front'.[16] The press largely ignored that part of the speech and concentrated on the conditions which the conference laid down for accepting war work. They were put to the conference by Margaret Bondfield and unanimously carried.

(1) All women who register for war service should immediately join the appropriate trade union. Membership of such an organisation should be a condition of employment.
(2) Where women do the same work as a man they should receive the same rate of pay.
(3) Any woman drafted to war service should be paid an adequate living wage. There should be no sweated conditions.
(4) Adequate training with maintenance should be given and preference should be given to normal women wage-earners now unemployed.
(5) In any adjustment of staffs which have to be effected after the war, priority should be given to workmen whose places have been filled by women.

To those points two amendments were added, one demanding that 'those trade unions which excluded women be urged to admit women as members', the other calling for adult suffrage. Two more resolutions were carried, one moved by Sylvia Pankhurst demanding that maintenance for women on training be not less than £1 a week, and one moved by Dr Marion Phillips demanding that women should be appointed to the Government Advisory Committee on workers.

The resolutions formed the basic principles which women workers fought for during the war. This principled position by the women trade unionists was radically different from the purely feminist reaction of the suffragette movement. The suffragettes saw the war as a great opportunity for women to serve their King and country (the country which up to the outbreak of war had imprisoned and tortured them) and as a situation which they could utilize to prove their equality with men. The leaders of the Women's Social and Political Union, mainly Christabel, Emmeline and Mrs Pankhurst, threw their energies and their oratorical abilities into supporting the government's call to women to register for war service. They were barely concerned, if at all, with wages or conditions of work. Their concern was entirely that women should, like men, have the right to serve their country.

This campaign reached its peak in a large 'right to serve' demonstration on 17 July 1915. Mrs Pankhurst was one of the main organizers. She had no qualms that women workers would be used to force men to the front, for she thought men ought to be at the front and regretted that her own son was not still alive and able to fight. Addressing the mass rally she said, 'Let England be really a nation at war. Let every man take his place in the fighting line if he could, and let every woman reinforce him at home in the factory, in the field or wherever else she could be used.'[17] Lloyd George shared the platform with Mrs Pankhurst and the old arch-enemies were seen to be close allies in the patriotic campaign to recruit women to work and men to fight. 'Without women', Lloyd George maintained, 'victory will tarry and a victory that tarried means a victory whose footprints are footprints of blood.'[18] Mrs Pankhurst, flushed with patriotism, assured the audience that the government would see that there was no sweated labour in the establishments which it controlled. Needless to say, the press reported the demonstration extensively and praised the women for their patriotism.

For the representatives of women trade unionists, it was one thing to pass resolutions demanding the conditions under which they would do war work, quite another to fight for those conditions. Organization of the substituted women workers in the government-controlled industries was a major problem. The federation was concerned about who would organize the women, since the ASE – the body representing most men workers in the munitions industry – continued to exclude women. Early in the war, at one of the ASE triennial delegate conferences, a motion to admit women for the duration of the the war was heavily defeated. Despite their realization of the dangers of a substantial body of unorganized women workers being introduced into their industry, albeit controlled by agreements, the ASE members thought that the dangers of accepting women were even greater. The federation had already managed to organize one or two branches of women in the munitions factories and, in the summer of 1915, a formal agreement was signed between the ASE and the federation, allowing the federation to organize women in the munitions factories and providing for mutual help and alliance between the two unions. This formal agreement meant that women munitions workers had a recognized trade union which they could join and that the government recognized the federation as a body negotiating for women.

This recognition of the federation was particularly important in the light of the extensive control of the munitions industry vested in the state by the Munitions of War Act, passed in the summer of 1915. The act gave the government extensive power over the workers in government-controlled industries, powers which controlled their mobility, pay, rights and conditions of work. It embraced many of the clauses of the treasury agreement. Strikes and lock-outs became illegal and courts of arbitration were established to deal with disputes. One of the clauses in the act, which was to cause workers the most grievance was the establishment of the 'leaving certificate' clause. A worker, man or woman, could not leave her place of work (munitions work) without a certificate of consent from the employers. If an employee thought that the employer had unreasonably withheld consent, she could appeal to the munitions tribunal. The effect of the act was that workers in munitions factories had no legal way of improving their wages except through the long tedious process of a tribunal. The no-strike clause was particularly hard on the workers, since the munitions industry was facing a boom and employers had little need to lock-out workers. Added to this, the 'leaving certificate' system meant that an employee could not easily move to another employer offering higher rates, which in a market demanding labour would have caused a natural upswing in wages. Another constant cause of grievance was the tribunal's power to fine and even imprison workers for breaches of workshop rules or other offences under the Munitions Act. The factory acts, which had controlled the hours and overtime which women were allowed to work, were suspended for the duration of the War: women could work for any number of hours and on any type of shift system including night shifts.

Between July 1914 and January 1917 about 150,000 women entered the national factories. When, in the summer of 1915, the federation started seriously to act on their behalf, it found its hands tied by the Munitions of War Act. A few women who were paid equal basic piece work rates earned good wages, but the majority were paid time rates, which were fixed at a lower rate than men received for the same work. Also, as the war progressed, new production lines were designed for female labour. For these new jobs there were often no existing rates by which women's pay could be fixed and a low women's rate was established in line with that paid to women in the traditional areas of 'women's work'. The federation sought to get a minimum wage for all women employed in the munitions factories. A deputation from the federation and the ASE went to the Minister of Munitions to make an immediate claim for £1 a week minimum for women munitions workers, except for those women who had worked in recognized areas of 'women's work' prior to the war. Already articles were appearing in the liberal press about the 'sweated conditions' of women munitions workers, many of whom were earning 10s. a week or less. Since they had no opportunity to move elsewhere or to strike, this was tantamount to government-enforced 'sweating'. Such a wage had been abysmally low before the war. It was worth even less during the war, when the cost of living rose sharply, largely owing to widespread profiteering in basic foodstuffs, fuel and rents.

Pressure from the unions and the need to release more men for the front led the government to set up the Labour Supply Committee to draw up a comprehensive scheme for dilution which would increase the scope and numbers of women employed in a way acceptable to men and women workers. Its first recommendations, issued in October 1915, were quite extensive. They ranged from listing the jobs which the committee regarded as 'within the limits of women's physical capabilities' to recommendations concerning health and welfare. Most important of all they recommended a minimum wage of £1 for all women in government-controlled employment. This recommendation was made in a circular known afterwards as the L2 Circular. The great drawback to the recommendations was that they were optional. They were implemented in those munitions factories directly controlled by the government, but those employers who contracted war work from the government ignored them and even other government departments refused to implement them. The Admiralty openly refused to pay women substituted labour the minimum.

In addition to the Labour Supply Committee, the government passed the Munitions of War (Amendment) Act in November 1915. The act answered the trade unions' demand for labour representatives on the tribunals. It also allowed for the appointment of women workers as assessors on the tribunals, particularly in cases concerning women workers. These were minor concessions compared to the government's refusal to abolish or modify the 'leaving certificate' system, which the trade union movement as a whole had demanded. Nor, although the act gave the government power to fix the wages of all women on war work, did the government meet the trade union demand that Circular L2 (£1 minimum wage for substituted women workers) and Circular L3 (a minimum for substituted male labour) be embodied in law. Although certain improvements in women's wages had been negotiated locally, most women working in munitions continued to be paid between 12s. and 15s. for a 53-hour week. Finally, in February 1916 the government used its power and made Circular L2 and L3 mandatory.

The result was a substantial improvement in wages. In a typical shell factory the women covered by the L2 Circular found that their basic rate rose, immediately, on average from 15s. a week to 23s. a week. Not surprisingly however, employers found ways of reducing the increase. Women who theoretically earned the same basic rate as men would find their wages reduced by as much at 25% on the ground that inexperienced female labour needed additional supervision and assistance. Women working on time rates only received the rate 'customarily' paid to men for the job and it was easy for the employers to argue that a woman was not doing exactly the same job as the skilled man she had replaced. There were continual tensions between those on piece work rates, who could earn a comparatively high wage, and those on time rates, who earned the bare minimum. In fact, for time workers, the £1 minimum became the standard and not the minimum. Women workers faced a further cut in their wages. A 25% reduction was allowed on a weeks' wage if breakdowns or air-raids stopped work; if the women were sent home they were not paid at all, even though men in such circumstances earned full pay. Nevertheless, women covered by the L2 Circular were more fortunate than those who worked in munitions establishments not controlled by the government. Their wages usually remained at the 'sweated labour' rate.

Despite the minor concessions of the Munitions of War (Amendment) Act, there continued to be considerable industrial unrest, particularly over the powers invested in the government to control and direct the process of dilution. The unrest came to the fore on Clydeside in the winter of 1915–16. The Minister of Munitions had been given the power to ascribe grades to jobs. Thus shell making was pronounced a semi-skilled job, although skilled men were employed on it. Fuse and cartridge making were pronounced 'women's work', yet men and boys worked on it in several areas. Government grading of jobs was a direct challenge to the trade unions, one of whose functions was to defend the skilled status of their members. The down-grading of certain jobs enabled the government to introduce substitute female labour, and frequently, with the introduction of women workers, employers would modify a job slightly, in order to avoid paying equal pay for equal work. The trade union leaders on the Clyde saw in all this, an attempt not simply to employ cheap female labour and to lower wages during wartime, but to lower wages and down-grade skilled jobs in the long-term. They had strong evidence to support their fears. *Forward,* the Glasgow workers' paper (later suppressed) quoted a report of the Scottish Law Courts Record of 8 April 1915. It revealed quite clearly the employers' hopes that dilution could be used as a long-term strategy to weaken the skilled men's unions –

> This is work that could and should be done by women, and boys, and girls, who could readily be taught, and would quickly learn,

and whose pay would be less than that of men. In this matter, however, we have set up a legislative barbed wire fencing under the Factory and similar Acts, which in many ways hampers the freedom of the manufacturers, and of those who are willing to work for him at low wages and for long hours. The war itself, as a great economic force, is helping us to solve this question; the shortage of men now, and still more after the peace, is giving their chance to working women, and even to boys and girls, in regard to our workers, whatever the Unions may do, and not withstanding any paper guarantees, employment, can and will, never be the same again. The inevitable operation of the law of supply and demand must bring more women and girls into the ranks of our workers. It is only by means of this freedom to hire cheap labour, that our manufacturers can hope either to capture or to keep some of the German markets in low priced goods of large and widespread sale.[19]

With that sort of knowledge of the capitalists' long-term perspective, it is not surprising that the Clyde workers stated that 'dilution of labour without workers' control in the workshops will speedily mean a permanent deterioration in working class standards of life'.[20]

When the men at Parkhead went on strike in the winter of 1915–16 Lloyd George visited the Clyde to try to persuade them to accept dilution. The men persisted in stating that they would only accept dilution if they could control it and their own workshops. 'Mr Lloyd George said this would be revolution and he did not seem disposed to favour it.'[21] The workers were not appeased by Lloyd George's visit. In January 1916 the men at Johnstones engineering firm stopped work for five days to demand that women workers brought in under any dilution of labour scheme should get the same rates as the men. The government speedily repressed the Clyde workers, banning their paper, *Forward,* arresting their leaders, and imprisoning and then exiling them.

The question of dilution continued to fester until the 'Clyde Workers Agreement' was negotiated. It was drawn up by the union shop committee at Parkhead Forge and put to the Clyde Workers Committee. The agreement rejected a £1 standard (or minimum) rate for dilutees. 'If employers can obtain the same results for £1 from the new class of labour as they do from us for 30s., nothing, except, perhaps, our force after violent struggle, can prevent a reduction of wages. Our suspicion that under the cloak of patriotism cheap labour will slip in arises from the fact that naturally, cheap labour is welcomed by the employers.' It then went on to state that 'the income of the new class of labour be fixed, not on the sex, previous training, or experience of the workers but on the amount of work performed based on the rates presently obtaining for the particular operation'.[22] It demanded that committees of workers be formed to see that this was 'loyally carried out'. In addition, the agreement stipulated that preferential treatment be given to skilled men who had become unemployed and that every dilutee must be organized in the appropriate trades union.

Of all the agreements negotiated with regard to dilution of war work the Clyde Workers Agreement won the best terms for the workers, thanks largely to the strength of the newly created Shop Stewards Movement on the Clyde. But although the Clyde Workers Committee put up a stubborn fight to win for dilutees, who were largely women, equal pay or the rate for the job, there is no evidence that this was done out of consideration for women workers. The motive was to protect the male rate at the end of the war, not to establish the rate for the job, regardless of sex, as a basic principle. Even on the Clyde, where the workers were making 'revolutionary' demands for workers' control, there was no interest in establishing a permanent principle of the 'rate for the job' to ensure that women could not be used to undercut men.

One of the first 'male' areas invaded by women during the war was public transport. Some districts accepted women conductors on the buses without protest, but the Salford branch of the Tramways Workers Union passed a resolution stating 'that we do not entertain the question of female labour and that we refuse to work with women'.[23] The management in Salford offered better terms for women conductors than most. They offered them equal pay for equal work, as a protection of the male rate, but did not offer them the same war bonuses as those paid to men. The men argued that the company should employ men who were over military age or unfit for service. At Hull, in 1915, the men threatened to strike and 'absolutely refused to work with women.'[24] But however hostile the men unionists were, sooner or later, they had to come to an agreement similar to the one reached in Newcastle. It guaranteed that priority of jobs would be given to ex-servicemen at the end of the war, that the admission of female labour should not affect adversely the rates customarily paid to men, that no man should be dismissed for the purpose of being replaced by a woman and the union should be consulted about all changes in employment, hours and shifts.

A year later the men workers were up in arms again, over the hiring of women as drivers. This caused even more hostility than their employment as conductors. Once again men went on strike and refused to work with women drivers. In York, the men returned blank a management questionnaire about working with women drivers. In May 1916 the annual conference of the Amalgamated Association of Tramway and Vehicle Workers passed a resolution calling upon the association to stop the employment of women as tramcar drivers. Nevertheless, area by area, the union was forced to negotiate agreements for the substitution of women drivers.

Like the bus and tramway workers, the Liverpool dockers also refused to work with women. They, however, were successful. Throughout the war women were not employed on Liverpool docks. In 1916 eleven women were employed as porters on the docks and the men refused to work with them. Their protest was entirely on sexist grounds, since the employers were paying the women the same rate as men. The dockers used every argument to hand to support their case. Women would be a positive danger on the docks. Since it was illegal to employ boys under the age of sixteen on the docks, it should be illegal to employ women. It would 'imperil' their lives to work with unskilled women. Moreover, as Mr Sexton, the dockers' union representative pointed out, there were moral objections.

> The docker is a man who has some rough work to do and has got to show some strength. He is also a man of morals and he resents very strongly the introduction of women to a sphere of industry where the sanitary conditions are simply abominable, considered from the point of view of the two sexes. For the men they are all right, but the moment you have men and women

working together these conditions do not conform to the Liverpool Dockers sense of decency.[25]

The Liverpool docker kept his sense of decency, his abominable sanitary conditions and his male preserve. It took another war for the bastion to be stormed.

The National Union of Railwaymen (NUR), faced with a larger influx of substituted women workers than most industries, took a less hostile and more realistic attitude. Women first appeared as carriage cleaners and sweepers, then as porters, booking clerks and ticket collectors. But although the latter jobs had been male preserves before the war, the NUR accepted women members for the first time and pushed for equal basic rates for the substituted women workers. Whilst the union demanded that jobs should go back to the men at the end of the war, it recognized that in certain jobs, particularly that of booking clerks, women were there to stay. At the annual conference of the NUR in 1915 Mr M. Thomas put the issue to the membership.

> As regards female labour experience would prove that in some of the branches in which females were engaged now the work would not be profitable from the standpoint of the employer. Notwithstanding this I am profoundly convinced that you have to face the fact female labour has come to stop. Therefore we have to make up our minds on one or two things – first, what grades would it be dangerous for female labour to be engaged in, secondly, female labour must not be used as a means of reducing the prices that we have secured for particular grades by years of agitation.[26]

Mr Thomas had touched on two questions which were of prime importance to male trade unionists. He expressed the belief, which many men workers and employers held, that women were less profitable to employers because they had a lower productivity rate, took more time off and did not have certain desirable qualities. Therefore, if the unions insisted on their being paid equally, employers would not wish to hire them. He also raised the perennial question of what grades it would not be 'dangerous' for women to be employed in – 'dangerous' for the men workers, not the passengers.

The NUR negotiated an agreement for the duration of the

war, giving equal basic rates to women employed on jobs normally done by men, despite the employers' efforts to prove that they were committed to an unfair deal. The employers tried to argue that women could not really do a job as well as men. 'A woman ticket collector, for instance, can never be as successful as a man. She cannot deal with an obstreperous passenger nor get passengers to show expedition. So to pay her the same seems a waste of money, yet to pay her less may create a bad impression.'[27] Despite the NUR agreement, women on the railways found, like women in other industries, that, thanks to the war bonuses paid to men, the equal pay they received was far from equal. In 1916 the NUR tried to negotiate equal war bonuses for women. The companies answered that the agreement to pay women the minimum rate for the grade, whereas previously they had been paying women 3s. to 4s. less than the male rate, was improvement enough in women's wages. The union did not pursue it.

In 1918 at the NUR annual conference, the president, Mr Cramp, commented on the effect women workers had had on the union.

> The introduction of female labour upon railways had not resulted in a proportionate decline in trade unionism. The women were amongst their most enthusiastic members. None could yet predict the extent to which female labour might be retained after the war, but he confidently believed that in any case they might be counted upon to resist any attempt to exploit their labour at the expense of men.[28]

That Mr Cramp should speak so highly of women members, after three years experience of them, reflected as much on the attitude of the NUR as on the women themselves.

Predictably, the craft unions, which had fought so long and hard either to keep women out of their trades and unions or to restrict them firmly to 'women's work', contemplated the prospect of women workers in skilled jobs with alarm. The alarm was duly expressed by the Printing and Kindred Trades Federation, which announced its opposition to the introduction of women to the skilled branches of the printing trades. Then, like so many other unions, the labour shortage forced it to bow to necessity. This they did on the condition that women were paid the same minimum rates for the job as men. However, despite the agreement, women were not always paid the minimum rates, and so the union appealed to the goverment to enforce them under the Fair Wages Clause. The government sided explicitly with the employers. This emerged clearly when a deputation of the Printing and Kindred Trades Federation consulted Mr Montagu, financial secretary to the treasury, on the unfair low wages paid to women for doing men's work.

> If you can show me [Mr Montagu said] that in a particular firm and at a particular place, women are being paid a rate of wages which is unfair for women, then I think you have a grievance and that is an infringement of the Fair Wages Clause; but I am not in agreement with you that it is our business in interpreting the Fair Wages Clause to insist that women should obtain the same wages as men. If we did so it would lead to women losing a considerable amount of employment . . . It may be that in certain branches of your trade there is a growing tendency, as female labour comes more and more into the market, for work which used to be men's work to be done now by women. That is a phenomenon which is going on in other trades and which it would be very unfair to use the Fair Wages Clause to put an end to.[29]

The government obviously thought a fair wage for women doing the same job as a man should be less. Cheaper female labour would be an inducement to employers to hire more women, which would release more men for the front. The women's suspicions that they were used as an economic lever for the enlistment of men were well founded.

One would have expected that unions with a long history of female membership, unlike the exclusively male unions and the old craft unions, would have had little difficulty in coping with the influx of extra female labour, even to jobs previously done by men. On the contrary, the cotton unions were as alarmed as any other. The threat of women being introduced as mule spinners caused the spinners unions to protest vociferously and to demand that the home office import Belgian boys rather than allow women to be employed on mules. They, too, used 'moral' arguments. 'I do not know one single spinner who would let his girl do the work. Apart from the moral standpoint (which is sure to be complicated where men and girls disrobe together), have the advocates of girl labour seen the consequences? We shall have the employers saying that there is nothing in spinning if a girl can learn it, and will pay accordingly.'[30] One might think from such outbursts that women were not members of the cotton unions. When the government did not import Belgian boys, the unions asked that the age at which youths should be classed as young persons be reduced from eighteen to seventeen to enable boys to be employed as adult labour. Eventually, in a series of agreements, the cotton unions negotiated terms under which they would accept substituted female labour on 'men's' jobs at first only in certain grades, but as the war progressed and demand for female labour increased, in almost all grades.

The worsted and woollen industries on the other hand drew up one agreement which applied throughout the industry. It was a complicated agreement, but the result of it was that most women, except those who received equal piece work rates, earned 'only four-fifths of the rate previously paid to the men'.[31] The National Union of Shop Assistants had difficulty in establishing even a four-fifths rate for women substitutes. The employers consistently opposed equal pay for women on the grounds which many other employers used that more women were needed to do the same amount of work as men. The facts rarely supported their argument. Mrs Bessie Ward, a member of the union who continually pushed for equal pay, denied the employers' argument.

> There had been a good deal said in the past about the necessity of fixing the women's minimum below the standard for men because the women are less efficient. That statement is absurd on the face of it, but it is made more absurd from the facts which can be obtained from the places where women are working as substitutes for the men who have been withdrawn for the purpose of war. In the North of England, in the Manchester District, out of 25 shops, there is not one where the staff has been increased during the past six-months; and yet the majority of the staff are women. In the London area, the same remark applies. The women are inexperienced at first, and that naturally causes a temporary increase in the staff. The same thing would happen if inexperienced men were taken on. But the strange thing is that it takes a very short time to train the women in the grocery trade.[32]

Unfortunately most shop assistants were either poorly organized or not organized at all, making the establishment of even a four-fifths rate almost impossible.

Besides massive recruitment of women to work in the war industries the government also employed some 150,000 extra women clerks in the civil service and a large number of women in the Post Office. In neither sector did the women get equal pay. Most of the 150,000 women clerks employed by the government during the war were given temporary status, which meant that they could easily be dismissed at the end of the war. It also enabled the government to pay them lower wages than they would to women on permanent staff. A 'responsible official', interviewed on the government's pay policy, said that 'women were not paid the same rate as the men because the latter, who were on staff, had been placed on a scale which gave them automatic increases'. He also claimed that women were unable to work as long as men, and trotted out the old government argument that women were not really dependent on their wage. 'Many of the staff were high school girls from middle-class families, who were anxious to do war work, or being engaged to men at the front, preferred to have something to do than mope at home.'[33] The government's low rate of wages to women partially rebounded on the government, since it suffered an acute shortage of clerical workers. Women found that private employers, particularly the banks and business firms, paid better rates. In Local Government, the union NALGO positively encouraged the employment of women on a temporary basis since the President thought widespread introduction of women on a permanent basis would lower the status of the service.

Women were disgruntled not only with the low rates of pay, but also with the barring of most grades in the civil service to them. Women were relegated almost entirely to clerical work. In 1915 a memorandum from the National Union of Women's Suffrage Societies was sent to the prime minister asking that the recommendations of the recent royal commission on the civil service be implemented, in particular the recommendation that women should be employed in higher and more varied grades. The government ignored the recommendation. The *Manchester Dispatch* wrote a perceptive and scathing attack on the government's attitude. It quoted a government official, who maintained that women were all right on routine work, but when called upon to deal with a case of unusual character 'they are floored at once and immediately rush off to a man'. This argument cut no ice with the reporter from the *Dispatch*.

> When 'women clerks immediately rush off to a man for guidance' [he wrote], it is not on account of a lack of a sense of responsibility but because they wisely realise that they are for the moment at any rate 'officially bottom dog' and must submit to the rules and regulations. They cannot show a sense of responsibility if responsibility does not rest on them. . . .
> To a reasonable person not steeped in Civil Service Tradition and prejudice it is perfectly and ridiculously absurd in these days when women are filling prominent posts in all walks of life to say they are not capable of filling higher positions in the Civil Service. The Royal Commission, it may be pointed out, recommended for it before the war, an increased admission of women into all grades of the Civil Service.[34]

To add to these restrictions on women's employment in the civil service, the government imposed a marriage ban, which meant that women, on marrying, had to resign from work.

Women clerical workers in the private sector received better wages than those in government employment. They could earn between £1 and £2 10s. a week with relatively little experience, whereas women in the civil service earned rates between £1 and £1 5s. The National Union of Clerks persisted with its pre-war policy of equal pay for equal work; but Mr Elvin, the president, admitted that trying to implement the policy in wartime was virtually impossible. Inexperienced women clerks flooded into offices during the war and, whilst a few experienced women could earn £3 a week, the inexperienced women had the general effect of lowering rates. The union was faced, too, with the problem of organizing women spread out in small offices, many of whom were middle-class, with no background or understanding of trade unionism. Although the National Union of Clerks, like almost all other unions, stipulated that jobs should revert to men at the end of the war, Mr Elvin expressed his concern, a concern voiced by very few, about the great suffering and misery which untrained women who became unemployed at the end of the war would suffer.

Not only did women keep the schools, hospitals, transport and postal service, munitions factories, shops and a whole host of other industries and services going during the war, but early in 1915 a great campaign was launched to persuade women to work on the land. Farm workers had been one of the first groups of men to enlist in large numbers, which left a great shortage of labour on the land. The press gave considerable coverage of the campaign and appealed to women to fight the war from the trenches of their native land. The *Daily Express* ran a service for farmers by keeping a register of farms needing work and a register of women prepared to work. By March 1915, the government realized that they needed a better scheme to ensure that there was enough labour to keep farms going and the population fed. County committees were set up, usually run by local women, to organize the recruitment of women for farm work. A few training schemes were organized and a dairy college was opened to instruct women in dairy farming and cattle-rearing. Most women employed on land work, however, had no training and found themselves doing every type of job, including heavy labour, milking, gardening, harvesting, fruit-picking and ploughing.

In 1916 a voluntary organization, the Women's National Land Service Corps, was formed with the blessing of the board of trade and agriculture. It tried to improve the county committees' organization and recruitment of women land workers. They were faced with several problems. The farmers were reluctant to employ women maintaining that women were lazy, unable to do heavy work and unprofitable to employ.

The National Agricultural Labourers and Rural Workers Union opposed the introduction of female labour unless women were paid the same district wage as men, but they were unable to implement their policy. The county committees were staffed by local ladies who were efficient at organizing accommodation and jobs but who appeared to care little about wages. One exception was a Mrs Mildmay, who did a survey in Devonshire for the Women's War Committee. She reported that she found that there was a great demand for female labour and that women were available for the jobs. Women, however, were not registering and she put this down to 'scandalously low' wages.

In 1917, to cope with the continuing shortage of farm labour, the government formed the Women's Land Army. Those who enlisted were to be 'Paid Soldiers Pay: Billeted like Soldiers and Uniformed like Soldiers'. By the end of 1917 more than 9,000 women had applied to the National Service Department of the land army. Free training was given and a minimum wage was fixed at 18s. plus free accommodation and food.

The government (except in the munitions factories) and other public sector employers refused to pay equal pay for equal work during the war, even to substituted female labour, maintaining that a fair wage for women was substantially less than a fair wage for a man doing the same job. In contrast, in those industries which were effectively organized by trades unions, agreements were negotiated to control the substitution of female labour for male labour. The central points of them were that the male jobs should be returned to men at the end of the war, with priority given to ex-servicemen. Women trade unionists supported their male colleagues. Their slogan for women workers was 'Don't blackleg your man in Flanders', and they fought hard to keep women from doing the same job for less money.

However, the lack of commitment of the trade union movement to real equality of pay for equal work soon became apparent, even though it had been the policy of the TUC since 1888. Employers, too, opposed it in practice, even though they may have agreed to it in substitution agreements. Mary Macarthur's comment about the attempts of the employers to evade equal pay could well have been made in the 1970s about the implementation of the Equal Pay Act.

> The theory of equal pay for equal work was accepted, but in practice we found that the work was scarcely ever recognised as equal. Some simple adjustment was made to machinery – a twist drill, perhaps, was replaced by a flat cutter, an automatic stop was fitted to a lathe and it was declared the work was not the same.[35]

The women, therefore, changed their demand from 'equal pay for equal work' to 'equal wages to workers of equal value'. Mary Macarthur tried to persuade the 1916 TUC conference of the importance of the principle not just for substituted labour, but for wage agreements in general. She warned delegates that the fight should not be man worker against woman worker, but workers against employers. With almost prophetic vision she predicted 'that it would be the prevention of unemployment which would be the task of the future'.[36]

The war experience had made other women sceptical of 'equal pay for equal work'. 'Melissa', writing in the *Railway Clerk*, gave trade unionists a clear way forward to avoid the problem of women worker against man worker.

> It is no good talking about 'equal pay for equal work' for that much abused doctrine provides too many loopholes for the evasive employer. In whatever trade or occupation women's labour can be used as alternative to men's, the trade union will have to fight for minimum time wage, which after any necessary probationary period for either sex is the SAME FOR A MAN AND WOMAN.[37]

Her voice, like that of other women, fell largely on the deaf ears of the trades union movement.

Besides the employers' evasions of equal pay there were other factors which meant that even where equal pay had been negotiated women's wage packets were substantially lower than men's. Throughout the war the cost of living steadily rose and war bonuses, intended to raise wages in line with the rising cost of living, became an increasingly substantial portion of the workers' wage packet. Women in government controlled industries and the private sector were paid war bonuses which averaged 50% of the male rate. Although a few trades unions, like the NUR, contested the unequal bonuses, most unions negotiated and accepted lower bonuses for women. Women protested but their protests did not erupt into militant action until 1918, when a group of women workers rejected the payment of an unequal war bonus and the first 'equal pay' strike was launched, fought and won by women.

In August 1918, 3,000 women tramway workers in London struck against the award of a further 5s. a week war bonus to men. Women had been given no bonus. The London tramways came to a halt and within a day or two the strike spread to Bath, Bournemouth, Brighton, Bristol, Folkestone and Hastings. Mary Macarthur warned that women munitions workers might also take action, since they received only 50%

of the male war bonus. The press did not fail to take the opportunity to write stories about the poor, suffering general public
who had this inconvenience inflicted on them. The *Daily
Telegraph*, true to form, did a particularly touching story on the
effects of the strike. 'Two soldiers on leave from the front and
carrying their weighty active service kit collapsed in Cannon
Street and were removed to hospital in an LCC ambulance.
They had tramped through the City because there were no
buses.'[38] The unions involved appear to have taken different
attitudes towards the strike. An official of the National Transport
Workers Federation was reported as saying that 'we are doing
all we can to avert a strike,'[39] whilst the Vehicle Workers Union
called their men out in support. Both unions tried to negotiate a
settlement with the government. At a meeting on 23 August
the union leadership asked the women to return to work, pending reference of their dispute to the committee of production.
Some women opposed, shouting 'sold out'; but the majority
voted in favour of the return to work. On 30 August the committee of production awarded the full 5s. increase to the women,
backdated to the date from which the men had received it. It
was not only a victory for the women transport workers. The committee of production, fearing that female militancy might spread,
hastily awarded a 5s. increase to all women munitions workers.

In war, as in peace, the major concern of the federation and
the Women's Trades Union League was wages. The 150,000
women workers in government-controlled factories were relatively
well protected by agreements and the £1 minimum was raised
to 24s. in 1917 for a 48-hour week. The estimated 100,000
women in war work outside government-controlled factories
were far less well protected. On the whole they were employed on
'women's work' and paid women's wages. The federation, assisted
by other general labour unions, tried to organize the women
and to pursue their wage claims through the tribunals. The
federation claimed a 90% success rate in the cases it pursued. In
the course of the war they managed to raise the rate for women
in private engineering firms from 2½d. to 5½d. an hour, which
was only a ½d. below the rate for substituted labour. On pre-war
levels this represented an increase of 200%, in real terms, taking
into account the rise in cost of living, an increase of 50%. A war

bonus had also been negotiated of 11s. a week. Women in other areas of 'women's work' fared less well, although the demand for their labour and the precedents set in the munitions industries did cause women's wages to rise generally.

The war also brought important improvements in the hours and conditions of work. The improvements were caused mainly by the government's desire for ever-increasing productivity to keep the war machine supplied. Owing to the suspension of the factory acts many women worked excessively long hours with no proper meals or breaks in bad conditions. Those interested in increased productivity and in the health of women workers were worried that such excessively long hours were not conducive to the highest possible productivity rates. In 1915 the Minister of Munitions set up a committee to study industrial fatigue, the hours of labour and other factors affecting the health of women workers. In September 1916 it issued a detailed memorandum on hours and output, which stated that the maximum number of hours worked by women should not exceed 60 hours a week. The committee also issued a memorandum which recommended the appointment of welfare supervisors, to look after the general care of the employees and help with housing and accommodation, travelling, food arrangements, canteens, general health, hygiene and cleanliness. Welfare supervisors were appointed in most government-controlled establishments; but the workers complained that their supervisors were essentially management and being middle-class, did not understand their problem. The federation led the campaign against the appointment of welfare supervisors in factories. At a conference in May 1917 organized by the Standing Joint Committee of Industrial Women's Organizations, a resolution was unanimously passed condemning the introduction of welfare supervisors and demanding much greater control of their own welfare. Their resolution was radical, and in many ways far in advance of its time.

> That this conference declares its conviction that the establishment of welfare workers in the service of the employers can never materially increase the well-being of the workers, and that, while it advocates the employment of women to supervise the work of women, it does not consider that such supervision should be regarded as having any other function than those of management.

It protests against any extension of control over the private lives of workers and asserts that in every factory the welfare – social and physical – of the workers is best looked after by the workers themselves.

With this object in view, this Conference urges that in every workshop and factory there should be a Trade Union Committee, not only to look after wages and similar conditions, but to interest itself in all concerns of the workers under their direction, and to make representations therefore when necessary, to the management.[40]

Most government-controlled factories appointed welfare supervisors but they were compulsory only in factories handling TNT. A hue and cry had already been raised about its lethal effects. The *Lancet* published long medical articles on the poisoning of workers handling TNT and the government introduced strict controls in establishments handling the explosive. Not only in factories handling dangerous chemicals, but generally conditions in factories were improved. Canteens were established in government-controlled factories and were then made compulsory. A department was set up in the Ministry of Munitions to deal with the question of protective clothing. Overalls were supplied as were gloves, hats and trousers, the last for women working in such places as shipyards. Cloakrooms, lavatories, rest rooms and first-aid facilities were introduced. For the first time it became obligatory on employers to supply a source of cold drinking water within easy access for all workers. In 1917 the government recommended the provision of stools with backs for women workers. Accommodation was a great problem, since many war workers were directed to work away from home. At first workers were billeted; later hostels were built for women workers. As in the factories, the conditions in these improved as the War progressed, since the government had to persuade more and more parents to allow their daughters to move away from home to areas which needed labour. Although women departed (usually forcibly) from the factories after the war even faster than they had been recruited, the men returning from the war found their workplaces better places to work in. As Lloyd George said, 'It is a strange irony, but no small compensation, that the making of weapons of destruction should afford the occasion to humanise industry. And yet such is the case.'[41]

For all that society redefined the roles of men and women during the war ('Men must fight : Women must work' or, more succinctly, 'Men Trenches; Women Benches') women continued to bear children. Part of the government's concern for the health of women workers was their concern for the health of the reproducers of the British nation. Lloyd George explained : 'The workers of today are the mothers of tomorrow. In a war of workshops the women of Britain were needed to save Britain; it was for Britain to protect them'.[42] Welfare supervisors were instructed to take pregnant women off night shifts and heavy work. For women with children day nurseries were established. The *Daily Mail* greeted them with patriotic fervour. 'Mothers Who Make Munitions' were applauded along with the establishment of day nurseries since they meant that 'at last the deplorable waste of the service of willing women workers, the mothers of young children, has been recognised'.[43] To help establish day nurseries the Ministry of Munitions gave a 75% grant to local education boards plus a 7d. allowance per day for the attendance of each child. The mother also had to contribute a small amount for each child attending the nursery. Women who had to work on night shifts could claim an allowance for finding night accommodation for their children. Woolwich became the model nursery. It was custom-built with special children's bathrooms, toilets, chairs, rest rooms and play spaces inside and out. During the war nowhere was it heard that women with children should be at home looking after their children. The press continually applauded women war workers with such headlines as '100,000 Joans of Arc : Victory in the Hands of Women War Workers',[44] 'How Women Saved a City: Lacelooms deserted for Shell Making'[45] 'Scarred Shell Girls' Disfigured Hands as Proof of Patriotism'.[46]

The influx of more than 1½ million into the labour force during the war was reflected in the figures of trade union membership. In 1918 the female membership of all trade unions, excluding teachers, was about 1,086,000, about 17% of all organized workers. Female membership had increased during the war by 750,000, an increase of about 160% compared to one of about 45% in male membership. Membership of the National Federation of Women Workers at the Armistice was about 80,000, about four times as many members as it had had in 1914. New unions were also formed to organize women who were still excluded from male unions. Such was the Society of Women Welders. The transport and general labour unions account for the greatest recruitment of women during the war. Sixty-eight thousand women joined the transport unions and the female membership of the general labour unions rose from 24,000 to 216,000. The clothing, printing, pottery, clerical and shop assistants' unions all recorded large increases of female membership. The textile unions had a smaller increase, but that was due to the higher percentage of women organized in the industry before the war. In 1918 the textile unions still had the highest percentage of women workers organized in industry – about 75% of women workers in cotton and 82% in textile dyeing and bleaching.

By 1918, 383 trade unions had women members, of which 347 were unions with mixed membership and 36 were restricted to women. Apart from the National Federation of Women Workers, the women's unions accounted for only a few members. Most of the mixed unions did not make any sex differentiation about the rights of men or women to hold office, yet almost all of them were run almost exclusively by men, regardless of the proportion of women members. There were equally few women organizers employed by unions. Only four of the mixed textile unions and eleven of the other unions employed any women organizers. Of those the only ones to employ a significant number were the United Garment Workers' Trade Union and the Workers' Union, both of which employed sixteen. The Union of Post Office Clerks employed five, the rest only one or two. Unions had a variety of policies with regard to mixed or separate branches for women, but mixed branches predominated. Even so, women attended as 'second-class' members, since most unions had lower subscription rates and smaller benefits for women. Almost all the mixed Unions had negotiated agreements which established a clear sexual division of labour, with women restricted to certain jobs, suspended only for the war. Women were under-represented at the TUC level as well. In the latter years of the war, about 30 women delegates attended the Trades

Unions Congress out of 800 or 900 delegates in all. In 1919 there were 32 women delegates out of a total of 851. That marked a great progress from the first two women delegates at the congress of 1875. Women had established a permanent presence at the TUC.

Wages, war bonuses, conditions and the drive to organize women were the prime concerns of women trade unionists during the war. It would be wrong, however, to assume that women did not take a wider social and political interest. In January 1916 Mary Macarthur started publishing and editing the *Woman Worker* again. It was a socialist organ. In the first number, January 1916, Isabel Sloan ended an article called the 'Right to Live' with a rallying call to women workers which used the language of the right-wing warmongers to express left-wing demands.

JOIN THE GREAT INDUSTRIAL ARMY
'Do your bit' for the country, do your bit for women and children of Britain. An Empire is not truly great unless the men, women and children have good food, warm clothing, healthy homes, leisure and joy.
Join the great Industrial Army which is marching forward to liberate the workers from poverty and pain.
Don't blackleg your man in Flanders.
If you do a man's work demand the man's wages.
Join the Union NOW, and be ready for the call when the war of nations is over.
The call will come to one and all to make England a better country for its people.[47]

That was fighting talk. The paper, like the pre-war one (also edited by Mary Macarthur), had articles on socialism, the fight for better wages and the rising cost of living. It supported the series of rent strikes and reported at length the struggle by Glasgow housewives to oppose rent rises and evictions. It applauded the direct link between workers and housewives when, in the struggle to oppose evictions, 4,000 munitions workers marched with the housewives to the Glasgow City Hall, where the housewives threatened to keep the munitions workers lodged with them 'in bed for a day or two if we do not get our rents reduced'.[48] The paper also supported the Russian Revolution and immediately after the war called upon the government to recognize the Soviet Union.

The National Federation of Women's Workers also took a Socialist line. At its 1916 biennial conference a resolution, passed unanimously, called for the conscription of all incomes over £1,000. It demanded that the money be used for

(a) guaranteeing generous treatment to the dependents of all soldiers and sailors who are incapacitated or killed.
(b) guaranteeing to all workers employment at trade union rates of wages or adequate maintenance until such work is found and
(c) taking over the railways, shipping and mines, and developing the land now in use for the preservation of game and sport, to supply wheat and other necessary foodstuffs.[49]

The conference also called for increased allowances for wives of soldiers called up, maternity benefit, state paid for two months before the birth and at least three months after for all women, and adult suffrage. At the Trades Unions Congress in 1916 the federation submitted three resolutions. They called for the nationalization of land, railways, canals and mines, the right to work at trade union rates or to be paid adequate maintenance, and state control of food prices. Throughout the war the federation continued to demand equal pay for equal work and a 48-hour working week with one week's paid holiday. It pressed for maternity benefit, condemned the Defence of the Realm Act 40D, whereby any woman could be compulsorily examined for VD, and demanded a better national educational system.

Many of the women leaders in the trade union movement and the labour movement were strong supporters of the International Labour Movement. In 1919 Mary Macarthur and Margaret Bondfield attended both the International Women's Labour Conference and the International Labour Conference in Washington. The women's conference took a much more radical position than the general conference. The British delegates, with their war experience and socialist commitment, knew exactly what they wanted from the post-war world and were influential in the passing of several resolutions. The Women's Labour Conference urged that the minimum age for work should be sixteen; the Labour Conference set a minimum age of fourteen. The women called for a 44-hour week and a maximum 8-hour day;

E

the Labour Conference opted for a 48-hour week with numerous exceptions. Finally the women called for the abolition of night work for all workers, men and women, except those in essential services, whilst the Labour Conference only sought to prohibit night work for women. The women of the trade union movement had high hopes for the post-war world. The battles they had won outweighed their fears of peace. Even those women with the greatest fears could barely envisage the blow which was to come.

1 Central Committee on Women's Employment: Interim Report. HMSO Cmnd 7848 1915 p.4
2 Sylvia PANKHURST *The Home Front* Hutchinson & Co Ltd 1932 p.54
3 Ibid p.54
4 Central Committee on Women's Employment op.cit. p.16
5 Quoted in G. D. H. COLE *Trade Unionism and Munitions* Oxford University Press 1923 p.54
6 Ibid p.54
7 Ibid p.67f.
8 Quoted in Henry PELLING *A History of British Trade Unionism* Penguin 1963 p.150
9 COLE op. cit. p.73
10 COLE op. cit. p.74
11 PANKHURST op.cit p.159
12 *War Service for Women* Board of Trade   March 1915
13 The Daily Chronicle 24 March 1915
14 The Daily Sketch 23 March 1915
15 The New Witness 25 March 1915
16 The Daily Call 17 April 1915
17 The Daily Telegraph 19 July 1915
18 Ibid
19 Forward 1 Jan 1919
20 Ibid
21 Ibid
22 The Herald 12 Feb 1916
23 The Daily Dispatch 3 May 1915
24 The Yorkshire Post 26 June 1915
25 The Evening News 16 March 1916
26 The Birmingham Post 21 June 1915
27 The Railway Gazette 2 July 1915
28 The Times 18 June 1918
29 Quoted in Barbara DRAKE *Women in Trade Unions* Labour Research Dept 1920 p.86
30 Ibid p.85

31 Agreement made the 4th day of February, 1916, between the Representatives of Employers and Work people engaged in the Worsted and Woollen Industries of the West Riding of Yorkshire for the purpose of dealing with the exceptional conditions arising out of the War.

32 DRAKE   op.cit   p.85f.

33 The Westminster Gazette   18 Jan 1917

34 The Manchester Dispatch   1 Aug 1917

35 The Christian Science Monitor – Boston, Mass USA 3 April 1916

36 The Bristol Times   9 Sept 1916

37 The Railway Clerk   15 Jan 1916

38 The Daily Telegraph   20 Aug 1918

39 The Daily Telegraph   17 Aug 1918

40 DRAKE   op.cit   p.103

41 Quoted in L. K. YATES   *The Woman's Part*   Hodder and Stoughton 1918   p.44

42 Ibid   p.37

43 The Daily Mail   16 Dec 1916

44 The Daily Express   1 Feb 1916

45 The Daily Mail   4 Dec 1916

46 The People   13 Aug 1916

47 The Woman Worker   Jan 1916

48 Ibid

49 The Woman Worker   June 1916

5

'Women Must Go' 1918-1923

FOR WOMEN WORKERS, particularly the war workers, peace brought immediate widespread unemployment. Six hundred thousand women were made unemployed in the first few months of peace. Most women assumed that high unemployment was merely a product of the rapid demobilization of the Forces and the war workers in the winter of 1918–19. With the hope that such high unemployment would be short-lived, women struggled to maintain the gains which they had made during the war. But the struggle to retain jobs at any level was not just against the employers (often the government); it was also a struggle against the demands of ex-servicemen to be re-employed or re-deployed. It was an emotive issue. Public opinion stood firmly behind the ex-servicemen who had fought for their country. The argument of the women that they too had worked for their country had less appeal. Few argued that all workers, whether men or women, should have a right to work. Women relinquished their jobs to ex-servicemen (freely or forcibly); but by the early 1920s it had become clear that female unemployment was the product of the economy, not demobilization. For women reconstruction meant the destruction of almost everything they had gained during the war years.

World War I, far from resolving any of the pre-war tensions between men and women workers, had been a catalyst for creating new ones. The introduction of women into areas of industry, white-collar work and the professions, in which they had not previously been employed fundamentally disturbed the accepted sexual divisions of labour. Although trade unions had negotiated agreements during the war for a return to pre-war *status quo*, not all employers honoured them. Women booking-clerks on the railways were by no means the only women who had been given a job for the first time during the war and were retained in employment in peace time. In most cases, they stayed because the employers realized that women could do the job perfectly adequately for less money. In industry, too, many unskilled and semi-skilled women workers were retained for the same reason. The trade union movement had ignored warnings from women like Mary Macarthur and had opted to resolve the problems caused by the widescale introduction of women workers for the duration of the war only. It had not taken the opportunity to introduce the principle of 'the rate for the job' regardless of sex. That failure, which reflected the male chauvinism of the trade unionists, divided the working class. It led some male workers to the dole queue, where they were to stand resentfully while women were employed to do their jobs for less pay.

The hope of the male trade union movement that peace would bring a reversion to the pre-war sexual division of labour was in conflict with the interests of employers and the hope of women workers. In the course of the war, 1,200,000 women had worked for the first time in their lives. Not all of them wanted to return to the home. Women who had been restricted to domestic work of one kind or another had experienced the comradeship and the better wages and conditions of industrial work. Many of them refused to return to domestic service. For the first time, women had had the opportunity to do skilled and responsible jobs. They were not keen meekly to relinquish those jobs to men on the assumption that men had a divine right to the better jobs. The representatives of women workers, moreover, had won the right to be consulted by the government on all matters relating to women war workers. Women workers, too, on the shop-floor level, had asserted themselves in numerous small disputes and had gained national attention in the equal pay strike of the tramway workers. They had joined trade unions in their thousands (about 750,000 joined) and they expected their unions to protect them after the war as it had done during it. Mary Macarthur had expressed this hope at the 1917 TUC conference: 'If we stand by the men for complete restoration let them stand by us for guarantees and indemnities for the women.'[1]

There was, too, a general feeling that women should be rewarded for the contribution they had made to the war effort by an increased recognition of their rights as citizens and workers.

Limited recognition was given to their rights as citizens. In 1918 the Representation of the People Act enfranchised women over the age of thirty but it was not until 1928 that full adult suffrage was granted. The 1918 act was quickly followed by the Parliament (Qualification of Women) Act, which allowed women to stand for parliament. In other small ways recognition was given to women. The Industrial Courts Act of 1919, for instance, specified that at least one woman should be part of court proceedings.

Women's rights as workers were accorded no such recognition. The Sex Disqualification (Removal) Act of 1919 was the one concession made to them. It opened up higher education and the professions to women, with the exception of the Church, the stock exchange and the civil service, over which the government retained the right to control the admission of women. The act related only to sex: a woman could not be barred from a job on the grounds that she was a woman, but she could be on the grounds that she was married. The act, too, did not apply, or was not applied, to trade union agreements which barred women from a variety of jobs in almost every industry. On the contrary, the Restoration of Pre-War Practices Act of 1918 compelled employers to restore the pre-war customs and practices of unions. The government passed the act in fulfilment of its promise to trade unions that if they suspended their restrictive controls during the period of war to allow dilution and substitution, the government would ensure that they were restored in peace time. Although pre-war practices were not completely restored the hostility to the women retained in jobs which men regarded as theirs was out of all proportion to the actual number of women occupying them.

Although women knew that peace would bring a restoration of pre-war practices in industry, they believed that it would also bring them better opportunities than they had had before the war. Their hopes were expressed, in a conservative form, in the Report of the Women's Employment Committee of the Ministry of Reconstruction and the Report of the War Committee on Women in Industry. The former committee was commissioned to:

consider and advise, in the light of the experience gained during the war, upon the opportunities for employment of women, and the conditions of such employment, in clerical, commercial, agricultural and industrial occupations after the war.[2]

The committee was slightly uncertain whether its brief included demobilization – 'the transfer of women from war to peace work' – or whether it was merely to make long-term proposals. It opted for the latter, leaving the question of demobilization to a sub-committee. The report did, however, realize that two aspects of demobilization could radically affect any long-term proposals. First, since so many women workers were employed during the war in the national factories, it advised the retention of at least some of them for a period after the war, so as to give peace-time employment to large numbers of women, who would otherwise be made unemployed. Second, it listed a variety of jobs which women had done during the war which the committee regarded as suitable for women in peace-time. This exercise in listing jobs suitable for women was largely undermined by the statement at the beginning of the report that the committee accepted the government's commitment to a return of pre-war practices.

> In other words, when we report that a certain industry is suitable to women we are not to be taken to mean that openings in such an industry are in fact, or ought in our judgment to be, available for women.[3]

Nevertheless, many of the committee's recommendations were radical. The report recommended training, apprenticeships and re-training for women war workers in industry and equal opportunity of entry to local government service. A separate report published in 1920 recommended training schemes for women in agriculture. On hours and conditions, the committee advocated the re-introduction of the factory acts and all protective legislation, a new legal maximum of a 44-hour week for women factory workers and legislation to restrict the long hours of shop workers.

The war had shown that women workers worked better if they were given better nourishment, conditions and shorter hours, and the committee recommended the retention and extension of the better conditions established in many factories during the war. The importance of trade unions for women was recognized. 'Organization should be encouraged in every way', the report stated, and in particular unions comprising both men and women, since they were 'stronger for bargaining purposes'.[4] A wide extension of trade boards, to secure adequate wages for unorganized trades, was also recommended. So was equal pay for equal work, whether in non-manual grades or manual grades, piece work or time work.

> The granting of equal pay for apparently equal work is not only a standard simple to enforce, but corresponds as well to an instinctive sense of equity and justice; and this principle alone gives hope of the final settlement of that old feud between men and women workers which is inspired by the fear of undercutting. It may not meet every individual case. But we confess we can find no other working principle. Further, it appears to us that anything less than equal occupational rates (known colloquially as 'the same rate for the job') for men and women on time work would tend to undermine the whole basis of collective bargaining and re-act injuriously on the standard of life built up by organised effort.[5]

A dissenting note was added to the recommendations on equal pay by two men who also dissented from the recommendations in favour of a 44-hour week, government retention of national factories in the post-war period and mixed trades unions. They argued that, since men were so prejudiced, women's interests would be best served by separate unions; but one suspects, in the light of their other attitudes, that they were also thinking of the employers' interests.

Despite these radical recommendations, the committee, comprised half of men and half of women, asserted that child bearing was the primary function of women and that the family and home should in all cases take precedence over work.

> As a general principle, we would suggest that the only differentiation between men and women which can be justified is such as has its basis in the need of preserving women's powers unimpaired for those primary activities which are connected with the family and the home.[6]

In line with that general principle the report included the recommendations (which some women on the committee dissented from) that 'the employment of married women outside their homes is not to be encouraged' and that 'factory crèches in normal times are not approved'.[7] To enable unsupported women with children to stay at home, it advised the paying of mother's pensions, with a possible extension of the payments to wives of disabled men. So, for all its other merits, the report accepted the view that the primary function of a woman was that of wife and mother, a view on which the whole discrimination against women workers has been based.

By the time the recommendations of the Women's Employment Committee had been drawn up and signed, in March 1919, and some time before the report was published, late in 1919, government policies with regard to the demobilization of both the Forces and the war workers and the restoration of trade union customs had already been put into effect. By March 1919 a writer in *Reynolds Newspaper* was claiming that there were 650,000 women out of work. Contrary to advice, the government speedily closed the national factories, making thousands of women unemployed. 2,000 women were dismissed from the Woolwich factory; women were dismissed at a rate of fifty a week from the Portsmouth dockyard until all 1,500 were discharged; in Liverpool, by February 1919, 5,000 women munitions workers had been discharged; a further 4,000 were discharged in Rotherham. The trend was repeated in national factories throughout the country. The board of trade's report on employment stated that the number of women employed in industry as a percentage of the total dropped from 36.1% in November 1918 to 28.8% in April 1919, a drop of nearly 600,000 women workers in five months. That was probably an under-estimate, since many women did not register for unemployment benefit. The women in the land army were given a few months' grace. They were not demobilized until November 1919. But many of the temporary women clerks employed in the civil service were dismissed by the government as pre-emptorily as the munitions workers.

The dismissals of government employees did not go without protest. When 700 women returned to work at the War Office after Christmas 1919, they found a week's notice waiting for them. Many were members of the Association of Women Clerks and Secretaries (AWKS), which organised a protest meeting and demonstration against the dismissals. Journalists dubbed it the 'Flapper Stunt'. Unfortunately Messrs Lloyd George and Bonar Law were in France and unable to meet a deputation from the AWKS. The women, undeterred, found a pilot prepared to fly them to France, and when bad weather prevented their flying, they booked nineteen berths on a cross-channel ferry. The prime minister arrived back in England before they had set sail and agreed to meet a deputation of women from the AWKS and other unions representing women civil servants. Having gained an audience with the prime minister, they took the opportunity to express a large number of grievances. They objected to being de-mobbed, arguing that whilst they did not mind jobs going to *active* ex-servicemen who had worked in the civil service before the war, they objected to their going to any man simply because he was a man. They demanded a month's notice and demobilization payment for dismissed temporary clerks. They complained of the exclusion of the civil service from the Sex Discrimination (Removal) Act and of the absence of equal pay for equal work. On this latter point it was reported that the conversation went as follows :

> Miss Withrington : 'Men and women are on identical work, and yet there is gross disparity in the scales of pay.'
> Premier : 'Is this the case? I don't see why this should be. How do you explain this?'
> Treasury official : 'Old established custom.'[8]

The government ignored the women's grievances and the treasury even rejected the demand for one month's notice of dismissal. The National Federation of Women Workers protested about the dismissal of women war workers and pressed the government to utilize the national factories for the production of peace-time goods and the employment of women. It was supported by many other bodies including the Rotherham Chamber of Commerce, which felt that, since Rotherham women had supported the country 'most loyally' when shells were needed, it was 'their duty to try and find suitable employment'[9] for them. They suggested that the National Projectile Factory in Rotherham be turned over to the manufacture of clothing, bicycles and motors to provide employment for women. The government also ignored these suggestions.

Throughout 1919 and 1920 the government continued to dismiss women, although neither quickly nor extensively enough for some MPs. Mr Macpherson, the minister of pensions, came under particular attack for the number of women in his department. On 8 July 1920 he was asked in the House of Commons whether there was any work done by women that could not be done by men. The minister replied that there were about 5,000 women employed on women's work. When asked what was women's work, he replied 'cleaning offices'.[10] In December of that year Mr Macpherson was again under attack and he claimed 'married women and pin money-workers' were being phased out.[11]

Not only the government dismissed women. The trade unions, whenever they could, quickly asserted the rights given to them in the Restoration of Pre-War Practices Act to restore the traditional 'men's jobs' to men. In many industries the majority of women introduced during the war were speedily discharged. A postscript in the *Electrical Review* of 22 August 1919 referred to dismissals from the Manchester Tramway Company.

> Out of a total 1,350 women and girls employed by the tramway department during the war only 24 women conductors remain on the books and in addition, there are about a dozen trolley girls; practically all women labour will be dispersed within this month.

The dismissals were, however, neither fast nor comprehensive enough for the tramway men. The annual conference of the Amalgamated Association of Tramway and Vehicle Workers in 1919 resolved 'Tram Men and Peace: Women Must Go'; and 'on the question of female labour on the trams, the conference declared itself in favour of the displacement of women, especially those whose husbands are working'.[12] The conference went on to express the belief that women chose to continue to work on the trams until they were dismissed, only in order to draw unemployment benefit.

After the first bout of dismissals in the months immediately following the declaration of peace, it became evident that some women were still employed whilst men were unemployed. In the continuing demand by men for the displacement of women, the married woman was in the front line of the attack. The Tramway and Vehicle Workers specified in their demand for the displacement of women 'especially those whose husbands are working'. The same demand was made by ex-servicemen in protest marches and demonstrations throughout the country. In Bristol 5,000 unemployed ex-servicemen marched in protest against the continued employment of married women. The press, which only a year before had applauded married women for working, now attacked them.

> The first essentially vicious feature of the situation is that many women whose husbands are capable of supporting them are keeping ex-soldiers or male civilians, with dependents, out of work. In some cases a married woman is keeping an ex-soldier out of work – he will draw unemployment allowance – while her husband is also drawing out-of-work pay. This is rather hard on the tax payer. And undoubtedly the birth-rate is depressed by the office or shop employment of wives who cannot assume domestic cares also, but the patriotic duty of the married woman who is not forced to work for her living is to rebuild her home life.[13]

Other trade unionists also called for the displacement of married women, but they were not always supported by their unions. The Railway Clerical Association had experienced a large influx of women to jobs which had previously been regarded as male preserves, and when, after the war, it became clear that women were there to stay, the men of the Westminster Branch protested. They passed a resolution expressing their concern 'about the employment of women in railway offices while ex-servicemen are unemployed. Recently an ex-serviceman died and his place was filled by a woman. The members feel they are only employed and retained because they are 'cheap'. They have unanimously resolved that no married woman should be retained in the Company's service if her husband is in a position to keep her.'[14] The resolution opened up a debate in the pages of the *Railway Services Journal*. The editors published a spirited defence of married women workers. They agreed that it was a disgrace that men should be out of work, but they argued that the government should provide work for men without putting women out of work. They claimed that almost all the men who had left the railway service to go to the front had been reinstated and that, since women war workers had done their bit for the country, they, too, had a right to employment. Most of the letters printed in the journal took issue with the editors. One man, Mr Brooks, wrote an outspoken attack on the editors. 'Women', he wrote, had merely served their country; 'they didn't bleed for it'. He continued : 'Again we read, "So it seems as though the claim is that because of their sex women should clear out". I answer, Yes. Dispense with the whole lot of the war-time girls and because of their sex too. What is wrong with the following occupations : dressmaking, shop assisting, nursing and household duties, all of which fit women for their proper station in life – that of marriage?'[15] In the same issue there was a lone letter from a woman member. She wrote to thank the editors for their splendid article. She explained that she had worked throughout the war, often for long hours, and then spoke of the unpleasantness of being a woman worker. 'I have to bear all kinds of insults, particularly these last few months, not only from members of the public but, I am sorry to say, also from those in the ranks of the RCA.'[16] The debate continued in the pages of the journal for some months. At the same time the journal campaigned for equal pay for equal work and, although the union did not negotiate them, substantial rises were negotiated for women railway clerks.

The attitude of the TUC and the Labour party towards the employment of married women was equivocal. It was expressed in a pamphlet published by the two organizations in 1922, entitled 'The Employment of Married Women'. The pamphlet was the work of a committee established as the result of dismissals by the London County Council. In 1906 the local authority had passed a standing order which barred married women from council employment, with the exception of teachers, medical workers and cleaners. After the war the council removed those exceptions. The dismissal of women doctors provoked especially strong protests.

'The Employment of Married Women' expressed outrage at the dismissal of highly-trained doctors, but said little in defence of less-skilled married women. It did not lay down the general principle that a married woman had as much right to a job as any other person. It objected to the marriage bar solely on the grounds that it was difficult to operate fairly, since it would require a means test to ascertain whether a woman was supported by her husband and would, therefore, entail invasions of privacy. In their concluding statement, the authors argued that

> the question is fundamentally an economic and not a sex one. The difficulties that have arisen today are due to widespread unemployment and failure to protect its victims. They can only properly be met by a scheme of widows' and mothers' pensions for all women who have dependent children and no bread-winner, by invalidity pensions and by the prevention of unemployment, or failing that the maintenance of the unemployed.[17]

Thus the report, drawn up by the Standing Joint Committee of Industrial Women's Organizations (comprised essentially of representatives of the TUC, the Labour party and the Women's Co-operative Guild) neatly eschewed the central problem of whether in a capitalist society married women, supported or unsupported, have the right to work. Necessary as were the benefits suggested and obvious as were the recommendations about unemployment, they still evaded the central issue. The report was generally accepted by members of the committee, with the exception of the Union of Post Office Workers, who thought a marriage bar should be applied to women in the Post Office, and the National Union of Clerks, who agreed with the report but stated that most of their members would probably take the same attitude as St Pancras borough council, which had dismissed Dr Miall Smith. The AWKS dissented. Theirs was the only voice on the committee to demand a more positive statement in favour of married women.

The report was attacked by some women delegates at the 1922 TUC conference, both for the attitude it expressed and for the fact that the general council had relegated such an important issue, not just to a sub-committee, but to the Standing Joint Committee of Industrial Women's Organizations, which did not necessarily represent the trade unionist point of view. Miss Bradley, of the National Union of Shop Assistants, accused the general council and its sub-committees of taking an 'out of date' view on questions regarding women, in particular the employment of married women. 'Why should a married woman leave her work? Did any of you want Mary Macarthur to leave her work?' she asked.[18] In reply, she received a 'lecture', according to another woman delegate, from Margaret Bondfield, who said that the critics of the report had failed to read it properly. It did not advocate restrictions on married women. She did not point out, as the critical women delegates had done, that whilst it did not advocate restrictions, nor did it defend married women's right to work.

In advocating mothers', widows' and invalidity pensions, the standing joint committee took the same attitude, though less explicitly, as the Women's Employment Committee of the Ministry of Reconstruction – that married women should not be encouraged to work out of the home. Pensions for mothers was not simply a demand that unsupported mothers receive assistance to enable them to stay at home to look after their children; it was seen as a way out of the dilemma of married women working. If married women were supported, either by their husbands or by the state, they would not need to work and the whole issue would be – so many trade unionists hoped – resolved. The fact that married women might want to work or want to choose between work or home was not only not considered, but was assumed by some people to be contrary to the natural wishes of women. This attitude did not face up to the problem of married women whose husbands did not earn enough to support the family nor to the problem of married women whose children were no longer dependent. The number of the latter was increasing with the steady decline of family size. In 1919 the average size was 2.53 live births, a dramatic change from 1845 when the average had been 5.71 live births. In 1845 married women could expect their married life to be dominated by child bearing and rearing. By 1919 the decline in family size and the increase in life expectancy meant that women could expect part of their adult life to be free from child bearing and rearing.

Despite such evidence, the trade union movement, by and large, believed that married women should be in the home and that unsupported married women should be paid pensions to enable them to stay there. At the 1922 TUC Conference a motion in favour of pensions for mothers was carried for the third year running. The mover of the motion claimed that the very fact of women working caused a general lowering of wages, which was, in turn, the reason that women headed to work, since low wages left their husbands unable to support a family. That was a tortuous argument, one which ignored the demand for equal pay and the general rise in women's wages. Mrs Fawcett, seconding the motion, claimed that there was 'no woman anywhere, no mother anywhere, who would not prefer to stay at home and look after it and accomplish all her desire for her little children'.[19] The demand for pensions for unsupported mothers was widened by the mover and other speakers into a demand for pensions for all women, in effect family allowances. Ernie Bevin supported the demand in a speech which could well have been taken from a present-day argument in favour of 'wages for housework'.

> It is a challenge to the State to recognise by law that the work the mother gives in the home is of definite value to the State. That principle has not been accepted. I have often argued in wages controversies that any industry has not only to get from the working classes the muscle and skill of the men, but that it claims also, or gets, the great unpaid services of the women as well. This is a contributory factor to our industrial prosperity.[20]

Representations were made to the government, but the government had no inclination to recognize, by law, the value to the state of the work of mothers.

The concept of payment to mothers for their contribution to society had further implications, which were expressed by a group of women in a pamphlet entitled 'Equal Pay and the Family: A Proposal for the National Endowment of Motherhood'.[21] Like Ernie Bevin, they argued that the state ought to recognize the contribution of mothers to industrial prosperity by paying them. They took, however, a different position on the effect this would have on wages. Payment to mothers would be a major step towards achieving equal pay. Since the opponents of equal pay argued that the male wage was a 'family wage', if women with children were paid by the state then the concept of the 'family wage' would no longer be defensible and the rate for the job could be paid.

There was, then, confusion over the whole issue of married women workers, women's wages and mothers. On the one hand, the man's wage was regarded as a 'family wage', which justified the lower payment to women. On the other hand, the lower payment to women was regarded as the reason for the general lowering of wages which left men unable to support a family. Pensions for mothers, or family allowances, would remove many women from the labour market, but it would also remove most of the man's argument for higher wages on the grounds that his wage was a 'family wage'. Behind this confusion was the fear, created by unemployment, of women undercutting men and men's belief that they were the breadwinners and had the first right to any job. In this confusion there was a striking absence, apart from a few unheeded voices, of any leadership based on a clear socialist analysis of the way forward for men and women workers. Mary Macarthur might have provided that leadership, but she had died.

In the debate about the effect of women's low wages and the employment of married women workers, the trade union movement maintained a curious silence about 'equal pay for equal work'. Although several individual unions and the TUC were committed to it in policy, the public demand for its implementation was limited to certain women's unions, most of them unaffiliated to the TUC. At the TUC conference of 1923 a carefully couched demand for equal pay was made in a resolution which deplored the increasing differential between men's and women's salaries, thus putting women in 'unfair competition with male workers'. To counter this trend, the resolution called upon the trade union movement 'to make every possible effort to remove differences in remuneration on the ground of sex that seriously menace the standard of conditions of all workers'.[22] In response to the resolution the committee of the Women's Workers Group sent a questionnaire to all affiliated trade unions to find out the extent to which women were doing the same work as men for lower rates. It reported its findings to the TUC conference in 1923. The report found that there were some women doing the same jobs as men for less pay, but that the vast majority of women did different work from men. 'In the great majority of cases where men and women are employed in the same industry the women's work is different from the men's and the women's rates are considerably lower than the men's'.[23] There was little evidence that differentials between men's and women's pay were increasing. The report gave little encouragement to the demand that the trades union movement should 'make every possible effort to remove differences in remuneration on the ground of sex', and in fact made no recommendations for action.

In the immediate post-war years the fight for equal pay for equal work was carried on almost entirely by the National Union of Women Teachers and the National Federation of Women Civil Servants, with the support of other organizations representing women workers in the civil service and local government. In 1918 the London County Council announced a new set of wage rates to which the NUT agreed. The new scales gave the 4,000 men teachers a rise, but either gave no increases or paid less to the 12,000 women teachers. The low pay of women teachers in 1918 can be assessed by the fact that a woman teacher for her first three years received less than a woman tram conductor after six months' service. The women drew up a petition, with 10,000 signatures, protesting against the new wage scales. Their protest did have some effect and a back-dated war bonus was awarded to the women.

In 1918 and 1919 mass meetings and demonstrations were held throughout the country by women teachers and civil servants demanding equal pay. In a referendum of 1919 the NUT voted in favour of equal pay for equal work. Article 427 of the peace treaty signed by the British government had asserted the principle 'that men and women should receive equal remuneration for work of equal value'. In 1921 a motion was passed in the House of Commons calling for the introduction of equal pay for equal work in all areas of government employment, but the government pleaded that, owing to the financial straits of the country, the treasury could not foot the bill. It promised to reconsider the situation within three years. The NUT, too, was forced to accept unequal wage scales from local authorities.

By 1923 almost all the gains women had made during the war had been lost. They had been returned forcibly to the home, the dole queue or to 'women's work'. The trade union movement had supported 'the return' against the opposition of women's representatives. However, in a sense, just as the government 'rewarded' women with partial suffrage at the end of the war, so the TUC 'recognized' them. In 1920 the TUC voted to form a general council, consisting of thirty-four representatives of seventeen groups of unions, grouped generally by industry and occupation. The National Federation of Women Workers successfully moved an amendment to include an eighteenth group of unions representing women workers, which guaranteed two seats for women on the general council. It was a victory for women workers. Had not women had those two 'reserved' seats, undoubtedly the general council would rarely have had a woman member. At the same annual conference the TUC agreed to take over the work and role of the Women's Trade Union League. So, after forty-seven years the league ceased to exist and a committee of the General Council, the Women Workers' Group, took on the role of looking after women's interests within the TUC. Of this recognition of women the *New Statesman* commented:

> Trade Unionism has thus definitely passed out of the experimental stage, in which some element of distinct sex organisation was inevitable and has achieved a recognised position in the general Trade Union Movement.[24]

Within two years of its formation the Women Workers' group came under heavy criticism for not sufficiently representing the interests of women. Ellen Wilkinson, in supporting a referral back of its annual report in 1922, complained that

> here we have a report which calmly tells us that what the women's group has done has been to draw the attention of the Prime Minister to the unemployment of women; it has held one conference on unemployment, and has had a deputation which went to Geneva, while all other matters have been relegated to the Standing Joint Committee.[25]

She argued that things were desperate for working women, that they faced rising unemployment, received virtually no unemployment benefit and were leaving their unions in the thousands.

Her move to send the report back was lost by only 20,000 votes.

Dissatisfaction with the work of the Women Workers' Group resulted in a motion at the 1923 TUC conference calling for the establishment of a conference for representatives of all unions catering for women. The debate which ensued is one which continues to the present day. Those members in favour of the motion argued that it would give women a place and a time where their issues could be discussed. Ellen Wilkinson pointed out that, although women formed one-eighth of the organized workers in the country, there were only about a dozen women delegates at the TUC conference. A separate conference would enable women to 'state their own case and discuss their own difficulties'.[26] Male delegates from the textile unions opposed separatism, stating that if unions did more for their women members, particularly in the field of equal pay, there would be no need for a separate conference. Miss E. Howse of the Union of Post Office Workers went further. She saw the establishment of a separate conference as a retrograde step which would accentuate sex differentiation, not lessen it. She argued that since the Labour party had established a separate women's conference, fewer women had attended the main policy-making conference. Despite opposition, the motion was carried and the first women's conference was held in Leicester in March 1925.

By the decisions of the early 1920s women were recognized within the TUC. Their position was an uneasy one between separatism and unity. They had secured two 'reserved' women's seats on the general council and therefore two seats on the Women Workers' Group. A separate platform, too, had been established for them at least to express their views. However, the women's conference had no power to make policy. The views it expressed could be rejected by the General Council.

Throughout the history of women workers' organization there has been considerable debate about the value of separate women's organizations. In the early 'experimental' days of trade unionism, women were forced, in most instances, to organize separately, since they were barred from male trade unions. Other women organized separately because they found that there was no appropriate male trade union or, where there was, that it did not represent their interests. There were certain male trade unions who continued, like the ASE, adamantly to refuse membership to women, although a chink in the male bastion of engineering unions was made in 1922, when the Association of Engineering and Shipbuilding Draughtsmen agreed to accept, albeit in a separate section, women tracers who had unsuccessfully tried to organize themselves. There was no clear policy with regard to separate or mixed unions. Both were able to affiliate themselves to the TUC. This was challenged in 1919 by the National Union of Clerks who opposed a request for affiliation by the AWKS, on the ground that the TUC ought not to foster separate organizations. It claimed that its own record in acting for women members had been good. It was an honest claim. The union had consistently fought for equal pay and the rights of women to equal opportunity. The AWKS was, nevertheless, accepted as affiliate members, after Miss Maguire had made a spirited defence of her union.

> Our union is not the only sectional or sex organisation represented at this conference. Surely Mr Elvin does not suggest that the ASE because it does not admit women to membership should therefore be evicted from this Congress.[27]

On that point, if on no other, the AWKS won its case.

Whilst certain unions like the AWKS and the ASE firmly maintained their sex barriers, the trend in the immediate post-war years was for mixed unions. There was a strong feeling among women that the 'experimental' phase was over and that the time had come for them to be equal members of mixed unions. This feeling had been expressed in the dissolution of the Women's Trade Union League. And in 1920 the National Federation of Women Workers voted to merge with the National Union of General Workers. Mary Macarthur, the founder of the National Federation of Women Workers, had always looked to the day when the women would be part of a large strong body representing both men and women. She had seen separatism as a necessity of circumstance, not a feminist principle. Speaking in favour of the motion to merge, she expressed her beliefs about mixed unions and the hopes she had for the role women would play within the mixed union.

I feel, and the Executive feel, that if this scheme is agreed to and we are all given the strength and enthusiasm to carry it out, we are convinced that inside the National Union we shall be able to demonstrate the possibility of a great industrial organisation of men and women, in which women are not submerged, but in which they take as active a part as the men. That will be a great thing in the history of this country for it has never been done before.[28]

By 325 votes to 13, the federation voted to become a 'District' of the National Union of General Workers. Unfortunately Mary Macarthur's hopes were not answered. The most militant union in the history of women's organizations, which had existed for a mere fourteen years and organized more strikes than most unions do in a long history, became a 'submerged' district of the national union. Far from the voice of women gaining the backing of a large industrial organization, by 1930 it had been so effectively silenced that the National Union of General Workers did not send one woman delegate to the TUC conference that year.

Mary Macarthur did not live to influence the position of women members in the national union. She died on 21 January 1921 at the age of forty, barely five months after the vote to merge. Her death was a great loss to women workers and to the trade union movement as a whole. No other woman in the history of women's struggle to organize had made such a significant contribution. In twenty years of trade union work she had shown a superb ability for organizing women, raising consciousness, raising money and fighting and winning strikes. She had changed the women's trade union movement from a small rather refined organization concerned largely with conditions and legislation to a full-blooded section of the trade union movement. Throughout she maintained a clear analysis of the way forward for men and women workers. It was, in her words, a case of 'knowledge and organization' which would 'mean the opening of the cage door'.[29]

Behind all the issues discussed and debated with regard to women workers in the immediate post-war years was the fact that at least 600,000 (official figures, 1919) and possibly as many as 1,500,000 (the *Times*, 25 March 1919) women were unemployed. The wide gap in figures is accounted for mainly by the fact that the government based its figures on those receiving unemployment insurance and many women for one reason or another were not insured or did not qualify for benefit. The plight of the unemployed women was very great. For the demobilized war workers there was a brief period of benefit, but that was cut to 12s. a week in 1919. The women who received any unemployment insurance or 'out of work donation' were the lucky ones. Besides those who were uninsured there were many thousands of women who had their benefit stopped because they refused to accept the only work offered to them – domestic work. The National Federation of Women Workers led a deputation to the minister of labour to demand government schemes to provide employment for women and to protest at the way women were forced, by having their benefit stopped, to accept domestic work. It was reported that they cited the following case as an example of the way in which labour exchanges tried to force women into domestic service.

> Mr W. T Kelly declared that one employment exchange official entered a room in which 40 women were waiting for offers of employment and asked 'Who is for domestic service?' As no one replied, each one was handed the usual form and told she was not entitled to benefit.[30]

In 1921 the government introduced a scheme of standard and extended benefit. Standard benefit was based on insurance premiums already paid; extended benefit required unemployed persons to pay back the extra money when they were re-employed. Since domestic service was an uninsured job, employment exchange officials refused women extended benefit on the assumption that they would be re-employed in domestic service and therefore unable to repay the money.

The ministry of reconstruction had expected a big drive to encourage women to return to domestic work, which they had left in droves during the war. A committee was established to report on 'the domestic service problem' and to 'indicate the general lines on which available supply of labour for this purpose may be utilized in the best interests of the Nation'.[31] The committee published its report in 1919. It made many recommendations which would, had they been acted upon, have greatly improved pay, homes, conditions and status of domestic servants. The recommendations were ignored and women, not surprisingly, continued to find domestic service unattractive.

Another committee was appointed, this time by the ministry of labour, to 'inquire into the present conditions as to the supply of female Domestic Servants and to look at 'the effect of the Unemployment Insurance Scheme in this connection'.[32] The press had been full of letters and reports from disgruntled potential employers of domestic servants that women would not accept domestic work because they were receiving unemployment benefit. Many of these letters were listed in an appendix to the report. An article in the *Daily Mail*, headed 'Paying Women to be Idle', had stimulated a large number of protests, most of them claiming, like this letter, that

> thousands of girls and women who might have good homes will not take domestic service because they get the dole and idleness, learning nothing to fit them to be good wives and mothers.[33]

The committee, comprised entirely of women, listed all the reasons why domestic service was unpopular. It discounted completely the claim that unemployment benefit caused women to refuse domestic work. To make domestic work more popular, they repeated most of the recommendations of the 1919 committee. They too recommended that domestic service be made an insured job and that pension schemes be established. These recommendations, published in 1923, were ignored by the government. Unemployment and the refusal of benefit to women who refused domestic work ensured a good supply of 'female Domestic Servants' for the middle and upper classes.

The post-war years brought women the vote (if they were over 30), the right to enter the professions (if they were unmarried and could get a job) and recognition within the TUC. Those were the chief gains which women made in the immediate post-war years; they had been won largely by the role women had played in the war. However, at work, almost all the gains women had made during the war had been lost by 1923. A few more jobs had been opened up, but they were almost all 'women's work'. Textiles and domestic work continued to be the major employers of women. In the immediate post-war years, women workers bore, quite disproportionately, the brunt of unemployment. The war experience had led to no significant change of attitude in society or the trade union movement towards women workers. The post-war years brought a return, with a vengeance, of the attitude that a woman's primary roles was that of wife and mother, that her place was in the home and that she had no right to a job whilst any man was unemployed. Men returning from the front did not find a 'home fit for heroes'; they found a 'home' of unemployment, wage cuts and homelessness. They demanded that 'Women Must Go' and the women of the home front went in their hundreds of thousands to the dole queue, to domestic service and back into their homes. The new 'patriotic duty' of the married woman was to 'rebuild her home life'.

1 Annual Report TUC 1917   p.258
2 Report of the Women's Employment Committee   HMSO Cmnd 9239 1919   p.3
3 Ibid   p.4
4 Ibid   p.43
5 Ibid   p.23f
6 Ibid   p.7
7 Ibid   p.58
8 The Woman Clerk   Feb 1920
9 The Sheffield Telegraph   25 Jan 1919
10 The Woman Clerk   Aug 1920
11 The Woman Clerk   Dec 1920
12 The Daily Herald   23 May 1919
13 The Evening Chronicle   16 April 1919
14 The Railway Service Journal 15 July 1920
15 Ibid
16 Ibid
17 The Employment of Married Women   The TUC and The Labour Party 1922   p.8
18 Annual Report TUC 1922 p.306
19 Ibid   p.70f
20 Ibid   p.70f
21 Equal Pay and The Family. A Proposal for the National Endowment of Motherhood   Headley Brothers   1919
22 Annual Report TUC 1923   p.44
23 Ibid
24 The New Statesman   10 Sept 1921

25 Annual Report TUC 1922   p.289
26 Annual Report TUC 1923 pp.315–319
27 Annual Report TUC 1919 p.206f.
28 The Woman Worker   Aug/Sept 1920
29 The Woman Worker   June 1908
30 The Daily Mail   27 March 1919
31 Report of the Women's Advisory Committee on the Domestic Service Problem   Cmnd 67 HMSO   1919
32 Report to the Minister of Labour of the Committee to Inquire into the present conditions as to the supply of Female Domestic Servants   HMSO 1923
33 The Daily Mail   12 April 1923

6

'Asking for Bread and Getting a Stone' 1923-1939

UNEMPLOYMENT PROVED TO BE a blight, not merely on the immediate post-war years, but on all the inter-war years. It had a profound effect on the trade union movement. In the 1920s and 1930s trade union membership figures fell and rose in almost inverse relationship to the rise and fall of unemployment. Trade union membership declined steadily from a record high in 1920 of more than 8 million members affiliated to the TUC (a figure not reached again until 1946) to slightly more than 4 million in 1933 at the height of the slump. By 1939, membership had once more increased to 6 million, the increase paralleling the beginnings of economic recovery and a decline in unemployment. Membership figures of the trade union movement cannot be explained simply by unemployment figures. The TUC's retreat in the General Strike and the defeat of the miners had repercussions throughout the movement. It was followed by a period of defensive, conservative leadership in most sections of the movement. The 1927 Trade Disputes Act, passed by the Conservative government after the General Strike, tried to restrict the potential strength of the Labour party and trades unionism. It made sympathetic strikes, outside a particular industry, illegal; it forbade civil servants to join trade unions affiliated to the TUC; and it introduced a 'contracting-in' system for the payment of the political levy. The TUC general council, too, attacked elements of militancy within affiliated unions. In 1925, it passed a resolution stating that it would not approve affiliation of the National Minority Movement and that any trades union attached to the movement 'shall not be accorded recognition by the General Council'.[1] The Minority Movement was an attempt by the Communist party to form a broad left movement within the trade unions to fight for socialist policies, in particular nationalization, a 44-hour week and a £4 minimum wage. Within the trade union movement, it called for 100% industrial trade unionism and a rejection both of the sectionalism of the movement and of its reformist leaders. Hostility to the Minority Movement and the Communist party continued and led the general council to issue a 'Black Circular'. It advised unions to exclude Communists from posts of responsibility and refused to accept into affiliation any trade union which had Communist delegates.

Unemployment and the lack of socialist leadership also had a profound effect on women workers. Their membership figures began to decline dramatically immediately after the war and the decline continued throughout the 1920s and 1930s. In 1939 only half a million women belonged to unions affiliated to the TUC, less than half the number in 1918, despite the fact that women workers as a percentage of the work force had increased from about 27.4% in 1923 to more than 30% in 1939. (The latter figures do not include the many women who worked as homeworkers, baby minders, cleaners, menders, home launderers or in a variety of unregistered jobs.) The need for unity between men and women workers to fight the attacks on the working class was never greater than in the inter-war years and yet at no time was it so lacking. Even the Minority Movement made no direct appeal for the equality of women workers. Indeed, as unemployment rose, the tensions between male and female workers became more sharply delineated and more openly expressed. Some people struggled for unity, but far too frequently men and women were divided. Men saw women, not capitalism, as the cause of unemployment and falling wages. Women frequently responded by seeing little in trade unionism to advance either their own interests or the interests of their class. Cheap female labour became a major threat, not merely to men's wages, but to their very jobs. The new light industries, particularly the electrical industry and light engineering, employed large numbers of women and men were frightened by this trend, just as they were by the trend towards increased dilution. Unemployed men often had to rely on the wages of their womenfolk who, throughout the slump, could nearly always earn something by doing domestic work, cleaning or baby minding. Men deeply resented women working while they were unemployed; they resented even more being dependent on women.

Trade unionists, men and women alike, were agreed that an increased recruitment of women workers was necessary as a first step toward arresting the undercutting and general lowering of wages which women's cheap labour caused. However, they did not relate organization to a specific programme of demands for women workers. They did not realize that unless they offered women improved wages, opportunities and conditions, women were unlikely to show interest. The recruitment of women dominated both the women's TUC conference and the Women Workers' Group throughout the 1920s and 1930s. The recruitment campaigns which they launched lacked any specific appeal made to women, except to be recruited. They were received with apathy by trade unionists. The main resolution of the first women's TUC conference, in 1925, instructed the Women Workers' Group to recommend ways of increasing trade union organization among women. The group submitted recommendations to the TUC general council for approval. The council agreed that trade unions should be advised to form women's sub-committees and that it should itself convene area conferences and send deputations to unions to impress on them the importance of organizing women. The council decided, however, to defer its decision on whether a chief woman officer should be employed by the TUC as secretary to the Women Workers' Group. It also thought that the decision to form branch or district women's committees should be left to individual unions. Some area conferences were held, supported by local trade councils and other organizations concerned with women workers, particularly the womens' section of the Labour party and the Women's Co-operative Guild. Leaflets stressing the need for women to organize were printed and a questionnaire was distributed to all trade union secretaries in an effort to ascertain the level of organization, the wages, hours and conditions of women members.

One of the leaflets circulated by the Women Workers Group, 'To Parents', was specifically addressed to parents who were trades unionists. It was part of the campaign to stress, not just to women, but to male trades unionists also, the importance of organizing women. Even in the textile industry, with its long tradition of organization of women, the point still had to be made. 'Non Union Wives: Trades Council Delegates as Offenders,' revealed the *Cotton Factory Times* in 1924. The story told of the Weaver's Association's motion at the Ashton, Stalybridge and Dunkinfield Trades Council, which demanded that if a member of the council was

> allowing his wife or daughter to remain outside the trade union whilst actually engaged in any occupation for which there is a trade union in existence the name should be read at a meeting of the Council and the question of his credentials raised.[2]

The chairman tried to move an amendment to delete the latter part of the resolution. Mrs Higson, the mover of the resolution, rejected it.

> We want the whole hog. If a chap has a wife who won't pay, let him pay for her and get her inside the union. He must dock it out of her wages and pay it for her (laughter). We had not long since a man who said his wife would not pay. We had a terrible lot of bother with her, but she would not pay. It finished by him paying before he would be shown up. She was very stupid. I quite admit women are stupid but there are ways and means of making them do things.[3]

A compromise amendment was accepted, which resolved that the names of delegates whose working wives and daughters were not members of unions should be read out in the semi-private meeting of the executive committee with the offending delegate present. It was also agreed that the word 'son' be added to 'wife and daughter'. The question of wives and daughters came up in 1926 when, instead of a separate conference, a meeting was convened during the week of the TUC conference for unions catering for women workers. A resolution was passed, advocating the formation of women's guilds for wives and women relatives of trade unionists 'as a means of linking them up with the Trade Union Movement and encouraging the study and spread of the principles of Trade Unionism among women'.[4]

Also debated at the 1926 meeting was the question of trade boards and their effect on the organization of women workers. Since the Trade Boards Act of 1909, subsequent legislation had established trade boards in a variety of industries. The Trade Board Act of 1918 had given the minister of labour the power to establish a trade board in any industry where the minister thought that no adequate machinery existed for the regulation of wages. It gave the trade boards themselves the power to deal with hours and conditions and fix minimum wages. Since trade boards were established in industries where wages were low, the majority of workers under their authority were women. The establishment of trade boards had been generally welcomed by the trade union movement, but doubts were beginning to be expressed about their effect on the recruitment and organization of women workers. Two motions relating to trade boards were discussed at the 1926 meeting. One, which was carried, deplored the government's closure of the Grocery and Provision Trade Board and called for its re-establishment. The other, which was defeated, called upon the general council 'to conduct an inquiry into those trades in which the Trade Unions have found it extremely difficult to organize, i.e. catering trade, hotels etc. and domestic service, and to urge upon the Government the necessity of instituting trade boards for such trades'.[5] The motions might appear to be almost identical. But the fact that the latter was not accepted revealed that whilst trade unionists saw the need for government protection of low-paid, unorganized women workers, they were not prepared to admit to failure to organize in difficult areas. During the debate on the second motion, one speaker put the case against the trade boards.

> I have had some experience amongst some of the workers referred to in this resolution and it is my experience that the Trade Boards do nothing more nor less than develop a false sense of security.... The workers say 'I do not want to join a Trade Union, the Government, Stanley Baldwin, or someone else will protect my wages.' I do hope this Congress will not do anything which will create a greater sense of security in the Trade Boards – because I am sure they are retarding Trade Union organisation. And they are doing something far worse, they are not in any way creating a sense of responsibility amongst the workers, and they are one of the greatest dangers and difficulties which we are up against in organising the women. We have to show these people that their only means of improving their condition is by industrial organisation.[6]

Although it is hard to imagine that any worker in the autumn of 1926 might look to Stanley Baldwin to protect her wages, there was no doubt that the trade boards hampered trade union recruitment of industrial workers.

This was confirmed in 1931, when the TUC annual report gave the findings of a survey on trade boards. The report conceded that trade boards had improved wages, or at least stopped them from falling, in the trades which they regulated. However, trade unions involved in those trades complained that once wages had been fixed, it was very difficult to improve them, since employers claimed that they had been negotiated by representatives of workers on the trade boards. Evidence from the unions also confirmed that trade boards were, in most instances, a hindrance to developing effective organization. The report concluded that existing boards should continue, but that the creation of new boards should be carefully considered.

Underlying the debate on the trade boards was the larger question, whether women ought to look to legislation or organization for their protection. The trade boards ensured a minimum wage for women; low as the fixed rates were, they did mean a marked improvement for many and protection against falling wages for the rest. But the belief that wages, hours and conditions were the province of free collective bargaining, not statutory control, has always been strong in the trade union movement. History has shown that organization has achieved more than legislation. Legislation has only ever given minimal protection and rights. There was, therefore, a tendency, manifested in the debate over the trade boards, to see legislation as the enemy of organization, instead of welcoming statutory protection, however minimal, and organizing to improve it.

In the late 1920s little was done by the Women Worker's Group to increase the organization of women; the annual conference of women's unions did not meet in 1928 and 1929. The campaign to recruit women was merged with the general recruitment campaign, since membership fell dramatically in the late 1920s. A women's conference was held in 1930, at which the need to recruit women was again the dominant issue. A set of proposals was drawn up, including one that the general council establish a Women's Advisory Committee composed of the Women Worker's Group and five representatives from women's unions. The proposal was accepted and the Women's Advisory Committee established. Another proposal was that unions should form branch committees to discuss the recruitment of women. The conference also recommended the establishment of local women's organizing committees, as sub-committees of trades councils, consisting of representatives from trade unions, the Labour party, the Women's Co-operative Guild and other women's organizations.

The main aim of these committees, as stated in the circular sent to the trades councils, was to recruit new members and maintain the interest of existing ones. The circular gave no advice as to how the committees should do either of those things and made no suggestion of any positive aims for women workers which would attract them to trade unionism. In 1932 the Women's Advisory Committee reported on the response from trades councils to the circular. Of 421 trades councils circularized, 286 did not reply, 65 reported no action taken, 35 were considering the proposals and 35 had formed a committee. The two main reasons given for not establishing a committee were

(a) general apathy, or fear of victimisation owing to the intense industrial depression.
(b) apathy of local officials of the Trade Unions concerned.[7]

In October 1934 the Women's Advisory Committee of the London Trades Council staged a five-day pageant of Labour at Crystal Palace. It was a big affair with 1,500 performers, the London Labour Choir and a full symphony orchestra. Other committees organized area conferences. Throughout the 1930s calls were continually made from all sections of the movement for the increased organization of women. 'The increasing displacement of workers by the introduction of automatic machinery and the increasing use of girl labour to replace skilled males,'[8] was a trend regarded with alarm by men; organization of women was seen as a means of controlling it. Criticism, too, was made of the TUC's method of recruitment.

The manner in which it is being done is wrong. Leaflets sent round by the TUC which have cost hundreds of pounds are a failure. Let us adopt the method that was adopted by the late Mary Macarthur at Cradley.[9]

F

The TUC did not take the hint to encourage militant action. However, by 1937 the TUC had become aware of the need to offer women some tangible gains from trade union membership. A new ingredient was added to the recruitment campaign – the fitness and beauty ingredient. In 1937 a leaflet was issued with a picture of a young beautiful girl in a two-piece swimming suit on the front. The caption read 'Health and Beauty – a word to women and girls earning their own livelihood'. The leaflet said that real beauty was based on nourishing food, exercise, fresh air and the avoidance of physical strain. 'NO BEAUTY PREP-ARATION OR MEDICINE CAN GIVE YOU THESE ESSENTIAL FACTORS.'[10] Trade unionism could, since it could give better wages for food and clothing, shorter hours, better conditions and safety at work. A second leaflet, published in 1939, had a picture of a glamorous woman waving from a train window. Its caption was 'Ticket to Health and Beauty'. Inside there was a picture of a woman sitting in front of a mirror making herself up. Women were told that 'Beauty prep-arations can help enhance the charms of womanhood, but there are even more important foundations of beauty'.[11] Interested women were asked to 'post this coupon (to Sir Walter Citrine TUC . . .) FOR REAL HEALTH AND BEAUTY'.[12] These leaf-lets are a reflection of the attitude of the TUC and the Women's Advisory Committee towards women. Health and Beauty were seen as the most tangible gains to offer women. Whilst better wages and conditions would have led to better health and, per-haps, more beauty, the campaign merely re-enforced the stereo-type of women as disinterested in anything but their appearance.

The result of all these recruitment campaigns was a con-tinual decline in women's trade union membership. In 1918 the number of women in trade unions affiliated to the TUC was 1,086,000; in 1930 it was 468,090 and in 1939 it was only 552,585.

Their lack of leadership in the matter of women's recruitment was a reflection of the general lack of leadership in the TUC general council in the late 1920s and 1930s. Women workers are often accused of apathy, but the cool response of the predominantly male trade councils to the Women's Advisory Committee's attempt to interest them in establishing local organizing committees was indicative of the general apathy by trade unions towards women. The treatment which women received within the unions was hardly designed to make them enthusiastic supporters of trade unions.

In 1922 The Boot and Shoe Operatives Union was once again faced with a disgruntled group of women members led by Mary Bell, the woman who had stayed with the union in the pre-war years, when Lizzie Wilson had formed her breakaway independent women's union. Frustrated by the union's refusal to negotiate wage rises for women, Mary Bell warned the annual conference that

> The sex-war in our Union is forcing women to look well after themselves. We are starting a women's social club in connection with our Branch for educational purposes, the need of combination and sex-consciousness . . . From our mass meeting we have our instructions. Past History may repeat itself.[13]

In the mid-1920s Mary Bell persuaded the union to commit itself to an 'equal minimum wage' and to the opening up of all departments to women provided that the full men's wage was paid. By 1930, however, these commitments, had become long-term objectives. Mary Bell bitterly attacked the conference. 'We want to be equal members of the Union, and I want to say quite frankly that we shall fight this to the bitter end . . . even to our extinction.'[14] Far from being won to her point of view, the conference overwhelmingly resolved that 'this conference reaffirms its determined opposition to female labour being engaged on operations hitherto performed by male labour'.[15] In the mid-1930s the union became worried by the low level of organization among women boot and shoe operatives and set about organizing women in a series of one-day area conferences. In 1937, it negotiated a new agreement which gave women increased wages and lessened the differential between male and female earnings by 7%. The result was a substantial increase in female membership.

Although the gains fell far short of Mary Bell's hope for equal pay and equal opportunity they showed that, when the union was prepared to negotiate even small gains for women, the women responded. Yet, the decision by the National Union of Boot and Shoe Operatives to re-affirm its exclusion of women from certain grades, in order to prevent women from doing 'men's jobs' for less pay, was typical of most unions' refusal to negotiate equal minimum rates. The Tailor and Garment Workers' Union campaigned in 1928 for an agreement with the employers to maintain strict demarcation lines between 'men's' and 'women's' work. In 1935, when the sexual division of labour was again threatened by changes in production methods, especially the introduction of the conveyor belt, motions were tabled at the annual conference demanding that the executive take all possible steps to ensure that men only were employed in various areas of work. There were no calls for equal pay. In the late 1930s similar alarm was expressed by the Railway Clerks Association.[16] At its 1937 conference a motion was carried viewing with grave concern the increasing employment of women clerks and the consequent displacement of men. Again there was no call for equal pay, despite the fact that throughout the inter-war years the journal of the Railway Clerks Association had frequently advocated it.

In the late 1920s, women's salaries in local government employment were on average between 60% and 70% of men's salaries. By 1931 it had become evident that part of the policy of cuts in local government spending was to cut the wages bill by employing more women and fewer men. Alarmed by this policy, the annual conference of NALGO discussed ways of trying to reverse it. Some delegates urged that the principle of equal pay be introduced, but the conference opposed it. 'Warned by C. J. Newman, town clerk of Exeter, that its adoption might lower men's pay to the women's level, they rejected both the motions and the amendments.'[17] This policy was reversed in 1935, when a motion for equal pay was carried despite the opposition of two Yorkshire women. One of the women opposed equal pay because she thought women ought to concentrate on advancing themselves in areas of 'women's' work, the other because she thought equal pay would mean either the exclusion of women from work altogether or the scaling down of men's rates to the women's level. At the same conference a motion against the employment of married women was carried by an almost unanimous vote.

The right place for a married woman, urged F. E. Fox, sponsoring this, was in her home. If she wanted work outside, there were countless voluntary organisations; she must not compete for salaried jobs with men. A woman delegate, Miss A. Noble, agreed, arguing that the employment of married women, willing to work for 'pin money', must depress the pay of their unmarried sisters.[18]

Opposition to the employment of married women was maintained by many unions and those unions without a marriage bar sought to introduce one. Unemployment not only divided men from women, but single women from married ones.

In contrast to NALGO, the NUT had been committed to a policy of equal pay since 1919; far from trying to pursue the claim, however, the NUT accepted wage cuts which increased the differential between men's and women's salaries. Teachers suffered a series of government-imposed salary cuts throughout the 1920s and early 1930s. The NUT was party to the negotiations about how to apportion the cuts and women suffered disproportionately. In November 1930 the *Woman Teacher* described what the 1925 NUT agreement had done for women's wages.

(1) It brought about a differentiation in the annual increments of men and women respectively. Whereas the increment had been £12 10s. for both men and women, it was reduced to £12 for men and £9 for women. THE MEN LOST 10s. THE WOMEN LOST £3 10s. WOMEN LOST SEVEN TIMES AS MUCH AS MEN.
(2) In every one of the four scales women certificated assistants lost; in three of the four scales men certificated assistants GAINED, and in the fourth scale, although the men lost, the women lost more than seven times as much as the men.[19]

It was not until 1935 that teachers salaries were restored to their pre-cut level.

Married women teachers were sacked: headmistresses were increasingly replaced by headmasters; and young untrained girls were allowed to work in elementary schools for the wages of untrained teachers, while trained teachers were unemployed. The National Union of Women Teachers continued to campaign for equal pay, for the right of married women to work, for an extension of nursery schools and for smaller classes and more teachers. Its stance was political. 'Having seen with concern the effect of Fascism on the position of women in other countries the NUWT is strengthening its feminist activities, and opposing economies in education, and by talks and lectures hopes to make clear what Fascism means for women.'[20] The NUT and the NUWT were divided and wage agreements accepted by the NUT had increased the rift between the two unions. Women who remained in the NUT had little reason to believe that it was acting in their interest. The disunity of the teachers left them in an even weaker position than other unions to fight attacks on their wages and living standards.

Unlike teachers, local government workers and some industrial workers, members of the skilled craft unions on the whole were not troubled by the problems of women being hired to do the same jobs as men for less pay. They continued to control entry through apprenticeships, which were barred to women. However, dilution, brought about by new automated production processes, did lead to the introduction of semi-skilled workers, often women, whose wages were less than would have been paid to skilled men. For the skilled male worker this trend was as alarming as women undercutting men in the same job. The alarm was sounded at several TUC annual conferences throughout the 1930s; in 1937 a demand was made to organize women and to establish a rate for the job, irrespective of sex.[21] There was little that the skilled craft unions could do about the problem, however, so long as they, in particular the AEU, continued to exclude women and so deny themselves control over rates for the jobs or the hiring of women in the new industries.

A change in attitude was evident in the ranks of the AEU in 1937. During the debate on the need for the 'rate for the job' a delegate from the AEU who supported the principle spoke of the need to organize women.

> I am of the opinion that it is not impossible to organise women. Everybody who has read the press for the last six months will see the growing number of strikes that have taken place by women alone in the Midlands, and which have ultimately led in some cases even to the organisation of men.[22]

Some women were not content to be unorganized simply because the relevant union refused them membership. Jessie McCullough organised the women at the Lucas Factory into the Transport and General Workers Union. Once again the women had to prove themselves before the union took them seriously.

> The union officials were very lax and they used to look at me amazed when I brought in the application forms filled up. They just didn't believe women would join the union. But every week I took down more forms, and eventually we had a big meeting outside the gates and most of the girls joined. When the strike came, all the girls walked out.[23]

For her pains Jessie McCullough was sacked; but she received victimization pay from her union and a gold medal from Ernie Bevin for her trade union work.

Those craft unions which did accept women, like the Boot and Shoe Operatives Union, tried to stop or control encroachments of women on men's jobs by asserting the sexual division of labour. On the whole they were successful, since they could control their industries through apprenticeships. Unions like the AESD had little difficulty, since women were organized only in the tracer's section. Although there were some male tracers who received higher rates, tracing was regarded as essentially a 'woman's' job. Draughting was reserved for men through the control of apprenticeships. The tracers' section had great difficulty in recruiting women because, like many unions, they offered them little in return for their 6d. subscription. Women members of the AESD stood to gain from union benefits, particularly unemployment benefit, but minimum rates for tracers were not negotiated until 1939, when dilution began to worry the AESD. (Minimum rates for draughtsmen had been established in the mid-twenties.) Restricted to the small tracers' section, they were barely involved in the main business of the union, a position which they sought to change. They opposed the suggestion that the union follow other unions' example and establish a dowry scheme for tracers.

> The Tracers' Committee have long held the view that tracers are members of the Association just as draughtsmen are, and may, in private life, be offered sugar plums, but in business life their attitude is sufficiently modern and robust to allow of them

becoming members of and retaining membership of their appropriate trade unions, because it is at one time the ideal and the practical thing to do.[24]

The tracers were also determined that a marriage dowry benefit should not be used as a means of pressurizing women to leave work on marriage.

Although the AESD did little for women in the 1920s and 1930s, they did publish, from 1927 to 1935, a supplement to *The Draughtsman* called *The Tracer*, one of the few attempts by any trade union to educate women. Most journals, if they included anything at all for women, aimed their message, like the TUC, at 'health and beauty'. *The Tracer* not only had articles on the importance of trade unionism, but also published a series of technical articles and mechanical drawings on such things as steam engines, surface condensers, centrifugal pumps, dynamos and diesel engines.

The disastrous effect of the division of men and women workers on the lowering of wages is most clearly shown in the history of the Union of Post Office Workers (UPOW). In 1926–27 the union drew up a comprehensive wage claim to be submitted to an industrial tribunal. Post Office workers, like other government employees, were under pressure to accept cuts in wages and staffing levels. Despite such pressure, the union persisted in its wage claim, which included a demand for equal pay for equal work. It cited the resolution passed by the House of Commons in 1920 and Article 6 of the Treaty of Versailles, both of which committed the government to a policy of equal pay. They also quoted the recommendations of the War Cabinet Committee on Industry, which had recommended that equal pay for equal work should apply in all the manipulative branches of government service, and to counter objections on the grounds of different hours for men and women, drew attention to the War Cabinet Committee report which had recommended

> in the case of Post Office duties, the question of men having late hours or night work should not be allowed to complicate that of the relative value of their work to the women's, but should be provided for by an extra allowance to persons undertaking common duties under disagreeable conditions, a principle that might also be adopted in industry generally.[25]

The Post Office would not agree to the principle of equal pay, and so the union dropped that proposal before its wage claim reached the tribunal, stating that the union, 'while maintaining that the principle was a just one, found it necessary to claim other scales of pay for women'.[26] The scales of pay negotiated for women maintained unequal rates for equal work. Less than ten years later, the male members of the union found that they paid dearly for failing to pursue the fight for equal pay. Women were increasingly employed in certain jobs, at lower wages, as part of the Post Office policy of reducing its wages bill. By 1935 the male members of the union had become seriously alarmed. Letters appeared in *The Post*, the union's journal, arguing that 'a woman's place was in the home' and that it was a scandal that married women should work while men were unemployed. As the situation worsened, the attacks widened to women workers in general. In February 1935, the general secretary wrote in his annual report that 'Division, segregation, de-amalgamation, redundancy, and most of our present ills are traceable to the policy of employing less men and more women'.[27]

Matters came to a head at the unions' 1935 conference. An emergency resolution, proposed by the general secretary, called for the immediate implementation of equal pay as a measure to counter the influx of women earning less pay for the same job and consequently generally lowering wages and displacing men. It was passed unanimously. At the same conference another motion was moved deploring the increasing ratio of women to men employed by the Post Office and calling upon the union to demand a halt to the trend. In the debate on the motion the previous vote in favour of equal pay was largely forgotten. In a flurry of emotional speeches, the male delegates attacked women as the cause of all their economic ills. Mussolini and Hitler were commended for their defence of the male against the female. The mover of the motion, to great cheers, argued that it was a case of 'national and moral standards'. The seconder went further. He demanded that the policy of 'breaking morally and physically the youths of the present generation had to cease'. To cheers of 'Hear, hear' he said that:

Even Mussolini and Hitler, dictators as they were had realised that no country politically and economically could afford to despise its male population. He thought they would agree with him that, if history proved anything, it proved that every country where the male population had been ignored had become a decadent nation.[28]

He even called upon women members of the union to support him. One man opposed the resolution pointing out that if they had equal pay for men and women there would be no question of any ratio. *The Post* records no cheers of 'hear, hear' for his speech; another speaker, however, received laughter for his statement that whilst women 'might get equal pay for equal work, there might be no men to have equal pay with women'. There was laughter, too, when the mover summed up.

> They all agreed about the emancipation for women, but, if they had a nigger working two hours a day for one coconut they would not emancipate the negress if they made her work four hours a day for one coconut.[29]

The resolution was passed with only two dissentients. It is not surprising that women members of the UPOW were not enthusiastic about trade unionism. In fact, as one woman delegate said at the conference, trying to get women's interests served was 'like asking for bread and getting a stone'.[30]

In the same year, 1935, the annual conference of the Union of Shop Distributive and Allied Workers (USDAW) discussed the problem of married women. A motion demanded that the union refuse to employ married women in any capacity, in the hope that it would set an example to employers. The delegates reacted in a wholly different way from the members of the UPOW. One speaker said they should be fighting not to get rid of women, but to improve their wages. He added that the motion contained 'the first seeds of Fascism'.[31] Another delegate said that, if they passed the motion, they would be a 'laughing stock inside the advanced movements which are working towards this object of equality between men and women'.[32] Some delegates trotted out the argument that women should be 'minding their own business at home', but the motion was overwhelmingly defeated.

It was not surprising that at both the UPOW and the

USDAW conference Fascism should be mentioned in relationship to the employment of women. In 1934 at Nuremburg Hitler had stated the woman's world was, 'her husband, her family, her children and her home'. In Germany unemployment had been reduced, according to Nazi propaganda, from 5 million to 2.5 million, but as Hilda Browning pointed out in her pamphlet, 'Women under Fascism and Communism',[33] the 'miracle' of reduced unemployment had been wrought largely at the expense of women workers, who had decreased from 11.5 million to 6 million. The National Socialist movement paid girls to get married, if they promised not to return to work. In 1934 a series of posters appeared in Berlin trying to persuade women to leave work to become full-time mothers and wives. The exceptions were to persuade working-class women to accept either domestic service or agricultural work. Such ideas, as we have seen, appeared also in Great Britain. A pamphlet by D. E. Swaffield entitled 'Work for 1,000,000 Unemployed. An Open Challenge for every M.P.', appeared in 1933. His scheme was to dismiss a million women from work and employ a million men in their place. He thought the scheme would 'mean the ultimate reinstatement of women in women's positions, that is, the home'.[34] For the women rendered unemployed by the scheme he advocated the dole, domestic service, household duties and marriage; the latter, he thought, would provide for a large number of women displaced from work. Although these ideas reflect the extremism of the right, it is a sad reflection on the trade union movement that, in times of economic stress, some men looked to Fascist ideas as an answer to unemployment. Throughout the inter-war years, there was a strong underlying current, sometimes openly expressed by male trade unionists, that if only the world of work could be restricted to men unemployment and low wages would disappear. Few outwardly attacked the single woman's right to a job, though restrictive practices denied equal opportunity to women. But married women workers were attacked unless they were employed on jobs which men regarded as too low paid and inferior for themselves. The situation was aggravated by the imbalance in the population of the ratio of men to women. At the end of World War I there was a higher ratio of women to men than ever before and in 1931 the census revealed that there were 1½ million unmarried women over the age of thirty-five.

The debates within trade unions about the trend towards increased female labour, the statistics which showed that in certain trades like light engineering, the electrical industry, food and clothing there had been a proportionate increase in women employed and the fact that the proportion of women in the labour force increased during the 1920s and 1930s might give the impression that women did not suffer from severe unemployment. Women who worked outside the new mechanized light industries, however, did suffer. It is difficult to get a precise picture, since many women worked in 'uninsured' work and did not register as unemployed. Only 1 woman in 8 worked in an insurable job. Many married women did not register because they were not entitled to benefit; those who did were struck off the register if they refused to take domestic service. The 1931 'Anomalies' Act deprived almost all married women of claiming benefit. Regardless of whether a woman had worked in an insured job before marriage and regardless of the number of contributions she had paid, she could not claim unemployment benefit unless she could prove that she had contributed stamps since marriage and that she was normally employed and available for work. The effect of the act was drastic: by the end of the year in which it had come into force more than 134,000 married women had been disallowed benefit. Pregnant women, too, were unable to receive any benefit except poor relief. In order to get benefit an applicant had to go before a court of referees and prove that she was available for work. Regardless of the state of pregnancy, pregnant women were refused benefit if they were not available. Health Insurance benefit did not cover pregnancy either, unless the woman could prove some other condition as a grounds for ill-health and inability to work. Despite all the male talk about women displacing them, women almost certainly suffered proportionately more unemployment than men. In 1931 Lady Astor claimed, that according to the latest figures received from the ministry of labour, in 17 out of the 25 trades enumerated, there was a higher percentage of unemployed women than men.

In 1928 the TUC annual conference passed a resolution calling for equal unemployment benefit for men and women. The TUC also made deputations to the government demanding training schemes to alleviate the plight of unemployed women. Their schemes for training women were somewhat limited. The 1933 TUC women's conference suggested training in 'plain cooking, mothercraft, hygiene and physical culture,'[35] schemes hardly designed to give women training for employment. Domestic service continued to be regarded by the government and the TUC as the one great area of potential employment for women. In the 1930s, more than one-third of employed women were in domestic work and there were continual attempts to increase that number. In 1930 the Labour party issued a pamphlet, 'What's Wrong with Domestic Service? We want to know what you think'.[36] One would have thought that the Labour party hardly needed to issue a questionnaire to find out why domestic service was so unpopular.

It did become clear to the Standing Joint Committee of Industrial Women's Committees, as it had been clear to the government committees which looked into the question immediately after the war, that a radical improvement was needed in wages and conditions to make the work more popular. Several attempts had been made to organize domestic servants since the late 19th century, when Jessie Stephens had first tried to organize them in Glasgow, but none of the attempts had resulted in permanent organization. The Standing Committee tried again in the early 1930s to interest existing unions in organizing domestic workers, but it too failed.

> The T&GWU were unfortunately unable to accept the invitation as they considered the difficulties in the way of organising these workers were too great at the present time. After further consideration the G&MW adopted the same view.[37]

Some more modest attempts were made, among them Hampstead Trades Council's guild for about 100 domestic workers. Pressure was kept up from all fronts throughout the 1930s to encourage, or force, women into service. In 1938 an exhibition on domestic service was mounted to 'put this calling on a definite footing'. The official guide to the exhibition claimed that 'good Domestic Service is the foundation of National Health and

Happiness'. In 1938 the TUC made another attempt to organize domestic workers. A National Union of Domestic Workers was formed and a Charter for Domestic Workers drawn up by the union laid down desired minimum wages, hours and conditions. It was, however, World War II, not organization, which was to relieve women from domestic servitude. That so many women consistently refused to accept domestic work was a remarkable assertion of self-respect in the light of the mass unemployment which surrounded them.

Against this general picture of disunity of men and women workers, the nine days of the General Strike stand out as a remarkable exception. In 1926 men and women workers united on class lines. Little attention has been paid to the role women workers played in the strike, partly because women railway clerical workers were the only large group of women called out by the TUC as members of a key union. The *Railway Clerk* described the men and women who responded 'bravely' to the call and came out on strike for the first time in their history. It also contained reports from organizers in different areas. In Scotland reported that

> From station, dock and depot men and women rolled up prepared to play their part in the great effort to see justice applied to an heroic and long suffering section of workers. . . . In days gone by strike was too frequently regarded as a man's affair. This time we saw a transformation. The womenfolk were devoted and solid too.[38]

Northumberland and Durham reported that men and women worked together to produce a Strike Bulletin and South Lancashire ended its report by saying that it

> would not be complete without mention of the women members who struck work with us. We cannot forget the splendid work our women folk rendered to us at this critical time in history. They took a full share in the work, were as eager as the male members; not only did they take their share of the humdrum work of the strike but in some instances took the platform and were very acceptable speakers. We must see that in future openings are made, so that these ladies can find their sphere in the R.C.A.[39]

In the news bulletins issued by the workers during the strike and sent to the TUC there were reports of the Rowntree's girls out on strike at York; in Scotland many textile factories employing large numbers of women were 'out'; women picketed at Reading 'with enthusiasm and effectiveness' and the Westminster Council of Action wanted 'men and WOMEN pickets'.[40] Ellen Wilkinson toured the country making speeches in support of the strike and was enthusiastically welcomed. At the TUC the two women on the general council were delegated to the Food and Essential Services Committee. In many areas of the country meetings were specifically held to explain to the strikers' 'womenfolk' the meaning of the strike. Many women workers in unions not called out, like the Rowntree's girls, spontaneously struck; others helped on picket lines and canteens, demonstrated and turned buses over in their non-working hours. Women in Hammersmith and Poplar received the same rough treatment from the police as the men and some Communist party women, like some Communist party men, were imprisoned.

Many middle-class women, like middle-class men, did help the volunteers; the response to the strike was essentially on class, not sex, lines. When the AWKS called its members out on strike, some of its members were critical of their executive's decision, and the union reported that 'members have even been heard to say that had they known that the Association was a Trade Union they would never have joined it'.[41] A special meeting to discuss the decision supported the executive, however, and after the strike the AWKS donated money to the miner's lock-out fund. At a more personal level, Bessie Dickenson, a weaver, not only helped to collect money for the miners but 'in the end I raffled all the stuff I'd collected for my bottom drawer, and my umbrella as well'.[42]

Unfortunately, it took the exceptional circumstances of the General Strike for men and women workers to act together. The nine days stand out as an exception, an experience remembered, but not as a basis for establishing a permanent unity of men and women workers. The TUC's decision to order a return to work, leaving the miners isolated in defeat, stunned men and women workers and left them disillusioned. The experience must have mystified women who had previously had little experience of trade unionism or militant action. Unfortunately, many women, like men, did not respond to the defeat by rejecting the leaders who had 'sold them out', but chose to reject trade unionism.

The defeat did not entirely crush militancy in women workers. A few working women did, remarkably, challenge the conservative leadership of their trade unions and their challenge erupted in unofficial strikes in the late 1920s. The first and most remarkable of these strikes was at the Rego Clothing Factory in 1928. Sam Elsbury, the organizer of the strike, wrote afterwards that

> when the Rego strike broke out, that of 600 workers, mostly poorly paid girls, against attacks on their already low living standards, trade unionists shook their heads and predicted an early defeat. Most of the girls were completely without previous experience of trade unionism and the fact that their strike was not only refused endorsement by their union's National Executive in Leeds, but was definitely attacked by it, made defeat tenfold certain. As an 'unofficial' strike no union funds were, of course available for strike pay, and the outlook for the strike was, therefore, about as bad as it conceivably could be. Nevertheless, this apparently hopeless venture lasted 12 weeks and terminated at Xmas, 1928, with the victory of the strikers.[43]

Deprived of strike benefit, the women had to raise their own money. This they did with great success. Some money came from the official trade union movement and for the first eight weeks of the strike the London Trades Council gave generous donations, but they were stopped when 'the Council felt that London Trades Unionists were viewing its prolongation with misgivings, as no attempt was apparently being made to reach a settlement'.[44] (There was little evidence that rank-and-file London trade unionists had misgivings about the strike. They supported the women generously throughout the twelve weeks.) Support also came from the Russian needleworkers who sent £216.

The strike must have had much of the exuberance of the strikes of women workers in the immediate pre-war years. The women, mainly girls between the ages of sixteen and twenty-one, marched, picketed and demonstrated. A collection of songs emerged from the strike which were later published. More than anything else, they give a feel of the spirit of the strike.

REGO

R stands for Rego, who don't know what they're worth,
E stands for Everything, they want the blooming earth.
G stands for Glory, when workers will be free.
O stands for what we Owe to Solidarity.[45]

As a result of the strike the Clothing Employers Federation approached the executive of the Tailors' and Garment Workers' Trade Union and requested that the London organizers be disciplined so that 'amicable relations' might continue between the employers and the union. The union complied. Sam Elsbury, the London organizer, was dismissed. The London members' then formed a breakaway union, the United Clothing Workers' Trade Union (UCW), of which Sam Elsbury was appointed general secretary. The union published its own journal, *The Red Needle*, in which it campaigned for industrial unionism in the needle working trade. It saw the urgent need to form a united body of workers which was not weakened by the sectionalism of the nineteen unions which, at that time, organized workers in the clothing trade. The first edition, at least, was printed in Hebrew and English in an attempt to reach the large number of Jewish clothing workers in the East End. The official trade union movement tried to crush the new union which was supported by the National Minority Movement and the Communist party. Ernie Bevin, of the Transport and General Workers' Union, threatened that bus and transport companies would be persuaded by the TGWU not to place orders with any company that recognized the new union. The clothing workers in London continued, despite such threats, to join the UCW and in May 1929 700 workers at the Polikoff factory, many of whom were women, joined the UCW 'en bloc'. The Polikoff employers issued a notice.

> Strikers, what do you hope to get from this strike except applause from the Red International? The strike is a Communist attempt to destroy the recognised British trade union movement.[46]

According to E. Mosshovitz the strikers answered that with a song.

> The TUC loves Mr P
> So Mr P loves the TUC;
> Both combined love the T&G and
> The whole damn lot love skinning me.[47]

With 'the whole damned lot', Mr P, the TUC and the TGWU against them, the strikers did not win recognition. The Union survived only until the mid-1930s.

Unofficial strikes and organization were not confined to the clothing workers; they erupted in other industries and often involved women. The high preponderance of women in the 'unofficial' unions seriously worried the General Council of the TUC. It was not surprising that women workers found much more in the unofficial 'red' unions to represent their interests than in the official trade unions. The 'red' unions, modelled largely on the aims of the National Minority Movement, were a challenge to the policies and structures of the official unions, in particular the craft unions, the sectionalism and restrictive practices of which had never been to the benefit of women workers.

The militancy of women like the Rego girls, Mary Bell and Jessie McCullough was rare. In the lean years of the early 1930s, the handful of women's unions failed to move motions at the TUC annual conferences, so that outside the annual report of the Women's Advisory Committee the problems of women workers were not discussed. The merger of the National Federation of Women Workers with the General Workers Union in 1920 had left a large gap in women's representation at the TUC. Unions like the AWKS and the Women Public Health Officers did not have the influence which the National Federation of Women Workers had wielded.

The main demand of women at TUC conferences in the 1920s and 1930s was an improvement in maternity and child-welfare services. Although women were having appreciably smaller families and infant mortality, though still high among the poor, had declined, maternal mortality rates remained high. In 1927 it was four times as dangerous for a miner's wife to give birth than for a miner to work in the pit. Small improvement in services had been provided for by the Maternity and Child Welfare Act of 1919 but, owing to cuts in local government expenditure, many of the provisions were not implemented or implemented only in part. The Women Public Health Officers moved several resolutions at TUC conferences demanding improved maternity and child-welfare services. They were supported by the AWKS, who also demanded 'benefits sufficient for the healthy maintenance of mother and child for six weeks before and after confinement'.[48] In response to pressure from Women Public Health Officers the TUC, in conjunction with the British Medical Association, drew up a scheme for a National Maternity Service which it explained in its report to the 1939 conference. The Women Public Health officers were opposed to the scheme, because it was intended to operate in the private sector, not the public municipal services. The average poor woman could not afford visits to a GP. The women were annoyed at not having been consulted in the drafting of the scheme, which sparked off the most heated debate on any women's issue at TUC conferences of the 1930s. Several speakers opposed the scheme on the grounds that it based the service in private practice, not in the public sector. The Medical Practitioners Union defended themselves and private practice. Mr D. A. Welply, a delegate from the Medical Practitioners Union tried to assert his full medical superiority over the women.

> I did not intend to speak on this but having just had a very excellent post-graduate course in mid-wifery from two ladies, I feel competent to speak. . . . The general practitioner has given up, to a great extent, doing mid-wifery. One of the ladies said he did not know anything about mid-wifery. I disagree with that. Very many of the General Practitioners are excellent, in fact they are the only people who are competent to deal with mid-wifery, but there are many who have given it up because it has been taken from them by the local authority.[49]

A compromise was reached when the general council agreed to take women's objections to the scheme into consideration. As with so many other issues it was the war and not trades union demands, which was to improve the situation for women. Under the special care given to pregnant and nursing women during World War II, maternal mortality, for the first time, radically decreased.

Other organizations of working women outside the TUC also campaigned for women. The organizations tended to be those based on professional working women and were concerned largely with equal pay, equal opportunities, the right for married women to work and the opportunities for older women to work. Middle-class women, except those involved in the trade union movement, had since the 19th century tended to regard the factory acts which restricted the hours, overtime and jobs of some women as a serious infringement on their rights to equality and equal opportunity. The factory acts had been suspended during World War I, but were re-implemented after the war with one change – the employment of Women, Young Persons and Children Act of 1920 allowed women and young persons to be employed in factories on a two-shift system. In the late 1920s, when women's job opportunities were being severely attacked in a variety of ways, there was a renewed demand by middle-class women for the abolition of the factory acts. A pamphlet prepared for the London and National Society of Women's Service, entitled 'The Woman Worker and Restrictive Legislation'[50] so argued that restrictive legislation was one of the major obstacles to women's emancipation.

The Open Door Council also campaigned for the abolition of restrictive legislation. The council was a movement formed to fight for the equality of women at work. Largely owing to its pressure, the government commissioned a study of the effect of protective legislation on women's job opportunities in 1930. Contrary to the assertion of the Open Door Council and the London and National Women's Service the report found that trade union restrictive practices, not legislation, were the chief restraint on women's opportunities. In the textile industry there had been a small increase in the proportion of women employed, partly because the tendency of restrictive hours was 'to assimilate the hours of men's employment in the industry to those of the women'.[51] In other industries the increase of female employment had been slightly greater and there was no evidence that restrictive legislation had affected it. On the other hand, the report found that in almost all industries trade union restrictive practices did hurt women. The report cited the example of the cotton unions, which, as a general policy, barred women from working on mules; but in Wigan, where most of the men worked down the mines, the trade unions agreed to women working on mules. It was the same with piecers. In Oldham, Stockport and Preston the unions barred women from working as piecers, whereas in

Manchester and Bolton they did not. Of the Potteries the report said that

> The Trade Unions have throughout opposed the introduction of women into processes which they regard as unsuitable for women by reason of the heaviness of work and other conditions of employment.[52]

The report accepted that there were certain 'natural' divisions of labour along sex grounds, the skilled and heavy jobs being equally 'naturally' the province of men and the light, unskilled repetitive jobs being equally 'naturally' the province of women. Despite that, the report showed that the distribution of women in industry was governed and restricted by trade union agreements as much as any other force.

There was also pressure from employers for modifications, if not the abolition, of restrictive legislation. (Those who opposed the factory acts called them 'restrictive', those who supported them, 'protective'.) The trade union movement had opposed the introduction of the two-shift system for women workers and called for its repeal. The employers argued strongly for its retention. In 1935 a departmental committee conducted an inquiry into the system. It took evidence from employers, unions, workers and social workers, but the report was loaded in favour of employers and dismissed the evidence submitted by the TUC, which claimed that the system depressed wages, injured health and brought many social and economic disadvantages to the worker. Of the injurious effects to family life of the two-shift system the report blithely stated that

> as regards the effect on family life generally, it is probably true, as Professor Sargeant Florence has suggested to us, that 'The home is not really the social centre nowadays, the young people usually go out to the cinema, and probably the old people stay at home and listen to the wireless.[53]

That statement reflected the hypocrisy of the government. When it suited the employers and government (a Conservative government) family life was unimportant. On the other hand, the establishment, in its attempts to oust unwanted women from the workforce, continually asserted that the family was of prime importance for the national well-being and that women should be at home. The report recommended the continuation of the two-shift system and the government accepted that recommendation.

A small consideration but one which, in a sense, completes the picture of the employment problems of women in the 1930s was the problem of older women who sought employment. There were in the 1930s more than 1½ million unmarried women over the age of thirty-five. Most of them had to earn their own means of survival and many of them had dependants. The number of working women with dependants was disputed. A Fabian Society survey claimed that it was as high as 51.13% whereas a survey by Seebohm Rowntree and Frank D. Stuart[54] found that for women over twenty-five it was 19.5%. Even the lower figure meant that many working women had to support dependants on a wage that was usually based on the assumption that women did not need a 'family' wage. Older women found particular difficulty in getting employment, especially in clerical work where young attractive girls were desirable both for their feminine attributes and for the fact that they were cheaper. In 1935 the Over-Thirty Association was formed 'in the interests of the old industrial and professional women workers, many of whom are suffering very severely from the effects of unemployment.'[55] Of the women registered at the London employment exchanges in 1935, 60% were over thirty. It is a sobering reflection that women workers in the 1930s were considered to be old if they were over thirty. A decade later the association became the Over-Forty Club.

1 TUC Circular No 28   25 March 1927
2 The Cotton Factory Times   10 Oct 1924
3 Ibid
4 Annual Report Women's TUC 1926   p.3
5 Ibid   p.359
6 Ibid   p.360
7 Annual Report TUC 1932   p.104
8 Annual Report of the Women's TUC 1933
9 Annual Report TUC 1934   p.237
10 TUC Recruiting Leaflet   1937

11 TUC Recruiting Leaflet 1939
12 Ibid
13 Quoted in Alan Fox *A History of the National Union of Boot and Shoe Operatives 1874–1957* Basil Blackwell 1958 p.484
14 Ibid p.484
15 Ibid p.485
16 The Railway Service Journal June 1939
17 Alec SPOOR *White Collar Union* William Heinemann 1967 p.467
18 Ibid
19 The Woman Teacher Nov 1930
20 A. M. PIEROTTI *The Story of the National Union of Women Teachers* National Union of Women Teachers 1963 p.38
21 Annual Report TUC 1937 p.242
22 Ibid p.246
23 R. A. LEESON *Strike: A Live History 1887–1971* George Allen and Unwin 1973 p.131
24 The Draughtsman May 1930
25 Quoted in Union of Post Office Workers Wage Claim and Evidence 1926–27
26 Ibid
27 The Post 16 Feb 1935
28 Annual Conference Report, Supplement to The Post 1935
29 Ibid
30 Ibid
31 Report of the Annual Delegate Meeting of the National Union of Distributive and Allied Workers 1935
32 Ibid
33 See Hilda BROWNING *Women Under Fascism and Communism* Martin Lawrence Ltd 1936
34 D. E. SWAFFIELD *Work for 1,000,000 Unemployed: An Open Challenge to Every MP.* Universal Publications Ltd 1933 p.20
35 Annual Report TUC 1933 p.104
36 *What's Wrong with Domestic Service?* Labour Party 1930
37 Annual Report TUC 1932 p.106
38 The Railway Service Journal June 1926
39 Ibid
40 TUC Collection General Strike Documents
41 The Woman Clerk July 1926
42 LEESON op. cit. p.97
43 *Rego and Polikoff Strike Songs* United Clothing Workers' Trade Union 1929 p.5
44 *Short History of the London Trades Council* By a Delegate London Trades Council 1935 p.92
45 *Rego and Polikoff Strike Songs* op. cit. p.8
46 LEESON op. cit. p.118
47 LEESON op. cit. pp. 188f
48 The Annual Report TUC 1936 p.415
49 The Annual Report TUC 1939 p.331
50 J. BLAINEY *The Woman Worker and Restrictive Legislation* J. W. Arrowsmith 1928
51 *A Study of the Factors which have operated in the past and those which are operating now to determine the distribution of women in industry* HMSO Cmnd 3508 1930 p.8
52 Ibid p.17

53 *Departmental Committee on the Employment of Women and Young Persons on the Two Shift System* HMSO Cmnd 4914 1935 p.17
54 B. Seebohm ROWNTREE and Frank D. STUART *The Responsibility of Women Workers for Dependents* Oxford University Press 1921
55 Pamphlet Over-Thirty Association 1935

7

'Woman Power' 1939-1945

THE YEARS FROM 1939 to 1945 are still remembered as the time when women not only 'proved' they could do any job but disproved many of the myths about women workers – that married women have a high absentee rate, that women cannot keep secrets, that men and women cannot work together, that women do not like responsibility and are not interested in training, that women are too emotional to be reliable under stress, and that women have a lower productivity rate than men, etc. They were years, too, when society concerned itself, as at no other time, with the dual role of women with jobs and homes. Not only were the problems of child care given national attention, but also shopping, cooking, washing and maternity. A new phenomenon, women part-timers, became a feature of women's employment. It was seen by the government as a way in which the demand for women's labour could be reconciled with the needs of homes and families. Conscription of women for war work and the Services, a radical innovation, put women on an equal footing with men in a completely new way. Conscription raised the fundamental question of the value of women and men. The fight for equal compensation for women injured or disabled in war service was a fight for basic equality. The years from 1939 to 1945 represent a brief surge forward for women, a bright interlude between the dark days of the thirties and the conservative days of the fifties.

The scale of women's involvement in World War II was much greater than it had been in World War I. Then about 1.2 million women entered industry and about 100,000 joined the auxiliary Forces. In World War II more than 2 million women entered industry and more than 500,000 joined the armed forces and civil defence. Nor was the difference simply one of scale. In World War I women were only required to register 'voluntarily' for war work; in World War II they were conscripted for war work and the services. This led to a difference in approach to women, particularly on behalf of the government. The demand for women's labour caused the government to encourage the maximum use of women's potential at work and to recognize their responsibilities at home. With regard to the latter, there was no official suggestion that men and women should share domestic work, but the government did introduce schemes whereby the state took on part of the burden of women's home responsibilities. There was another important difference between the first and second wars, which affected quite strongly the response of trade unionists to government measures. World War I started with a groundswell of patriotism, but as the war progressed workers expressed increasing discontent at what they regarded as the unnecessary prolongation of the war. The appalling suffering and death rate of the men at the front and the suffering at home caused by rising prices, profiteering and, relatively, falling wages were the main causes of the discontent. Smaller losses and less blatant profiteering meant less discontent in World War II. The British population as a whole throughout the second war was much more committed to the belief that the war against fascism was imperative.

However, the different reactions to each war are not sufficient explanation for the smoothness with which 2 million women were introduced to the work force, many to the jobs of men, when in the first war a smaller introduction had led to strikes because men 'utterly refused' to work with women. In 1939, men had the experience of history to draw upon. History had shown that, despite the influx of women into men's jobs during World War I, those jobs had, by and large, returned to men in peace time. The war had caused no fundamental change in the sexual distribution of labour. Given the right safeguards, men assumed that history would repeat itself. Women, too, had remembered the history and many of them were determined that it should not repeat itself.

In the late 1930s the government began to re-arm in preparation for the war. The manufacturers were reluctant, however, to switch production from motor cars to aeroplanes, and so in March 1938 the government assumed powers to direct industry to manufacture what was necessary for re-armament. On the following day, 23 March, the TUC leaders were invited to No. 10 Downing Street, where they agreed to relax trade union restrictive practices in the engineering industry. It was their first visit to No. 10 since 1926. This agreement, made eighteen months before the declaration of war, paved the way for substitution in the munitions industry. Few other steps were taken by the government, even in the first few months of the war. Although the TUC resolved at the outbreak of war that 'Congress, with a united and resolute nation, enters the struggle with a clear conscience and steadfast purpose',[1] it was reluctant to enter into any agreement with the Chamberlain government, of which it was deeply suspicious. The situation was radically changed in May 1940 when, after the collapse of the Chamberlain government, Churchill formed a coalition government with Labour representatives in the cabinet. Ernie Bevin, a Labour MP and trade unionist was appointed minister of labour. It was a job which involved negotiating with the TUC widescale dilution and substitution and extensive state control over labour and the rights of trade unionists. Throughout 1940 and 1941 a series of acts was passed which gave the government powers to direct and control labour. Labour could be engaged only through employment exchanges or through approved trade unions. Skilled workers could not, without permission, leave their place of work nor be dismissed. Strikes and lock-outs were made illegal and a National Arbitration Tribunal was established to settle disputes when normal negotiating machinery failed. (As in World War I, making strikes illegal did not prevent them. The strike by the Betteshanger miners in 1942 showed the difficulty, in extreme cases, of enforcing the law.)

It was soon realized that these measures were not sufficient; there remained a critical shortage of labour. In the early months of the war unemployment of women rose quite sharply owing to the curtailment of non-essential occupations. But women were soon re-absorbed into the labour force as war work developed. By the summer of 1940 the government realized, just as it had done in 1915, that women were the great untapped source of labour. The difference in 1940 was that single women, from both the middle and working classes, were already working, leaving married women as the pool from which the government would have to recruit its war labour.

Bevin's plan was to utilize women to the maximum. Single women with no ties were directed to move into men's jobs; childless married women were moved into single women's jobs; married women with young children and even grannies were expected to work at least part-time. The registration of women began in April 1941 with women born in 1920. Registration of women continued until by October 1942 all women from the age of forty-five downwards had registered. It was then extended to include women up to the age of fifty. Although registration was not the same as conscription, the distinction was fine. A registered woman could be directed to work on any job at any place. The National Service (No. 2) Act, which became law in December 1941, made single women between the ages of twenty and thirty liable to be conscripted. A conscripted woman could choose between either one of the Women's Auxiliary Forces or full-time work in one of the essential industries.

Of the restriction of conscription to single women *Time and Tide* commented that

> the attitude towards married women – they are not compelled to serve even if they are childless – evinces a form of discretion that is certainly not even the better part of reason. There is every reason for going carefully with compulsion in respect to the women with infant children. But there is no more reason that the childless married woman or the one with children of school age should be left outside the national effort than the widow in the like case should be. Incidentally this dispensation to married women as such is likely to encourage the making of irresponsible marriage contracts.[2]

The economic needs of society had once again caused the concept of 'women's role' to be turned on its head. It was no longer the patriotic duty of women to be at home, but rather to be at work.

Turned, too, on its head was the concept of 'women's work'. Men workers, as always, were wary of any change in the sexual distribution of labour and tried to negotiate agreements which would ensure protection of their jobs and wage rates at the end of the war. The agreement made between the TUC and the government before the war had marked the first step towards agreement between trade unions and employers over dilution and the substitution of labour. The main concern of the trade unions was that relaxations should be statutorily removed at the end of the war. Clauses to that effect were incorporated in agreements made in the early years of the war, but the trade union movement was not satisfied until the passing of the Restoration of Pre-War Practices Act in 1942. Men were nervous, too, of the inevitable dilution of skilled jobs by the development of new production processes more compatible with a predominantly female work force.

Bevin's skill at negotiating and the precedent of World War I enabled substitution in the munitions and war industry to take place relatively smoothly. A typical agreement covering the substitution of women for men was the one signed between the Shipbuilding Employers Federation and the Confederation of Shipbuilding and Engineering Unions.[3] It stated that women under twenty-one were to be paid the rate for 'youths'. Women over twenty-one were to get that rate for the first eight months of their employment. Women doing unskilled and semi-skilled work were to get the full-time rate and full war bonus 'where the woman is able to perform the whole of the male duties without extra supervision or assistance'. Where the woman needed extra supervision or assistance, the basic rate and bonus were to be lower. The agreement was for the 'duration of the war only' and it did not apply to occupations 'in which women were employed before the war'. The agreement was made with the interests of male members, the male rate and the male jobs essentially in mind. There was no attempt to fix a 'rate for the job'. Women's rates in 'women's' jobs remained the same and the male rate in male jobs was protected for men. The loopholes in the agreement, in particular the clause 'without extra supervision or assistance', gave employers ample scope to argue that women did not warrant equal pay since they could not do the work equally. Small changes in production methods also gave employers justification for not paying equal pay for equal work and new production processes were designed to be worked by women at 'women's' rates.

In their evidence to the Royal Commission on Equal Pay

(1944) employers and trade unions admitted that, despite the agreements, women rarely received 'equal pay'.

> In the Engineering Industry, for example [one employer testified], women who are employed on the same work as men during the war and who carry out the work by the same method and with no more supervision or assistance, are entitled, under a war time agreement, to receive the same rate as men, but it is found that, in practice, these conditions are not satisfied in the majority of cases, with the result that only a minority of the women are able to qualify for the full time rate.[4]

Employers claimed that piece rates were normally fixed at an equal rate for 'men and women doing the same work under precisely the same conditions' and that the lower average wages of women piece workers reflected their lower output.

The claim made by employers that women who did the same jobs as men under the same conditions were paid equal piece rates was contested by the TUC, in a case which revealed the illogicality of the sexual division of labour. At an engineering firm in Bristol, in which no women had been employed before the war, 'women's' piece work was paid at women's rates. The firm argued that since that job had been done by women in other parts of the country before the war, for pay purposes it was a 'woman's' job. When questioned by the royal commissioners as to whether the trade union concerned could not have claimed equal pay for the women under the 1940 substitution agreement, Dame Anne Loughlin, speaking for the TUC, replied that

> the position was so difficult, and the employers were faced with the possibility of a stoppage by the women because they were so incensed, that we had to make an agreement with the employers. They were not prepared to make a written agreement, because they were afraid of prejudicing the national position, but they did arrive at an understanding with us whereby the women had after so many weeks 1d. an hour above the women's rate and then 2d. an hour, and eventually 3d. an hour. But the woman's piece rates were still based on her time rate and not on that additional 3d. that we were able to procure for her.[5]

Women substitutes in other industries or professions fared worse than those on war work. Women employed in the civil service received unequal pay and unequal war bonuses. In both areas there was a large influx of women workers into the non-manual and manual grades. NALGO tried to negotiate equal cost of living bonuses (war bonuses) for women, but the local governments persistently refused on the ground that the government did not pay equal bonuses in the civil service. In 1944 local governments finally made a minor concession to the union's demand and awarded equal bonuses to women earning over £700 a year, which benefited only a handful of the higher-paid. The Union of Post Office Workers once again put in a claim for equal pay, in particular for women doing men's jobs and night work. The postmaster general refused to concede equal pay even for women directly substituting for men, fearing that, if the principle was established in war, it would be impossible to oppose it in peace-time. His view was

> that the somewhat increased measure of employment of women during the war on duties normally done by men provides no justification for interference with the existing wage structure.[6]

In industry generally the agreements for substitution tended to follow the pattern of those negotiated in the engineering industry : the man's rate for the man's job, provided that all the conditions were the same, and relaxation of normal practices only for the duration of the war. Equal war bonuses for women were rare, a fact which many women trades unionists resented deeply. To women like the women railway clerks, denied equal pay for equal work, the unequal war bonus (men 16s. and women 12s.) added 'insult to injury, as women have to meet the same rise in the cost of living as men'.[7] The government and private employers consistently justified unequal pay to women for equal work on the grounds that women had a lower productivity rate, that they needed extra supervision or that a lower women's rate was custom and practice. It was harder to justify the unequal war bonuses except on the ground that it was the custom to pay women less. Women workers and trade unionists challenged the view that women achieved lower levels of productivity. Ernie Bevin contradicted the claim that it took three women to do the work of two men. In 1943 he maintained that the output of women instead of being that of three women to two men was slightly the other way compared with production in 1939![8]

Unequal treatment of women did not go uncontested. Women used the nation's dependence on their war work to push forward their claims for equal pay and recognition of their skills and to publicize the problems of working wives and mothers. As in World War I, demands for equal pay for equal work and for a higher standard rate of women's pay were foremost. At the 1940 TUC conference a motion was passed calling for equal pay for women 'substitutes'. There was little debate allowed on the subject, since cries of 'Vote' were shouted from the floor after the third speaker. It was evident that the majority of delegates regarded the passing of equal-pay motions as a matter of form, however little they related to practice. At that conference, too, women pushed for a repeal of the marriage bar in all areas of employment and a repeal of the 'Anomalies Regulation' whereby most married women were ineligible for unemployment benefit. In contrast to pre-war days the motion concerning married women, moved by the AWKS, was carried with no one speaking against. The only concern about married women returning to work was voiced by a representative of the insurance companies who claimed that employers were already taking married women back into employment, but were paying them lower rates than single women.

At the TUC conferences of 1941 and 1942 the main issues which concerned women workers were given more time and consideration than they had previously received, while at the TUC women's conferences they were discussed in a more radical and comprehensive manner. Questions of women's dual role and the role of the state, particularly with regard to child-care, but also with regard to the provision of other services like school meals, national restaurants and laundries, were, in addition to the primary issue of equality of pay, debated as part of the whole pattern of women's position in society.

Of course, equal pay for equal work and a higher 'women's' rate remained the fundamental issues throughout the war, especially since the differentials between men's and women's rates increased rather than decreased, thanks to smaller pay rises and unequal compensation for injured or disabled women.

Women were sceptical, despite unanimous votes, of the men's commitment to equality. At the TUC women's conference of 1941 some openly said that they hoped for little support from the men. One woman delegate claimed that their attempts to get rises in the munitions industry had been undermined by the AEU. Another, Miss Walker (CAWU), told delegates that

> the problem could not be left to the male section of the movement. Nor could it be left to the Government. The rates of pay in the defence services and the different rates of compensation between men and women, proved that the Government still accepted the recognised fact that there are women's rates.[9]

Not all women blamed the male section of the trade union movement. In 1941, Miss Hancock, speaking for the general council, put the blame on the women's failure to organize. 'I am not,' she said, 'prepared to ask men to help women unless women are prepared to help themselves.'[10] Since she was speaking specifically of the engineering industry, her remarks were particularly inappropriate, for although some women in the industry were organized by the general unions, the main trade union in the industry, the AEU, did not admit women. The AEU did not change its rule until 1942. Miss Hancock's attitude had been expressed by the TUC general council and many of the women on it since 1920, and it continues to be expressed to the present day. It is an attitude which does not do justice to the reasons why women have had a low level of organization.

The one campaign which was waged successfully by women in World War II was the campaign for equal compensation for women injured or disabled in war service. It received support, not just from the trade union movement, but from many sections of society, including the press. Under the Workmen's Compensation Act compensation was based on earnings and the same principle was applied in the Personal Injuries (Civilians) Scheme. Women in the forces and in civil defence were paid between two-thirds and four-fifths of the male rate. For industrial injuries women had accepted a lower rate of compensation, but women who were compulsorily called up to jobs in which they ran the risk of injury saw the question in another light. In the Commons' debate on the conscription of women, the question of equal pay

G

and equal compensation was raised by women MPs. Dr Edith Summerskill wrote of the debate

> the only organised protest in the Lobby of the House of Commons against it (conscription for women) came from women who demanded that in the event of conscription becoming law the Government should undertake to give men and women equal pay for equal work and equal compensation for injuries received as a result of enemy action. . . . Although a woman may be called upon to serve and perform the same duties as a man, her monetary value is assessed at four-fifths of her male colleague. If, in the course of her work, she is disabled and loses a limb or an eye, the loss is reckoned as being worth only four-fifths of that of a man. The Government has never explained how a woman earning a living with her hands suffers less than a man through the loss of an arm.[11]

In the summer of 1942 the question was again brought up in the House of Commons and once again women opposed the call-up of women for fire-prevention and fire-fighting without equal pay and equal compensation. Women in the fire service received two-thirds of the male rate and consequently two-thirds of the compensation rate. Herbert Morrison, speaking on behalf of the government, hoped that women would not be 'sticky or troublesome'. 'Only last Thursday,' the *Sunday Times* commented, 'Mr Morrison hoped that British women, with their fine war record, would not be "sticky" or "troublesome". While compensation for women remains at two-thirds the amount for men, his choice of adjectives is not very gracious.'[12]

Over this issue the women of Great Britain were decidedly sticky and troublesome. The TUC, like the women MPs, took the view that women should not be made to do fire-prevention and fire-fighting work unless they were paid equal pay and equal compensation. At first the government tried to maintain the position that in the Personal Injuries (Civilians) Scheme it was merely following the precedent of the Workman's Compensation Act. In 1943 it modified its position and appointed a select committee on equal compensation. The TUC argued before the committee that the Personal Injuries (Civilians) Scheme was designed for all people injured through enemy action and that the unequal rate of compensation implied that:

any woman is of less value as a citizen than any man. One would have thought that in these days of declining population and the way in which women have demonstrated their capability to do every type of war work, that the contrary would be the more correct argument.[13]

The TUC argued that compensation was paid to maintain a person during a period of disability; in the case of permanent disablement it became a pension. Since extra allowances were paid for dependents, there was no justification to pay women less on the ground that the rate was a family rate and not an individual rate. In fact, the only reason the TUC could find for the lower rate of compensation was the invalid one, that a woman was less valuable to the state than a man.

> Woman's life is at least as valuable as a man's and her physical well-being is just as important.[14]

In the end, equal compensation for women injured by enemy action was won.

One of the major breakthroughs made during World War II, and one of the few sustained after the war, thanks to the establishment of the National Health Service by the Labour government, was the dramatic reduction in maternal mortality rates and a significant reduction in infant mortality. The improvements in state maternity services, which the Women's Public Health Officers had demanded throughout the 1930s, were made in the light of threats of German bombs. Before the war, alarm had been expressed about Britain's declining birth rate and it was realized that, if it was not to decline even further during the war, maternity services had to be quickly and radically improved. Maternal and infant mortality were closely related to poverty. Both would probably increase if women produced babies in bombed slums on a poor war-rationed diet. The government therefore established maternity homes in rural areas and encouraged pregnant women to spend the latter stages of their pregnancy under professional care. Special rations were provided to ensure that pregnant women had an adequate diet and pregnant women workers were given time-off to attend ante-natal clinics. The result was a dramatic decline in maternal mortality from 497 per 100,000 to 232 per 100,000. Infant mortality declined by 28%.

The government also wanted women with children to work. At the outset, when Ernie Bevin announced the registration of women for war work, he promised that the government would provide adequate child-care facilities for working mothers. The government went part of the way towards fulfilling its promise. In the pre-war period there had been only about 100 nurseries, most of them voluntarily run and financed by charity. At the peak period of women's work during the war, in 1943, there were 1,182 nurseries, of which 912 were day nurseries and 270 nursery schools, financed by government grants. In addition some factories ran nurseries and a few charity nurseries and nursery schools survived. Nevertheless, the representatives of women workers thought that the government had fallen short on its promises. In 1942 a conference was held by the Standing Joint Committee of Working Women's Organizations to discuss nursery facilities. A motion was carried declaring that 'the care and supervision of young children whose mothers enter employment is a national responsibility'. It went on to protest

> against the circular (Ministry of Health 2535) sent on December 5th (1941) to local authorities, which suggested that most of the young children of married women at work outside their homes must be cared for by means of private arrangements made by the mothers. The Committee regards this suggestion as an attempt to evade promises previously made by the Government that the children of mothers volunteering for war work would be properly looked after.[15]

This resolution was remarkable. For the first time a body representing women workers had stated that the care and supervision of young children of working mothers was a national responsibility. The ministry of health's circular revealed that the government wished to evade its commitment to provide child-care facilities and place the cost and burden on the working mother. The conference drew up a comprehensive list of demands concerning state provision of nursery and child-care facilities. They demanded that local authorities provide child-care facilities for all women war workers with children under the age of five; that nurseries for children between the age of two and five should provide education; that some residential nurseries should be established in 'safe' areas (away from bombing); that enough nursery nurses and teachers should be trained; and that baby-minders should be registered with the local authority, supervised by health visitors and paid for by the local authorities. At the 1943 TUC women's conference it was further demanded that there should be day centres, open from 7 or 8 am until 6 or 7 pm, for children of school age, to care for them before and after school hours and during the holidays. These demands were unanimously supported by the TUC women's conference and the TUC conference. It was clear, however, that the government's commitment to providing facilities for working women was limited to war-time.

The government's concern to increase productivity and to recruit women as extensively as possible caused it to consider workers' well-being in a new light. Research had shown that in World War I productivity was greater when workers did not work excessive hours, when they were well fed, had good conditions and relaxation, and when external worries were minimized. For women workers 'external' worries were far greater than for men. Women shopped, cooked, cleaned and washed, besides caring for children. The government realized that, in order to enable women to work well, it had to minimize those problems which either hindered women from working or, if working, caused absenteeism and a lack of concentration. Suddenly, besides nurseries, shopping hours, travelling, communal laundries, school meals and national restaurants became government concerns. At work, welfare, canteens, recreation and health were all seen as vital components in the struggle for ever-greater productivity for the war machine. Although it was in the government ordnance factories that these changes were most discernible, the change in attitude filtered through to many employers and trade unionists.

Recognition of the special needs of women workers was also expressed by the TUC. Even a spokesman for the general council recognized that women performed two jobs and that they not only had to work for long hours, sometimes having to travel long distances to and from work. 'In addition, in tens of thousands of cases, they had domestic duties' – at which it is recorded that a voice called out 'and shopping'.[16] Shopping was a major issue for women workers. Long hours and travelling often meant that women did not get an opportunity to shop during normal shop-opening hours. Since a frequent cause of absenteeism was that women left work early to do their shopping, employers were often prepared to negotiate a 'shopping hour' whereby employees were released earlier. Some shops altered their opening hours, but the practice was opposed by the trade unions concerned, which did not wish to see an extension of the long hours many of their members already worked. The difficulties women faced in finding time to shop were discussed at the 1941 TUC conference as part of a general motion concerning the problems of working women. This was remarkable. Delegates to the TUC had to consider questions previously considered as the sphere of women at home, having no place in the world of work and collective bargaining.

Long hours and long journeys were also central issues which concerned women workers. Widespread dispensation from the regulations covering women factory workers was given. The restrictions on overtime, hours and night work were lifted in most areas. Since women were often 'directed' to work at places far from their homes, they frequently demanded that transport be provided. Hostels and billets were organized for women who were directed to work in munitions factories in different parts of the country. Workers, too, were entertained like the troops, both in their canteens and while at work. 'Workers Playtime' was broadcast to cheer them up and to push up productivity.

The myths about women workers were quickly shattered during the war years and the government, out of necessity, was at the forefront of encouraging women to train, to become skilled, and to take responsible jobs. It set up and financed training schemes and issued leaflets to try and persuade women to forget their conventional role of unskilled worker and enter a variety of jobs. The Technical Service Register was established for women to be trained as draughtsmen, electrical technicians, engine testers and laboratory technicians. Women were trained to be supervisors. There were agricultural courses for women in the land army and women were encouraged to go to university to study subjects which the government regarded as essential, including engineering, pharmacy and agriculture. The government had not only to negotiate with the trade unions for the widescale introduction of women into 'male' areas, but also to persuade employers that women could do 'men's' jobs. In 1942 the ministry of labour produced a pamphlet for employers in the shipbuilding and allied industries. The aim was to persuade employers that women 'can do almost every job a man can do except those requiring sheer physical strength'.[17] Employers were urged to hire women for a far greater variety of jobs; the government claimed that, 'subject to proper safeguards, women have tackled really heavy work, especially in loading vehicles, trucks and machines'. The government advised how jobs could be broken down or lifting tackle used to enable women to do them. The pamphlet also dealt with other fears which employers might have. It was explained that the provision of separate cloakroom and welfare facilities was a minor problem and that, since relaxation of the factory acts with regard to hours and overtime was normally readily granted, they should be no obstacle. A list was given of areas of work where women had already been successfully employed, including forewomen, electric welders, crane drivers, joiners, fitters, machinists and boiler workers.

In 1943 the government published a large glossy magazine called *Women in Shipbuilding*. The magazine contained photographs of women doing almost every kind of skilled or heavy job in shipbuilding. By the pictures were captions to hammer home the point to reluctant employers – captions such as 'Women's skill in welding is now acknowledged in engineering firms where they have been employed on this work – over a much longer period than in shipyards' or 'Their natural conscientiousness combined with their love of making a neat job makes them ideal "wiremen".'[18] The government also tried energetically to persuade employers to change their work routines in order to employ women part-time. In 1942 it published a leaflet, 'Mobilisation of Woman Power: Planning for Part-Time Work', in which it explained the advantages of employing women part-time.

> Women may tackle monotonous or heavy jobs better and with more energy for half a day than if they were working all day. Under such conditions of work the output of two part-timers is often greater than that of one full-timer.[19]

The employer gained the further advantage of less absenteeism and better time-keeping among women part-timers. Employers gradually did come to see the economic advantages of women part-timers and during World War II it became a major feature of women's employment.

There was also considerable evidence that low rates of pay were a disincentive to women applying for jobs. Mr Kershaw, from the Colne Weavers Association, commenting on the Women's Report to the TUC conference in 1941 thought that conscription for war work had had to be introduced because, without equal pay, there was no incentive for women to go into industry.

> As an employee at a Government Training Centre, I may tell the delegates present that I feel it very keenly, probably more keenly because I have come from an industry where equal pay for equal work is an established principle, when I see young women at the Training Centre, who have to pay anything up to 30s. a week in Leeds for board and lodging – girls who have come from Scotland or from Wales or from other places – who although they do identically the same work as I do, receive only 38s. per week, while I receive 60s. 6d. It is my opinion that this is a situation in which we shall not get the response from the women of this country until we make attempts to alter such a state of affairs.[20]

An Irish welfare worker in one war factory not only thought that low pay was one of the main reasons for the difficulty in recruiting women to her factory. The absence of a 'rate for the job' was another.

> The rate for the job would stop a lot of ill feeling, you wouldn't believe! As it is, the men are frightened of cheap labour; it stands to reason. And why shouldn't they be? And all the while the girls feel cheated.[21]

Other women claimed that men were the major stumbling block to the recruitment of women, since many men were not prepared to let their womenfolk work even in a state of national emergency. Some women even organized meetings to try to explain to husbands and fathers the national necessity of women doing war work.

Despite low pay women did almost every conceivable type of

work during the war, surprising employers, men workers and even themselves. War is often seen as a time when men can fulfil their unrealized potential. World War II was a time when women, too, found that they could do things which even they themselves had regarded as impossible. They also found out that comradeship was not a male prerogative.

Peggy Scott, in *They Made Invasion Impossible,*[22] described how women in every sphere found that they were capable of doing almost anything, jobs of enormous responsibility, of great danger, of an arduous physical nature, of great skill or merely of a nature which had led society to assume that only men could perform them. She also demolished many of the myths attached to women workers and to women. One which had been perpetuated since the 19th century, by moralists and trade unionists, was that allowing women and men to work side by side was both unproductive, since neither sex would be able to concentrate, and morally dangerous. Experience in the war showed that both assumptions were untrue. Women and men in the mixed batteries of the ATS, for example, worked together well. There was no evidence of diminished concentration. The ATS mixed batteries also showed that women were prepared to take responsible jobs and that men were prepared to accept orders from women.

Besides proving that they could do responsible jobs, work with men, do dirty or heavy jobs and remain calm under stress, women 'proved over and over again in the war that they can keep a secret. A thousand women kept the secret of radio-location for many months before its use was made public.'[23] Another myth, conveniently upheld by employers and male workers, that women like boring repetitive jobs and have no ambition, was disproved time and time again. Ex-parlourmaids and shop assistants found themselves doing skilled or qualified jobs during the war and thoroughly enjoying them. Women enjoyed their new-found skills, the interesting nature of their work and the comradeship of working. For many of them it was their first experience of comradeship, one which they relished. Finally, it was a government report which went part way to dispelling one of the major myths about women workers – particularly married ones – that they have a high absentee rate. The report was based only on a study of women with no male control group in only two factories. But although it was limited, it reached some interesting conclusions. Older married women lost less time than young single women, a fact which has been confirmed by several other more recent studies. Absenteeism was much higher in factory A than factory B, partly because factory A was isolated. Its employees therefore had long travelling hours. Factory A was also five times larger than factory B and had grown to that size very rapidly. The report concluded that these differing factors were a major reason for the differing absentee rates. Implied in its conclusion was that absentee rates had as much to do with the position, nature and conditions of the work as the fact the workers were women. The report also asserted that the results of the inquiry lent 'little or no support to the view, which was fairly widespread at the time of the inquiry, that in each factory there were a number of workers who persistently took one or two shifts off each week for no valid reason'.[24] Not surprisingly, much of the time taken off by women was in order to perform domestic duties.

The fundamental change in society's attitude towards the role of women caused concern and speculation about what would happen to women when peace came. Women had bitter memories of the hopes World War I had held for their future, hopes which had been destroyed almost overnight. Many of them were resolved that history should not repeat itself. They felt they had earned the right to an equal place in society and, having made great strides towards it in the war, they were determined to defend their gains. With regard to job opportunities their hopes were limited, since in many spheres the pre-war practices act guaranteed the re-instatement of trade union restrictive practices. The old job demarcations on sex grounds would inevitably return.

As early as 1941, women were concerned that women conscripted to war work should have at least the same guarantees as men conscripted to the Forces, namely that they would be re-instated in their former employment. In 1942 the Women's Advisory Committee drew up a comprehensive memorandum on post-war resettlement in which they made it clear :

that all classes of women who have contributed to the war effort irrespective of whether they have been transferred, directed, conscripted or have volunteered, have an equal right to employment.[25]

Women who had worked before the war should be given priority, either in re-instatement in their pre-war jobs or in new employment. Those women who had entered work for the first time during the war should either be given a lump sum (if they wished to leave employment) or be allowed to have their claim to a job considered by a tribunal. The committee also recommended that the school-leaving age should be raised to fifteen to avoid flooding the labour market with school-leavers. Behind its recommendations lay two basic fears, which stemmed from the experience of the post World War I years: that widespread unemployment at the end of the war would hit women workers most severely and that, in that eventuality, women workers would have less claim to re-instatement than men.

In 1943 the Women's Advisory Committee repeated its demands for post-war resettlement and added that greater opportunities for training in industry and the professions should be given to women. In its memorandum published that year it made a much more radical recommendation, one which came directly out of the change in attitudes towards working women which had taken place during the war. The state had taken several measures, however piece-meal, to ameliorate the burdens on women who were workers and housewives. The memorandum pushed for the continuance and development of those measures in peace-time.

> Furthermore, as the demands made upon women by the war have increased, it has been necessary for the State to take responsibility for the establishment of public services to cover work which has hitherto been confined to the home; they have included communal feeding, the setting up of nurseries, the provision of school meals on a larger scale, factory canteens etc. . . . The Women's Advisory Committee favours the continuance and extension of these services.[26]

In their hopes for a post-war world in which women workers should have equal pay and equal opportunity and the state should be shouldering some of the burden of their responsibilities for home and children, the Women's Advisory Committee was not alone. Women writers of the period echoed the same thoughts.[27]

But Peggy Scott, while hoping that peace would bring a new world for women, saw that women were not united in what they wanted from the post-war world.

> It is among the older women that the new life is stirring; that the new ideas have taken root; among the women who have had homes of their own, who have tested their limitations and their loneliness. Emancipation from drudgery, from individual isolation, is most likely to come through them. They have found freedom by working part-time outside their home and earning their own money; they have found inspiration in working for the community; these are the women who appreciate the aid of Day Nurseries and Communal Restaurants.
>
> The girls in the service who have never tasted domestic drudgery make it plain in their Brains Trust that they do not want anything communal after the war; neither blocks of flats, nor communal meals, nor laundries, nor nurseries. They want a home with a garden, their own husband and child. And the women who speak for women, most of whom have seen women leap forward in two wars, pressing on to preserve the new freedom from drudgery that has come to women in this war, the new rights and responsibilities with men that have become theirs, are not depressed; they know this isolationism will not last. The girls, unlike their older sisters, have tasted freedom first; they have experienced the wider interests of employment and their own pay packet; of social clubs and variety of companionship; and they know that one man and a child are not going to take their place exclusively for long.[28]

The younger women got their men, their children and, some, homes with gardens; but nurseries, communal feeding, laundries and play centres were to be a war-time memory.

The attitudes of working women towards post-war employment were fairly systematically tabulated in a survey done in the autumn of 1943 for the ministry of reconstruction.[29] This survey and a report of the ministry of labour in 1945[30] were much more accurate in their speculations on the post-war situation for working women than the hopes expressed by the women writers and women trade unionists. Both reports predicted a return to the pre-war situation, both in the types of jobs women would do and in the number of women who would wish to work. In a sense their predictions were self-fulfilling, since neither report made any recommendation for the training of women, the retention of such things as nurseries nor any other recommendations which would enable women to alter their position at work. The 1943 survey at least recognized the problems; the 1945 report appears to have been based on the assumption that a return to the pre-war position of women was desirable.

The 1943 survey was based on a fairly wide sample of working women. It found that the largest group of women entering war-time employment consisted of married women over the age of thirty-five. Beside this great influx of married women, the main changes in women's employment were the significant increase of women receiving some kind of training and the movement of women away from traditional areas of work, such as domestic service and textiles, mainly into engineering. The survey found that married women under thirty-four did not, by and large, want to continue in employment and would be the most 'reduced' sector. The type of occupation in which women were employed greatly affected their attitude.

More than three-quarters of the professional and administrative workers wanted to continue work in the post-war world, compared to less than half of the labourers and packers. Those with the best paid jobs with career prospects least wanted to give up working.

In assessing women's attitudes to work after marriage the survey found very much what Peggy Scott had found – that experience changes women's attitudes. Far more single and widowed women disapproved of work after marriage than married women. Generally, women thought that married men with dependents should have first right to a job, but more single than married women thought that a job should go to the person best qualified to do it. There was evident, not just a difference in experience, but also a hangover from the days of unemployment, when many single women had, with men, opposed the employment of married women. What is particularly revealing about this survey, done in the middle of the war, was that most women saw their war-time situation as abnormal. They expected a return to normality. Although radical changes had transformed their position, traditional beliefs, in particular that a married woman's place was in the home and that men had a first right to employment, remained strong. The report concluded that, although a percentage of older women would wish to stay in employment after the war, 'when final adjustments have been made there will be no more women in employment than might have been expected if normal increases had occurred since 1931'.[31] It also predicted that women would return in the main to 'peace-time industries and employment'. If men earned enough to support their wives and children, women would be prompted to work in later life only by

> boredom and lack of company at home. Few women, even now, appear to look upon work as a career so long as all the disadvantages attaching to their sex, and to work after marriage remain.[32]

The report made no recommendation that those disadvantages should be minimized or abolished. The 1945 report did not even consider those 'disadvantages'; it assumed that, although there might be some re-adjustments needed due to new processes in industry, women would return either to the home or to pre-war work roles.

Not only in government reports, but also in the words of the prime minister and some of his cabinet ministers, the government was noticeably non-committal about its proposals for the position of women in post-war Britain. A National Conference of Women was called by the government in 1943 at the Albert Hall. Women representing all sectors of women, including several women trade unionists, were invited. The morning session was devoted to speeches by ministers; in the afternoon ministers answered written questions from women. Many of the questions dealt specifically with war-time problems, but some were general questions on the rights of women and others were on the government's proposed policies for reconstruction, with regard to health, education, housing, equal pay, job opportunities and rights to re-instatement for women. The government gave many positive answers to questions relating to war-time problems, such as improving transport for workers, requisitioning large houses to ease the housing shortage and extending food rationing. On the other hand it was either evasive or non-committal on almost all questions relating to equal rights for women. Ernest Brown, the minister of health, defended the unequal National Health Insurance benefits to married women paying the full rate on the ground that it was the law, but he did say that change would be considered by the Beveridge commission. Herbert Morrison claimed that it was impossible to change British nationality laws to enable women marrying aliens to retain British nationality until all the Dominion governments had been consulted, although he personally thought the law should be changed. The answer to a question on why it employed so many young women, which was no doubt driving at the marriage bar, merely committed the government to employing older women if younger ones were called up to the Forces.

The crucial questions relating to equal pay, equal opportunities and rights to re-instatement at the end of the war were answered by the chancellor of the exchequer and the minister of labour and national service. Their answers promised nothing. To the question, 'Will the government show their appreciation of the work done by women in the war by conceding equal pay to those employed in government service?', the chancellor took six sentences to answer 'no'. He stated that in the industrial sphere government rates were based on 'the fair market rate, regard being had to general practice in outside employment'; in the non-manual grades, 'the government does not see its way to alter the existing position'. The minister of labour was less outspoken, but his answer to whether the government would 'insist on the rate for the job being paid throughout industry' and on whether they would 'encourage equality of opportunity regardless of sex' was equally negative. He stated that the rate for the job was a matter for trade union agreements, not the government; he passed over equal opportunity, except to mention the pre-war trade practices act, which was tantamount to pledging the government to a restoration of unequal opportunity. With regard to re-instatement, he said that no guarantees could be given to women, but that he recognized the need for some re-training of women 'to facilitate the resettlement of women released from the Forces or from other forms of war service'. In the words of the minister the overall policy of the government for reconstruction 'will be to maintain employment at the highest possible level and yet to interfere as little as possible with the speedy restoration of home life'.[33]

Male trade unionists were as concerned as women about the post-war world; but their hopes often lay in a diametrically opposed direction. In the early years of the war there had been considerable interest among trade unionists in women's wages and conditions of work. Their concern for wages was dominated, as in World War I, by a desire to protect male wage rates in peace-time. Although many unions had passed resolutions for equal pay and some had expressed concern about the increasing differentials between men's and women's rates, only a few unions negotiated equal pay for women 'substitutes' without including an agreement that those jobs would return to the men at the end of the war. Some unions, like the Union of Post Office Workers and the Railway Clerks Association, did try to use the war to win general equal pay claims, but they failed. The establishment of the royal commission on equal pay in 1944 diverted trade unions from immediate action and enabled them, temporarily, to await the conclusions of the royal commission.

The interest of trade unions in the problems of women workers waned during the war. Agreements having been signed on substitution and guarantees gained that any relaxation of restrictive practices would only apply for the period of the war, most trade unions believed that the problem of women workers had been solved and that in peace time things would return to normal. Fear that peace would bring widespread unemployment concerned men workers, too, and they reverted to their attitudes of the 1920s and 1930s. During the war the marriage bar had practically disappeared. Married women were employed and encouraged to be employed, although often on discriminatory terms. Some married women were paid lower rates than single women; others were employed on a temporary basis and were thus deprived of many of the benefits of staff status. The latter was the practice of the Post Office during the war. In 1944 the Manchester delegation to the Union of Post Office Workers, concerned about post-war employment, said that although 'in principle' there should be no marriage bar, 'the removal of the bar might lead to an intensification of the unemployment problem by reason of the additional number of women seeking industrial employment'.[34]

In the TUC there was an equally clear 'cooling off' in concern about women. The Women's Advisory Committee and the women's conference continued to push for a consolidation and extension of the gains they had made in war-time. However, at the TUC annual conferences interest in women's questions fell dramatically even though a motion in favour of equal pay was carried unanimously in 1944. In 1943, the year Dame Anne Loughlin was in the chair, not a single motion was discussed concerning the problems of women. An insight into the apathy towards women workers was given in 1945 by a delegate from the Bank Officers' Guild. She stated that in the past year the Women's Advisory Committee had invited all unions catering for women clerical workers to participate in discussions on the problems peculiar to women in clerical occupations. She said she had come to the rostrum 'to express the disappointment of my delegation that only three unions circularised saw fit to accept the invitation'.[35]

The Women's Advisory Committee assumed that after the war many women would have to return to domestic service and it drew up a memorandum offering suggestions as to how women could be persuaded to do so. The memorandum recommended training, better hours, wages and conditions. The assumption that many women would be re-deployed in domestic service was one which they shared with the government. In 1944 a pamphlet issued by the ministry of labour claimed that 'domestic work is a priority job'. Domestic workers were called the 'community's housewives', who 'are the band which holds the national family together, without them the community could not live'.[36] Just as housewives were morally exalted, but given a low status and no remuneration, domestic workers were praised and given a very lowly status and equally low remuneration.

Whilst the TUC and its affiliated unions showed a marked apathy towards women workers, particularly in the latter half of the war, women were much less apathetic about trade unionism. They joined trade unions in their hundreds of thousands. In 1939 out of a total TUC membership of 4,116,601, women accounted for 552,585. By 1943 women's membership

had risen to 1,219,543, by 1945 to 1,340,729. Given the great
increase in female membership and the fact that in some unions,
as a delegate to the 1946 USDAW conference claimed, 'many
of our womenfolk have kept the trade union movement going
throughout the war',[37] it is surprising that trade unions showed
so little interest in women. Women had to continue to fight for
recognition and equal rights in their unions.

The women members of the National Union of Boot and
Shoe Operatives campaigned throughout the war for a woman
officer, but the executive council argued that experience in
branch officership was necessary for an organizer and that the
few women who held branch offices, as in the Leicester Women's
Branch, were too valuable to be spared for the job of an
organizer. In 1943 the council agreed to appoint an area woman
officer 'whenever the opportunity presents itself';[38] throughout
the war the opportunity did not present itself. The women
members of NUPE (National Union of Public Employees) also
demanded that a 'female organiser be appointed forthwith',[39] but
their resolution was lost. An amendment to the motion, which
demanded that two more organizers be appointed to organize
the large number of clerical and female public employees, was
also defeated. The general secretary said that in the last few
months the union had 'experimented' with organizing clerical
and female workers and that the experience had not been
encouraging. In contrast the 1945 NALGO conference was more
encouraging. The conference voted to abolish the two reserved
seats for women on the national executive council and in the
elections eight women were candidates and two were elected.
In the following year three women were elected.

Two unions which had particularly large increases in female
membership during the war were the National Union of General
and Municipal Workers and the Transport and General Workers
Union. Although both recruited women, and in some areas
negotiated agreements for minimum wages for women, they were
curiously silent on the problems of women workers. In 1939 the
TGWU had published a series of pamphlets on the union, its
work, role, policies and problems. Part VI was on women
workers and it laid out quite clearly what the union regarded
as the main problems concerning women workers and what its

policy was regarding them. The section opened with the assertion that women in industry were there to stay, but claimed that whilst women had particular qualities of manual dexterity their main attraction to employers was the fact that they were cheap labour. On this question the union maintained an equivocal attitude. On the one hand, it opposed women as cheap labour, particularly with regard to dilution and the trend towards employing women on new processes. On the other hand, it argued that if they were to demand equal pay 'there would be a danger that the women would be discharged and only the men retained, at least in certain sections of the industry'.[40] Likewise, whilst arguing that the view that men should receive higher wages because they had greater family responsibilities was outdated, they criticized the increased employment of girl labour at the expense of youths. In all, the pamphlet revealed a very confused attitude towards women. However, the TGWU was quite clear that it was of great importance to encourage their organization.

> The modern tendency for women and young persons to participate in organised leisure should not be ignored. This enthusiasm for dancing, cycling, rambling, football, gymnastics and other organised sports and pastimes can usefully be directed into Trade Union Channels.[41]

Although the pamphlet was published in 1939, there was no radical change in the union's attitude towards women during the war.

Despite men's assertions to the contrary, many women became active trade unionists during the war, especially at the local and branch level. Women found they could not only organize themselves effectively, but also improve their rates and conditions, as one shop steward explained.

> Conditions have been better since we organised. Women have been given one early night a week, stopping work at 6.0 pm instead of 7.0 pm, and on Saturday we finish at 12.30 pm instead of 1.0 pm so as to give us time for shopping. We try things out in our factory and tell the shop stewards in other factories, and they follow. When women are put onto a new man's job we demand the same rate as the men – and get it. The women gave the men a lead in our factory. They said 'If you can arrange things like this, so can we,' and organised too.[42]

Union membership brought women other benefits besides better wages and conditions. Going out to work gave women a new confidence. It widened their horizons and gave them more self-respect. Women were not only in better health, in better spirits from being released from the isolation of the home, they were also 'learning freedom by going into the factories'.[43] It is a reflection of the oppression of women that they found factory work in the capitalist system a step towards their liberation.

One of the most significant gestures of recognition of women workers by the trade union movement was made by the Amalgamated Engineering Union, when in 1942, they at last voted to accept women members. In World War I it had evaded the issue by coming to an agreement with the National Federation of Women Workers that the federation would organize those women entering engineering during the war. In the absence of the federation in World War II, the AEU was faced with the choice of organizing the women themselves or leaving them open to be organized by another union, as had already happened in some areas. The rank and file of the AEU, worried by the enormous influx of women into the engineering industry, did not regard the national substitution agreement as sufficient protection for their jobs and wage rates. They feared, too, that, as in World War I, the war-time situation would be used to break down skilled jobs, create more 'women's' jobs and generally erode the status and wages of the skilled men. They looked upon the organization of women and the application of equal pay for equal work as a means of arresting this trend. No less than seven motions on the subject of women were sent from divisional committees to the AEU conference in 1942. The motions called for the admission of women to the union for the duration of the war, equal pay for equal work, and the raising of the women's rate from 75% to 95% of the men's rate. Another motion called for clear definitions of the work women should be allowed to do and for clarification of the phrase in the national agreement, 'work commonly performed by women in the industry'.[44] The national committee put forward a resolution declaring that 'the opening of the ranks of our Union to women will safeguard the wages and conditions of all engaged in the engineering industry and we ask our members to note this when recording their votes in the ballot at present being taken'.[45] The motion was carried by 50 votes to 2. The committee also moved and carried a resolution seeking changes in the war-time relaxation agreement, such as a reduction in the qualifying periods, an elimination of the supervision clause and the firm establishment of the principle of equal pay for equal work. Had they been negotiated, those proposals would have improved the position and pay of women covered by the agreement, since they would have minimized the ways in which employers could evade equal pay. In speaking in favour of the motions, Jack Tanner, the AEU president, said that the position of women was 'a reflection, I believe, of the unwillingness of organised men workers to appeal to women as equals and to show them the way they can best defend the interests of the men and themselves'.[46] Despite the president's words, the ballot on whether to accept women members had a very low poll and the executive's report stated that 'though the results showed a majority in favour, the total vote was a disappointing one demonstrating a lack of enthusiasm'.[47]

On January 1st 1943 women became eligible for membership of the AEU. The new rules provided for a separate annual conference for women delegates and for the right of women to have female shop stewards represent them. Women were also given the right as members to vote in all elections, but 'the Branch Offices that can be held by women and girls are limited and will require as a qualification at least 12 months membership with the exception of door-keeper who may be a non-free member'.[48] The first women's conference was held in May 1943 and there were twenty-six sister delegates present. The conference passed resolutions affirming the women's war effort, welcoming the AEU's decision to accept women into membership, calling for the women's adult minimum rate to be no less than the male labourer rate and expressing concern for certain aspects of women's health and welfare. Jack Tanner addressed the meeting in words full of promise for the women workers in the engineering industry. He repudiated

> the narrow and prejudiced view that women are merely 'make-shift' workers incapable of doing the job required and on sufferance in our industry. In point of fact we are of the view that

many capable and intelligent women today are doing jobs below their individual capacities.

Because we believe that women are fully able to carry out the innumerable new processes which have become an integral part of modern engineering we believe wholeheartedly in the 'rate for the job'.[49]

He also believed that there should be no economic discrimination against women and that women should receive more opportunities for training. 'We have told our male members, and we shall tell them again, that they have got to help you women, that they have got to pass on the knowledge and skill they have acquired through long apprenticeship and long experience'.[50] Jack Tanner paid tribute to the burden of 'two jobs' which women carried.

> More than three-quarters of those present . . . are married women. And for me, as a man, it is a matter of admiration and respect that women with household responsibilities should not merely be working in industry but should become the elected spokesmen and trusted representatives of their fellow workers. We men, of the AEU, know what an active member's life and shop steward's duties mean; the endless, sometimes tiresome detail work, the patience, the tact, the resoluteness, all voluntarily expended; but we do not also have to think of the house-work, the washing and the shopping, the kids' breakfast and the old man's tea.[51]

Jack Tanner conceded that women did have a higher absentee rate than men, but there were 'very practical reasons for it' – reasons like shopping, the old man's tea and the care of children. He advocated more day nurseries and nursery schools, shopping 'time-off', preferential treatment for women workers in shops, better transport and better conditions at work. With regard to the role of women in trade unionism, he saw a future in which women would be equal and active members who would help to build a strong union for the men to return to from the Forces. However, he did reveal that past experience had shown that the joint production committees had little interest in the problems of women workers. A survey recently done on the joint production committees had found that women's problems had been discussed at only 6% of all committees. Only 19 of the 49 committees had any women on them.

Yet the questions discussed by those committees not only affected women equally with men but afforded conspicuous opportunities for women to take hand; canteen questions, questions of lighting, heating, sanitation, first aid posts, protective clothing.[52]

The speech is interesting for two reasons. It reflects very much the spirit of the war, the feeling that women's talents and skills were grossly undervalued and that the time had come for women to be equal members of trade unions. On the other hand, many entrenched attitudes are apparent, especially the notion that the 'home' job was a 'woman's job'. Although Jack Tanner thought that the burden should be lightened for women, he did not suggest that men share the 'home' job. He looked entirely to the state and employers to make provisions to enable women to do their two jobs. He also stated that the place of women in the workforce was essentially in the engineering processes which were designed and rated as 'women's' work. It was clear that skilled jobs and apprenticeships would continue to be mainly the province of men. Within the union, although he talked of equality, there was a strong indication that he saw 'conditions', not 'terms', as the main province of women members. One woman, at least, was sceptical about the motives behind the AEU accepting women members, but her belief in the importance of trade union organization outweighed her scepticism.

> I've been thinking about it, us joining the AEU. And I see it like this; if they hadn't let us in and didn't make a fuss to raise our wages, we'd be as skilled as the men by the end of the war and yet working for smaller wages. See? And the boss would want to keep us on after the war instead of taking the men back. If we get into the Union, and get the men's pay, the boss will prefer to take the men on after the war. There wouldn't be a proper reason to keep us on now would there? But that's not really important in the long run compared to what it'll mean for us women to be in the Union.[53]

At the close of the war, women felt that they had earned for themselves a place as equal citizens and as equal members of trade unions. The election of a Labour government in 1945 with a large majority gave even greater hope to women that they would get equal pay, and that nurseries, school meals and communal restaurants would be retained. The Labour govern-

ment was party to the ILO convention which had pledged itself
to equal pay for work of equal value and equal opportunity for
all regardless of sex or race. The number of women trade
unionists had almost trebled during the war and more women
than ever had been active in their unions, especially at shop
and branch level. The decision by the AEU to admit women
members meant that all the major unions had women members,
although many smaller unions had either virtually no women
members or no women members at all, since they organized in
industries in which women, apart from briefly in the war, were
not employed. A few unions continued to organize on sex
grounds, but they had become very much a minority.

The history of women in the two World Wars shows that a
few years of exceptional circumstances do not change attitudes
profoundly. There were no basic changes in the normal trade
union agreements, which were based on a sexual division of
labour and unequal pay. Since the substitution agreements
applied for the war only, the training and skills women had
acquired would find no place in the post-war world unless there
was change in trade union agreements. Government measures
to ameliorate the burden of women's dual role were introduced
in the interest of war-time productivity, not women's rights.
There was no fundamental change in attitude towards women.
The home remained their province, one which men were not
expected to share responsibility for. There was no re-evaluation
of the position and responsibilities of men, women and the state.
World War II left little permanent mark on the position of
women workers. As in World War I, the one legacy of the
enormous influx of women into industry was a leap forward in
improved conditions at work. Remembering the experience of
women in World War I Anne Loughlin said in 1941 that

> in the last war, as in this, women were praised sky high for the
> work they performed. Those of us old enough to remember the
> last war know that women got very little more than lip service
> when the war was over.[54]

History was in that respect to repeat itself.

1 Quoted in Henry PELLING *A History of British Trade Unionism* Penguin 1963 p.209

2 Quoted in Margaret GOLDSMITH *Women at War* Lindsay Drummond Ltd 1943 p.35 Time and Tide 6 Dec 1941

3 Agreement between The Shipbuilding Employers' Federation and the Confederation of Shipbuilding and Engineering Unions. Signed 17 July 1941

4 Royal Commission on Equal Pay 1944–46 Appendix VI p.54

5 Royal Commission on Equal Pay 1944–46 Minutes of Evidence 27 July 1945 p.208

6 Annual Conference Report Union of Post Office Workers 1943

7 The Railway Service Journal Feb 1943

8 Quoted in Peggy SCOTT *They Made Invasion Possible* Hutchinson and Co Ltd 1944 p.8

9 Annual Report of Women's TUC 1941   p.19f

10 Annual Report TUC 1941 p.219

11 Fortnightly March 1942

12 Quoted in GOLDSMITH op. cit. p.130f

13 Annual Report Women's TUC 1943 p.7

14 Ibid   1943 p.8

15 Annual Report Women's TUC 1942 p.14

16 Annual Report TUC   1942 p.208f

17 *Wartime Employment of Women in the Shipbuilding and Allied Industries* Ministry of Labour 1942

18 *Women in Shipbuilding* Ministry of Labour 1943

19 *Mobilisation of Woman Power: Planning and Part Time Work* Ministry of Labour and National Service 1942

20 Annual Report TUC 1941 p.217

21 Quoted in A. Williams ELLIS *Women in War Factories* Victor Gollancz 1943 p.45

22 SCOTT op. cit.

23 SCOTT op. cit. p.68

24 S. WYATT, R. MARRIOTT and D. E. R. HUGHES *A Study of Absenteeism Among Women*   HMSO Medical Research Council : Industrial Health Research Board 1943

25 Annual Report Women's TUC 1942 p.4

26 Annual Report Women's TUC 1943 p.20

27 See ELLIS op. cit.

28 SCOTT op. cit. p.147

29 Geoffrey THOMAS *Women at Work. Wartime Social Survey* An Enquiry made for the Office of the Minister of Reconstruction June 1944

30 *Women in Industry* Ministry of Labour and National Service 1945

31 THOMAS op. cit. p.2

32 THOMAS op. cit. p.2

33 National Conference of Women Called by H.M. Government. Report of Proceedings 28 Sept 1943

34 Annual Conference Report. Union of Post Office Workers 1944

35 Annual Report TUC 1945 p.339

36 *Domestic Work is a Priority Job* Ministry of Labour 1944

37 Report of the Annual Delegate Meeting of the National Union of Distributive and Allied Workers 1946

38 Quoted in Alan Fox *A History of the National Union of Boot and Shoe Operatives 1874–1957* Basil Blackwell 1958 p.564

39 Report of the Annual Conference of the National Union of Public Employees 1945

40 Transport and General Workers Union Pamphlet Part VI 1939 p.4
41 Ibid p.9
42 SCOTT op. cit. p.112
43 SCOTT op. cit. p.113
44 Report of the Proceedings of the 24th National Committee of the Amalgamated Engineering Union June 1942
45 Ibid
46 Ibid
47 Report of the Proceedings of the 25th National Committee of the Amalgamated Engineering Union 1943
48 Ibid
49 Minutes of the First Amalgamated Engineering Union Women's Conference 20 May 1943 p.7
50 Ibid p.13
51 Ibid p.8
52 Ibid p.9
53 Quoted in GOLDSMITH op. cit. p.205
54 Annual Report TUC 1941 p.293

8

'Liberty on Your Lips'
1945-1950

THE QUESTION women inevitably ask about the post-war years is, 'What happened?' What happened to the nurseries, the equal pay, the skills, the responsibilities, the 'shopping hour' and the status of women workers? The theory of economic necessity cannot be neatly used to explain 'what happened' after World War II. It was followed by a labour shortage, not high unemployment. Married women, instead of being attacked for working as they had been in 1919, were encouraged to continue or to return to work. The election of 1945 brought to power a Labour government. In 1919 Lloyd George's coalition government had no Labour representatives in the cabinet. It was expected that a Labour government would be much more committed to the equality of men and women than a coalition of the right. Yet by 1950, as had been the case by 1923, women had either returned to their homes or to their old jobs, mainly as unskilled and semi-skilled workers. This 'return' was aided to a considerable degree by the Restoration of Pre-War Practices Act which guaranteed the enforcement of pre-war practices particularly in terms of job demarcation on sex grounds. Other trade union agreements which had not been concerned with the substitution of women for men, had during the war maintained their pre-war policies of job demarcation on sex grounds, unequal pay for equal work and low minimum women's rates.

Besides the effect of the Restoration of Pre-War Practices Act, the chief reason for women returning to their homes and unskilled work was, as the ministry of reconstruction's war-time social survey had stated, that

> few women, even now, appear to look upon work as a career so long as all the disadvantages attaching to their sex, and to work after marriage, remain.[1]

The war had provided ample evidence that where 'the disadvantages attaching to their sex' had been ameliorated, women workers were not only prepared to work, train and take responsibility; they also enjoyed work. Where women workers had to bear the full burden of 'two jobs', where they worked at unskilled jobs for low pay, where they were denied training and jobs with career prospects or where they did equal jobs for unequal pay, there was little incentive for them except for sheer economic necessity. In the light of the war experience, it is surprising that the post-war labour shortage did not lead the government and the TUC to remove 'the disadvantages' which discouraged women from working. On the contrary, they made it more difficult for women by closing nurseries, by retaining restrictive practices and by refusing to give women incentives such as training or equal pay and equal opportunities. Whilst some women did throughout the period make demands and fight for greater equality, some of the women in leadership positions in the trade union movement, by accepting the TUC general council's policies, hindered women.

The government's refusal to remove 'the disadvantages' of women workers was disastrous for its campaign to encourage married women to work and produce more babies. Great Britain's dwindling birth rate and the return of women to the home meant that in the 1950s the government had to look to the colonies for cheap labour. Equal pay, training and recognition of their skills would have given women an incentive to work. Equality in social security benefits, pensions and tax status would also have helped. Not only did the years 1945–1950 see women forced back into their pre-war roles; the Labour government also allotted an unequal place to women in the welfare state. The social security system was based on the concept of the family, with the male as main breadwinner; so the welfare state perpetuated the traditional position of women as second-class citizens.

Nurseries, equal pay and equal opportunities, a reduction of the differential between men's and women's rates, equal benefits and the right of married women to equal employment were the main issues for women trade unionists in the immediate post-war years. A study of these issues shows clearly the lack of commitment by the trade union movement to act in the interests of women's equality. The fight over nursery schools and day nurseries revealed most starkly the dominant attitudes within the trade union movement. The day nurseries and nursery schools established during the war by a 100% government grant to local authorities was one of the major gains women workers made during the war. Although nursery provision had fallen far short of the government's promise to provide adequate child-care facilities for all mothers engaged on war work, a start had been made. Day nurseries cared for pre-school children of all ages for the full working day, sometimes providing nursery education, but at least providing skilled care for all children attending them. Nursery schools on the other hand were for children aged two to five. Whilst they gave nursery education they were of less help to the working mother, since they usually took children only in the mornings or for a short school day and had normal school holidays. During the war, more than two-thirds of nursery places had been in the day nurseries. The 1944 education act provided for an extension of nursery schools, a measure supported by both trade unionists and the Labour party as a means of improving the education standards and opportunities of working-class children. Despite the act, few local authorities used their powers to establish nursery schools, even though the Labour government expressed a desire to see an expansion of nursery schools.

In 1945 the ministry of health and the ministry of education sent a joint circular to local authorities advising them of the government's attitude towards day nurseries, which was radically different from their attitude towards nursery schools. The government hoped that local authorities would not prejudice the expansion of nursery schools by the provision of day nurseries.

> The Ministers concerned accept the view of medical and other authority that, in the interests of the health and development of the child no less than for the benefit of the mother, the proper place for a child under two is at home with his mother. They are also of the opinion that, under normal peace-time conditions the right policy to pursue would be positively to discourage mothers of children under two from going out to work.[2]

In 1946 the government reduced the day-nursery grant from

100% to 50%. The reduction proved to be an effective disincentive to local authorities, which either closed their day nurseries or passed the extra financial burden on to the mothers. For most working women earning an unskilled woman's wage, it was not worth working and paying the high cost of having their children cared for at a day nursery. They therefore fell back on baby minders, whose standard of care was usually inferior, or opted not to work. The cut in the grant fell most harshly on those women who for one reason or another had children and had to work. As a letter to *The Times* (3 July 1945) from the honorary secretary of The National Society of Children's Nurseries pointed out, the poorest districts, where state-run, grant-aided day nurseries were most in need, were the very places where they would disappear, since they would be too expensive for the mothers.

The government's action did not go uncontested by women trade unionists, but sadly their fight to save day nurseries and to get the 100% grant restored was hindered by the TUC general council, including its women members. In 1946 Miss Harrison, of the Fire Brigades Union, moved the following resolution :

> This Conference believes that adequate nursery provision, i.e. Nursery Schools and Day Nurseries, are a vital social service beneficial both to parents and children and call upon the Local Authorities to fully implement the joint Circular of the Minister of Health and Minister of Education on Nursery Provision. It further believes that in the light of the Government's appeal to women to play a full part in production it is imperative that the 100% grant to Day Nurseries should be restored and that there should be no increase in the charges to parents. It also urges that the 'Means Test' qualification should be withdrawn.[3]

Miss Harrison pointed out that since the war 349 nurseries had been closed and that 99 of them had been closed as a direct result of the reduction in the grant. Meanwhile costs had escalated. During the war the usual charge had been 1s. per day, but the charges had risen to between 16s. 6d. and 26s. a week. Several delegates spoke in support of the motion, but one or two expressed reservations about a restoration of the full 100% grant. The issue was taken to the 1947 TUC conference where the Women Public Health Officers introduced a motion which, whilst agreeing with the government that women with young children should not be encouraged to work, nevertheless called for more day nurseries for the children of mothers who had to work. It was a muted resolution but it did at least call for a recognition of the fact that some women with young children had to work. The delegates to the conference took little interest in the motion and one speaker 'found it very difficult sitting in the Hall, to hear much of the debate, owing to the constant noise and walking out'.[4] Although the motion was passed, it by no means reflected or influenced the view of the general council.

The position of the general council, stated in the 1947 report to the TUC women's conference and in its annual report to the TUC, was 'that the case for day nurseries must be proved in each locality after an examination of all the circumstances and that they should not press for a general extension of them'.[5] So day nurseries continued to be closed. By 1948 the general council had moved even further in its opposition to state-aided day nurseries. It opposed calls for the restoration of the 100% grant and argued that if local authorities thought day nurseries were necessary, they should foot the bill. It also advocated private day nurseries and argued that factory-run nurseries were convenient for the mother, without asking the employer to bear some of the cost or understanding that employer-run nurseries tied the mother in an insidious way to her employer. While the government was enacting legislation to establish the welfare state, the TUC was advocating private enterprise for child care. Underlying the general council's attitude to day nurseries was its attitude towards the place of women in society.

> There is no doubt in the minds of the General Council that the home is one of the most important spheres for a woman worker and that it would be doing a grave injury to the life of the nation if women were persuaded or forced to neglect their domestic duties in order to enter industry particularly where there are young children to cater for.[6]

There had been little change since 1875, when Henry Broadhurst had stated that he believed the proper sphere of women was 'at home'.

All sections of the TUC publicly supported the government's

appeal for women workers. Women trade unionists, however, realized that, unless women were offered tangible gains for working, they would be unlikely to respond to the call. The general council merely suggested that employers consider employing more women on a part-time basis to enable them to work and keep up with their 'household responsibilities'. It recommended short shifts to encourage women to work in what they regarded as the traditional areas of female labour – clothing, hosiery, wool and worsted, cotton, laundry, nursing and clerical work. In 1947 the ministry of labour, as part of the campaign to encourage married women to work, issued a leaflet called 'Call to Women' in which it claimed that women were the 'only reserve of labour left to draw upon'.[7] The leaflet pointed out that since 1943 1,150,000 women had left industry, causing an acute labour shortage, particularly in the traditional areas of women's work. Magnanimously, but dishonestly, the ministry of labour declared 'that all that can be done in the way of provision of day nurseries, nursery schools and other child care facilities is being and will be done',[8] but meanwhile the cost of child-care was placed on the working mother. Hints were made in the leaflet that some work could be done by foreigners, but it claimed 'there is a vast unsatisfied demand for British Women Workers'.[9] Hints about importing foreign workers were also made in the 1948 annual report to the TUC women's conference, in which it was stated that the government had been considering importing women of Germanic origin to England on two-year contracts to work in the cotton and textile industries.

The royal commission on population, which reported in 1949, confirmed that the average family size had fallen since the turn of the century to 2.2 children per married couple. They commented that whilst the birth rate had fallen to sub-replacement level, a deficiency of about 6%, 'the deficiency is not nearly as great as the pre-war reproduction rate calculations suggested'.[10] The report posited a variety of reasons for the declining family size, including the wider use of contraceptives, the diminished need for large families to support the elderly and the sick and the change in 'woman's status'. Woman's status had been severely undermined by the Industrial Revolution and the 'movement for the equality of the sexes was in part a revolt against

the conditions that tended to restrict women to the role of pro-
ducer and household drudge'.[11] The movement towards equality
had also encouraged women to restrict the size of their families.
More pertinent than their reasons for the declining family size
were the recommendations made by the royal commission for
increasing family size at least to replacement level. They recommended increased family allowances and an extension of allowances to include the first child. With a blatant middle-class
bias, the commission advocated supplementary children's allowances for professional workers and the introduction of allowances
for officers in the armed services. On the same grounds as the
government, they opposed day nurseries but thought that there
ought to be more home helps, nursery schools and play centres.
To make childbirth more attractive they recommended better
maternity services. Anaesthetics should be freely available to
women at childbirth and the National Health Service should give
contraceptive advice. 'Preparation for family life should be given
a more prominent place in the education system'. To prepare
children, particularly girls, for family life, they recommended 'a
wide development of sex education in schools' and 'adjustments
of the curricula to raise the status of the practical crafts of home
making and subjects related to married life'.[12]

> It is also suggested that the preponderance of unmarried women
> teachers tends to a deprecation of the subjects that relate to
> marriage and family life; if this is so, the removal of the marriage
> bar may go some way as a corrective.[13]

It was an extreme irony that the commission recommended the
lifting of the marriage bar, not so that married women as of
right could work, but so that they might encourage girls to
marry and have children to supply the labour market.

The government's refusal to implement equal pay, supported
by the TUC, was another indication of the lack of commitment
by both parties to encourage women to work. Although the royal
commission on equal pay was set up in 1944, those giving
evidence were aware that the report would influence government policy in peace-time so the evidence was based on pre-war
experiences. Examples from war-time were seen more as
examples of abnormality than as a blue-print for a new restruc-

H

turing of wage rates. Evidence was given by employers, trade unions, women's groups, government departments, academics, doctors and a few individuals. Not surprisingly, few women gave evidence, although many men claimed to speak in their name.

The brief of the commission had its limitations. It was only to 'examine the existing relationships between the remuneration of men and women in the public services, in industry and in other fields of employment; to consider the social, economic and financial implications of the claim of equal pay for equal work; and to report'.[14] It was not to make recommendations. The commission also chose a narrow definition of 'equal pay for equal work' and proposed 'to leave inequality in respect of overall value out of account in deciding whether work should or should not be called equal and to this extent at least "equal pay for equal work" will not, as used by us, have the same import as "equal pay for equal value to the employer"'.[15] A large part of the royal commission's inquiry was therefore to ascertain the extent to which women and men did exactly the same work and thus the extent to which equal pay would be applicable if implemented. The commission found that, although there was much equal work done in non-manual grades in the public sector and the professions, there was very little equal work in private industry. The latter fact they attributed partly to custom and practice, but mostly to trade union agreements. The fact that so few men and women did the same jobs in private industry enabled the TUC to agree with employers that there was little claim for equal pay. In summing up the attitude of the TUC, the report stated that the TUC 'made it clear in their view the introduction of equal pay, if it were to come, should be brought about not by any fiat of the Government but through the ordinary machinery of negotiation'.[16]

The AEU document put forward outspoken demands for equal pay. It was the only trade union submission concerning private industry which attacked, not only unequal pay for equal work, but also the whole structure of 'women's' work and 'women's' rates. In its opening statement the AEU stated that women had shown during the war that they were as efficient, as productive and as capable of performing a variety of skills as men when given the opportunities for training and that 'the public scandal of their exploitation as cheap labour in this industry is a menace both to general wage levels and to any policy of industrial expansion'.[17] With regard to the question of labour wastage it argued that 'so long as women work in engineering they produce and so long as they produce they are entitled to a decent wage'. On women's high absenteeism, turn-over and sickness rates, the AEU was equally forthright.

> The rate of wages paid to women in industry provided them with no incentive to remain at work and very strong reasons for not doing so when they felt inclined. We believe that the high incidence of sickness amongst women arises from their low wages, the poor nutrition which they can afford, the lack of all these means to food, health and resistance to disease which are taken for granted in higher income groups.[18]

They elaborated the point by pointing out that not only did many women earn low wages, but before and after their working day they had to 'clean and dust and sweep and cook', and therefore it was not surprising that they needed to take days off to recuperate. The AEU had no objection 'to women entering the industry upon the same terms and conditions as men'. The employment of women on unequal terms gave rise to 'grave social and industrial consequences . . . from the antagonism to the employment of women amongst male workers whose wage levels are thus threatened and a retrograde tendency on the part of organised male workers to limit and oppose technological progress'.[19]

Since there was general agreement that the government should not interfere with the normal machinery of wage negotiation in private industry, the main debate regarding equal pay centred on the public sector. But the treasury's policy of 'fair relativity', pegged wages in the public sector, especially the civil service, to wages in private industry. The wage fixers were caught in a 'Catch 22' situation. The treasury agreed that their rates merely reflected the inequality of rates in private industry. The TUC argued that, until the government gave a lead by implementing equal pay in the public sector, private industry had no example to follow. It was clear that the government would have to make the first move by implementing equal pay in the non-manual grades of the civil service.

Another issue which was raised frequently at the royal commission's hearings was whether a man's wage was a 'family wage' in relation to a woman's wage or not. Many still chose to believe this was the case, even though their arguments had been severely undermined by the introduction of family allowances. One of the main arguments used by trade unionists for paying men more than women had been the notion of a 'family rate'. Employers happily went along, since it enabled them to pay women derisory wages.

The TUC did recommend that the government should implement equal pay in the public sector: 'That the Government should support the application to industry of the principle of equal pay for equal work by applying it with the least possible delay to their own establishments.'[20] In addition it urged the government to encourage local authorities to introduce equal pay and to use its influence on those bodies, mainly the newly formed wages councils (the old trade boards), which had the power to fix minimum wages. So whilst the TUC was quite prepared to recommend that the government and local authorities implement equal pay, they were opposed to any such direct action in the private sector – the sector which, in those days, they mostly represented.

The repeal by the Labour government of the 1927 Trade Disputes Act made the civil service unions free to affiliate to the TUC, as some immediately did, including the Union of Post Office Workers and the Civil Service Clerical Association. The affiliation of those unions to the TUC was to assist the campaign for equal pay. The Union of Post Office Workers in their evidence argued before the royal commission that equal pay should be immediately implemented in the Post Office. Night work had been the main argument against giving women equal pay, despite the fact that women had done night work during the war. The UPOW countered that argument by saying that night work should be reduced to a minimum and that women should be made eligible for night work. Men and women should be paid an equal basic rate as well as an equal extra payment for doing night work.

Outside of the Post Office, the arguments for equal pay were all on behalf of the professional grades in the civil service and local authorities and teachers. The two most cogent claims were made by the Civil Service National Whitley Council (Staff Side) and the Council of Women Civil Servants. Both gave considerable space to discounting the argument that men were paid a 'family wage' and that equal pay for women would give them a higher standard of living than men. The Council of Women Civil Servants stated that the 1921 census returns showed that only 39% of the total adult male population supported children. A survey of 151 of their own members showed that 17% were responsible for total dependants and 41% for partial dependants. The Staff Side of the National Whitley Council pointed out that

> differentiation between men's and women's scales in the Civil Service can only be said to be related to family dependancy in the crude sense that there is a conventional idea of the standard of living an officer in a particular grade ought to have and that this may include some notion in the case of a man of what he needs in order to marry and have a family. Since, however, the same rate is paid to single and married men, those with large and those with small families, the dependance principle cannot be said to operate. In the case of women the differentiation applies universally without any regard to family dependancy. The notion of the 'average family' and the idea that single women never have obligation are both fallacious.[21]

Both unions were eloquent in their criticism of the marriage bar. It supplied the treasury with a constant source of cheap labour in the clerical grades, but the treasury's view of marriage wastage was inconsistent.

> We may perhaps be forgiven if we find it strange that the State should both pay women less on account of the risk of loss of their services on marriage and at the same time force them to retire on marriage.[22]

The public sector employers, to a man, opposed the implementation of equal pay. The treasury gave the lead in its stalwart opposition – a position it had maintained since the introduction of women into the civil service. The outspoken male chauvinism of the treasury outstripped even that of private employers. Since little overlap in work occurred between men and women in the industrial grades of the civil service, the treasury evidence to the royal commission dealt specifically with the non-industrial grades. Whilst not arguing that women's work was inferior to men's, the treasury argued that women were of less value since they had higher sickness rates, higher ill-health retirement rates and a high rate of wastage due to marriage. The higher marriage wastage rate was, the treasury conceded, a mixed financial blessing.

> Among the higher grades certainly, the marriage wastage is a serious disadvantage, since the training period is long and costly, and marriage bar or no marriage bar, half to two-thirds of the women can be expected to resign during their training or fairly soon after. If they are retrained after marriage, the employer is likely to suffer inconvenience and cost due to interruptions of service for childbearing. It must be added, however, that among the lower grades in the Civil Service the marriage wastage is an advantage since a great deal of the work is better done by young people, and further, reasonable prospects could not be provided for the career staff without the turnover caused by marriage of the women.[23]

The crux of the treasury argument lay not in the advantages or disadvantages of employing women with regards to health or marriage, but 'in the question of why women in general receive lower wages than men'. The treasury answered the question: 'as a class, women need less than men. For this reason, to put it quite crudely, they will take less'.[24] It discounted the argument for family allowances by arguing that there would be 'formidable budgetary and economic difficulties inherent in an attempt to restore the man's differential by allowances in respect of his family responsibilities'.[25] In summing up, the treasury said that it opposed the implementation of equal pay in the non-industrial civil service, because it would mean paying rates higher than those 'needed to recruit and retain the women required'. Equal pay would result in a situation where 'the average woman employed would be on a higher standard of living than her average male colleague' since 'most women can maintain a given standard of living on a lower wage than is possible for most men'.[26]

Other public sector employers used similar arguments. Sir Thomas Gardiner, speaking on behalf of the Post Office, said that he agreed with the basic principles of the treasury memorandum. So did the Burnham Committee, which had fixed unequal rates for teachers in 1919 and had perpetuated them since. It maintained that in order to attract more men to teaching it was necessary to pay them a higher rate. The Rushcliffe Committee used the same argument for paying unequal rates to nurses.[27] The Armed Forces paid women two-thirds of the male rates, except for women doctors and dentists, who were paid, after protest, the same rate as men on the principle of 'fair relativity' – civilian women doctors and dentists receiving equal pay. Women in the police force, all unmarried since the marriage bar still operated, were paid 12% less than the men, the home office arguing that police women were merely supplementary to and not a substitution for men. The only public sector area in which certain inroads into equal pay had been made was in some local government employment. In January 1946 an agreement had been signed by the National Joint Council recommending equal pay for those doing equal work in the administrative, technical and professional sections. In this agreement, as in the whole question about equal pay, the unions and the employers had agreed that in the clerical and industrial grades there was more or less total job segregation on sex grounds and therefore no basis for a claim for equal pay. The unions' refusal to argue for equal pay in the clerical grades or for a re-evaluation of the 'women's' jobs, like cleaners and canteen workers, meant that the vast majority of women workers in the public sector were excluded from the debate about equal pay.

The British Employers' Confederation went to great lengths to justify lower payment to women. It argued that women were confined to lighter jobs, had high sickness and absentee rates and, even where they were not regulated by law, could not be subjected to the long hours of work which men could do. The confederation complained that the statutory 'requirements for the protection of the health and welfare of workers are in many cases more onerous in the case of women',[28] that women were less changeable in their work than men, that they were not prepared to take on responsible jobs, that they had limited training and experience, and that they produced less than men. All the myths about women workers which the war-time experience had disproved, were trotted out. Like the treasury, the employers thought that to pay women equal pay would mean 'placing women in a privileged position to men',[29] although they conceded that where all things were identical men and women should receive equal pay. They ended their evidence with a plea to be allowed to employ cheap female labour to enable Great Britain to compete in the world market at competitive prices.

The medical profession were called in to give evidence, particularly in relation to the physical differences between men and women. Economists were also asked to give their opinion on the economic effects of implementing equal pay. Curiously, almost all the medical evidence was in favour of equal pay and almost all the evidence from economists against. The medical profession argued that there was no evidence to support the claim that physical differences between men and women were a justification for unequal pay, except in a few jobs involving severe muscular work. They disposed of the claim that menstruation affected women's work and efficiency. Most pointed out that the higher sickness and absentee rates amongst women were due more to the fact that most women did two jobs or did jobs which were boring and low paid. Prof. E. M. Killick commented.

> I know of no inherent physiological reasons for the high sickness rate amongst women. The low sickness rate amongst certain groups of women, e.g. clerical workers, suggests the amount of sickness is largely influenced by conditions of work and the complications of home life.[30]

The economists, in contrast, mainly opposed equal pay. Sir Hubert Henderson, Professor of Economics at Oxford opposed it in the public services on the ground that it would imperil the recruitment of men to those jobs.[31] Another eminent professor thought that to encourage women into industry by improved pay and away from their function of 'home-making, child rearing and child bearing' would have far-reaching social implications. Other economists either hedged or thought that equal pay should only be implemented in non-manual grades.

The final section of the report, on the General, Economic and Social Consequences of Equal Pay, reveals what the Royal Commission would have recommended if it had been so briefed. Generally, it concluded that the effects of equal pay in teaching and in the upper levels of the civil service would be beneficial; but it saw little to justify equal pay in the industrial grades or in private industry. There were reservations to these main points, mainly the fear that equal pay might adversely influence the recruitment of men to teaching and that the payment of equal pay in the civil service might upset the Treasury's principle of 'fair relativity'.

Three women, Dame Anne Loughlin, Dr Janet Vaughan and Miss L. F. Bettleford, who had sat on the Royal Commission, drafted a memorandum of dissent from the main body of the report. They challenged the findings of the report, which agreed with the employers' argument that women were of inferior value to employers. They also accused its author of double thinking. On the one hand, the report argued that equal pay would drive women out of industry since men, at the same price, would be preferred. On the other hand it argued that equal pay would encourage more women to work and so neglect their main role at home. The minority report apportioned much of the blame for women's low wages to trade unions which had negotiated job demarcation between the sexes on wage grounds. It rejected what the main report saw as a conflict between 'exact justice' and 'oiling the wheels of economic progress'. The women who signed the minority report saw no such conflict.

> On the contrary the claims of justice between individuals and of the development of national productivity point in the same direction.[32]

In 1946 the findings of the Royal Commission were submitted to the government, which announced in 1947 that, whilst it agreed with equal pay in principle and supported the justice of the claim for equal pay for their own employees, it thought that the application of the principle would be inflationary. It therefore could not afford to implement it. The principles of equal pay and equal opportunities had been reaffirmed at both the 1928 and 1944 conferences of the International Labour Organization. In 1944 the Labour party had refrained from ratifying those principles before publication of the Royal Commission's report. After the report, it continued to withhold ratification, pending a change in Great Britain's economy.

The trade union movement was divided in its response. Early in 1947 the Standing Joint Committee of Women's Organizations, at a meeting in Caxton Hall, passed a resolution supporting the minority report. It called for representations to be made to the government by the TUC, for unions to make greater efforts to negotiate equal pay, and for women to organize to demand it.

The women soon found that they had to fight, not only the government, but also the TUC General Council. A delegate from the Civil Service Clerical Union at the 1947 TUC conference attacked the General Council for its 'weak and unconvincing attitude . . . on the question of equal pay'.[33] She accused it of delay in going to see the prime minister on the question and criticized it for not challenging the government's stand. 'Why,' she asked, 'are our Socialist Ministers holding hands with every reactionary Minister of the last 25 years, doling out the same reactionary arguments which have been condemned by conference over and over again?'[34] Apart from seeing the prime minister and issuing a pamphlet on equal pay, the general council did little to support the campaign for equal pay. At that same conference a motion was carried calling for the end to the marriage bar and for the general council to press for a policy of equal pay for equal work and equal opportunities for women. Unfortunately, the motives behind the motion, as expressed by the mover, a delegate from the National Union of Vehicle Builders, were somewhat mixed. An important part of his argument was that women should be hired at the expense of 'the non-working Poles'.[35]

In 1948, the TUC took a step forward in its support of the principle of equal pay, but practically no steps towards putting it into practice. A pamphlet called 'Q and A of Equal Pay'[36] was issued by the TUC. It stated clearly that the TUC thought the government should implement equal pay in the public sector and that in the private sector equal pay should be reached through negotiation. In isolation, the pamphlet reads as a clarion call to government and unions to implement and negotiate equal pay. Unfortunately the pamphlet and the action taken by the general council were at odds. The subject was obviously an embarrassment to the general council, for in 1948, when Florence

Hancock was in the chair, she omitted any mention of equal pay in her opening speech to the conference.

It was a point not missed by Miss Jones of the Civil Service Clerical Association. She pointed out the contradiction in the platform's position – calling women to enter industry, but doing nothing to encourage them by negotiating for better or equal wages. She ended her attack with a parody of a poem by Goldsmith.

> When lovely women stoop to folly
> And find too late that men betray,
> Ah what can soothe their melancholy
> And boost production? Equal Pay![37]

In 1949 the general council finally came out into the open. In its annual report it stated

> that in the present economic situation the General Council should not press for immediate and comprehensive implementation of the principle and the responsibility for submitting claims for equal pay in particular industries or occupations rested with the affiliated Unions concerned and not with the TUC. . . . In the light of the above and of the continuing need for counter-inflationary policies the Committee decided that a further approach by the TUC to the Government on Equal Pay would be inappropriate at the present time.[38]

Its attitude to equal opportunities was the same.

> There was further agreement that as regards the reference to equal opportunity for women to acquire special skills and to continue to use such skills as were acquired during the war, this was a matter involving trade union agreement and practices which should be dealt with at an industrial level.[39]

So, in 1949, the TUC general council washed its hands of equal pay and equal opportunity for women. It sided with the government and accepted that to implement equal pay in the public sector would be inflationary. The general council did not go unchallenged, but the challengers lost. The annual report was accepted by a vote of 3,835,000 to 1,765,000.

The responsibility for pursuing women's equality was thus left to the discretion of individual unions. There had been a substantial increase in female trade union membership during the war – an increase of about three-quarters of a million. Despite the fact that more than a million women left industry in the immediate post-war years, their trade union membership remained at about 1¼ millions between 1945 and 1950. This increased membership was not reflected in an increased commitment by individual unions to their women members. The presence of a large, outspoken body of women members was evident in some white-collar unions, but not in the majority of unions, even those which had had a substantial increase in women members. Most unions, like the TUC, supported equal pay in principle but failed to pursue it in practice. As for equal opportunities for women, few unions were committed to it in principle and most opposed it in practice, both in the agreements they negotiated and in their own structures.

The AEU, in contrast to most unions, had made a clear policy statement to the royal commission on the way forward for industrial equality for women. In practice, although they put in a claim for equal pay, they failed to negotiate it. Without equal pay it was impossible for the union to push forward for women to enter the industry 'on the same terms and conditions as men'. The restoration of the Pre-War Practices Act had restored the old job demarcations on sex grounds and since women continued to be excluded from apprenticeships there was no move made towards equal opportunity. Within the union, the new women members, of which by 1950 there were about 44,000, were organized in a separate women's section with a separate women's conference. Although women could be elected to office in the main body of the union, it was not until 1951 that women gained full equality within its ranks.

In the Association of Engineering and Shipbuilding Draughtsmen women also continued to be organized in a separate section, the tracers' section. Through apprenticeship, the job of draughtsman was reserved for men. As in many unions, whilst there were continual complaints about the low level of organization among women, there was also considerable feeling expressed in the Tracers' Column in the journal, *The Draughtsman,* that the union did not do as much for the women tracers as it did for the male draughtsmen. The differential between the minimum London rates for draughtsmen and those for tracers increased by 8s. between 1944 and 1948. The Union of Post Office Workers, the other union besides the AEU which had argued a clear case for equal pay for women outside the non-industrial civil service and local government employment, also failed to negotiate it. The postmaster-general remained adamant against it. Within the union calls for measures to give women greater job opportunities were opposed. At the 1948 conference of the union a motion called for equal opportunities for promotion for a section of women. The executive opposed the motion on the grounds that, whilst they were for equality of opportunity, they could not support the resolution because it only called for equality in a piecemeal way and 'one must do it on a broader basis'.[40] The motion was defeated. A similar resolution, calling for the right for women to enjoy the same privileges as men 'on writing and supervising',[41] was also defeated. It was opposed on the grounds that it 'did not go to the root of the problem' and more pertinently, perhaps, that if women were included in the rotation scheme, men would have four years on writing duties and twenty years on counter work. Married women employed by the Post Office also continued to be discriminated against. They were given only temporary, not staff, status.

The gap between policy and practice was sadly evident in a large number of unions. In 1947 the president of the National Union of Boot and Shoe Operatives stated that the union was 'committed to the policy of equal pay for men and women, not in the distant future, but . . . in the more or less immediate future'.[42] In that same year the union signed an agreement which increased the differential between men's and women's pay from 73% to 72%. When women challenged the agreement, the union complacently replied that 'the women's rate was higher, compared with the men's in shoe-making, than in four-fifths of the industries where comparable minima existed'.[43] Of this the historian of the union, Alan Fox, commented:

> But the discrimination against women in the boot and shoe industry has been greater than a surface impression would suggest. Women's contract rates tend to be distributed closer to their minima than men's contract rates to theirs, which means that the sex differential between average contract rates is considerably larger than the sex differential between minima.[44]

The picture was much the same in the tobacco industry despite the fact the industry was suffering a shortage of labour. The Tobacco Workers' Charter, drawn up in 1947, called for an equal basic minimum wage for all adults over the age of twenty-one regardless of sex. Nevertheless, an agreement reached that year gave women about two-thirds of the male rate. In 1947 women had also called for a free cigarette allowance to be given to women in the factories which gave it to men.[45] The executive opposed the demand on the ground that it would endanger the equal pay claim. As events turned out, women got neither free cigarettes nor equal pay. Despite many good articles in the *Tobacco Worker*, the union's journal, both arguing the case for equal pay and pointing out that strong rank-and-file organization was the best means of achieving it, the increases negotiated by the union in 1950 were 5s. 6d. for men and 5s. 0d. for women. The differential between men's and women's basic rates was thus increased. Another industry facing an acute shortage of female labour was the clothing industry. The Tailor and Garment Workers Union also saw equal pay as a means of attracting women to the industry, but equal pay remained a principle and the industry had to devise other means to attract women. In 1945 the Transport and General Workers Union came out in favour of the 'rate for the job'. Ernie Bevin, speaking to the annual conference, said 'that where women were engaged in what had hitherto been regarded as women's work, the union would endeavour to secure the standard commensurate with the basic wage for men in the same industry. This meant that wages would not be fixed for women because they were women but on the value of production.'[46] Whilst upholding a policy of the 'rate for the job', the union accepted the government's concern about inflation and therefore did not press for it.

In many unions there was a lack of commitment not only to equal pay and equal opportunity, but to their women members generally. In the USDAW the women laundry workers were up in arms and, in some cases, out on strike in 1946 over the executive's failure to negotiate improved rates and conditions. The union had had a big campaign to recruit women laundry workers and then, having recruited them, signed an agreement which worsened their terms and conditions. In some areas women led unofficial strikes against the agreement with some success; but the success was confined to those areas, since the agreement still stood and the union made no attempt to negotiate better rates nationally. Women in the National Union of Public Employees were also sceptical of their union's commitment to them. Throughout the 1940s they continued the battle started in the war to get the union to appoint a woman organizer. Since more than half of NUPE's members were women, it did not seem an unfair demand. The general secretary consistently opposed the demand by arguing that the union could not afford to appoint a woman organizer who, he thought, would inevitably bring a low return to the union in terms of women members, since women were so apathetic. A delegate to the 1949 conference of NUPE went further and asserted that women did not want to have women organizers or supervisors 'because they regarded them as "too catty" '.[47]

The women railway clerks, who had quite a long tradition of speaking out for their rights, took up an issue which they had been fighting since they were first organized in World War I. It was the issue of the marriage bar. The demand for its abolition was debated at the 1946 and 1947 annual conferences. In 1946 the resolution to abolish the marriage bar was amended by delegates from Glasgow to read that women should only be allowed to continue work after marriage 'in exceptional circumstances'. The argument the men put forward to support the amendment was that

> if true family life was to be restored in this country and a halt called to the falling birth rate and the growing number of unhappy marriages women must leave the service on marriage and devote themselves to the very important task of home-making.[48]

In addition, the movers of the amendment claimed that the rise in juvenile delinquency was caused by married women working. It was an argument that was to be used extensively in the 1950s. Despite a plea from Miss Lewisham of the executive council for married women to be given the right to decide whether they could best serve 'the country by remaining at work or at home',[49] the motion was passed as amended. In 1947 another resolution, supported by the executive, called for the abolition of the marriage bar and the right for women to continue in employment after marriage, forfeiting only their rights to superannuation. The Glasgow delegates moved an amendment similar to the one they had moved a year earlier. Speaking for the amendment, Mr Ross said that he 'doubted if the resolution represented the real views of the married men on the Executive – they looked a hen-pecked lot'.[50] Speaking against the amendment, another male delegate eloquently claimed that if the amendment were passed 'you will have liberty on your lips but tyranny in your hearts'.[51] The amendment was lost. The change of attitude and voting between 1946 and 1947 was probably largely influenced by the change of position of the executive. In 1947 a motion, too, was carried calling for equal pay for equal work.

The demand for the retention of the marriage bar was not confined to a few men from Glasgow in the Railway Clerks Association. It was a demand which tended to be voiced whenever unemployment or redundancies were threatened. Although there was a residual fear that unemployment would rise, labour shortage was, in the late 1940s, a much greater problem. It was acutest in the traditional areas of female labour, revealing the reluctance of women, after their war-time experience, to return to their pre-war unskilled low paid jobs. This reluctance was most evident in the shortage of domestic workers. Before the war more than a third of all working women had been employed in domestic work, the majority being employed privately whereas during the war most domestic workers were employed in the public sector in schools, hospitals, canteens and the services. The campaigns to recruit women during the war showed that, given a choice, they did not readily choose domestic work, and both the Women's Advisory Committee of the TUC and the Labour government were concerned about how to attract women back to private domestic service after the war. The Women's Advisory Committee argued that proper training and decent wages and conditions should be offered to domestic workers. The Labour government took the hint. In 1947 the National Institute of Houseworkers was established, sponsored by the Labour government. Its function was to train women and girls in domestic service, much of which was expected to be private. As Ernie Bevin wrote,

> we have also to think of our housewives in all sections of the community who need help to run their homes, and the Institute has to see that they get this help to maintain our home life, on which so much depends.[52]

Whilst the government was hoping to encourage women back into domestic service, they were also trying to encourage them to have more children. How domestic workers were to maintain their own home life while helping more privileged women to maintain theirs was not considered by the government. A report by the Standing Committee of Working Women's Organizations considered the problem in 1945. It published a report on Population Problems and Post-War Organization of Private Domestic Employment in which it suggested that the government institute a variety of services from day nurseries to communal meals services to enable women both to work and to care for their own families without undue strain. The recommendations went unheeded. The report also pointed out that

> young people will be willing to have more children if they have confidence in the future, confidence that the nation will need their work in peace as in war; that there will be security against ill health and other contingencies.[53]

Full employment and the benefits of the National Health Service and Social Security did give young people more confidence. But apart from the immediate post-war baby boom, young people did not show a greater willingness to produce more children. Nor did women show a great willingness to go into private domestic service. The long columns of situations vacant on the back page of *The Times,* advertising for parlourmaids, housemaids, nannies and domestic help showed that the demand consistently exceeded supply.

The period 1945–50 was a period in which the main bodies representing women workers and the government had 'liberty on their lips' but not in their actions. The reality was a gap between male and female average earnings of 50% and agreements which, far from narrowing that gap, often increased it. The absence of women in leadership positions with a clear policy for the way forward meant that women fighting for change received little support from the top. The forces that were determined to return women to their traditional areas of employment and the home were much stronger than those against them. Many women continued to be unorganized and had no voice; in many unions women were either so outnumbered, or the executives so male-controlled, that their voice was not heard, let alone acted upon.

By the end of the 1940s, World War II might never have happened for women workers. It had become a mere memory. Although more women were organized than before the war, they found their position within unions much as it had always been. Despite the labour shortage, the home was still seen as the place for married women. Nothing was done to make it easier for women both to work and have children and much was undone by the closure of day nurseries, national restaurants and communal laundries. The only concession made to the dual role of women was the continuance of the employment of women in industry part time, and part-time work was as beneficial to the employers as to the women. One gain was made – the abolition of the marriage bar in the civil service and most local government employment. Some private firms still applied it and it remained in men's minds a weapon to be kept in reserve as a means to control the supply of female labour. Restrictive practices had quickly re-asserted themselves and women were once again barred by union agreements, as much as by custom and practice, from entering or continuing to work in skilled employment. The wastage of the skills women had acquired during the war was one of the prices the country paid for the government and trade unions' obstinacy.

1 Geoffrey Thomas *Women at Work. Wartime Social Survey* An enquiry made for the Office of the Minister of Reconstruction 1944 p.2
2 Circular 221/45 : Ministry of Health. Circular 75 Ministry of Education 14 Dec 1945
3 Annual Report Women's TUC 1946 p.32
4 Annual Report TUC 1947 p.414
5 Ibid p.249

6 Annual Report TUC 1947 p.247
7 *Call to Women* Ministry of Labour 1947
8 Ibid
9 Ibid
10 *Royal Commission on Population Report* HMSO Cmnd 7695 1949 p.221
11 Ibid p.40
12 Ibid p.231
13 Ibid p.211
14 *Royal Commission on Equal Pay 1944–46* HMSO Cmnd 6937 1946
15 Ibid p.5
16 Ibid p.44
17 Royal Commission on Equal Pay op.cit. Appendix VIII p.76
18 Ibid
19 **Ibid**
20 Quoted in *Equal Pay: Memorandum of Evidence to the Royal Commission* TUC p.30
21 Royal Commission on Equal Pay op. cit. Appendix III p.33
22 Royal Commission on Equal Pay op. cit. Appendix IV p.46
23 Royal Commission on Equal Pay op. cit. Appendix II p.28
24 Ibid p.28
25 Ibid p.29
26 Ibid p.30
27 Royal Commission on Equal Pay op. cit. p.42
28 Royal Commission on Equal Pay op. cit. Appendix VI p.55
29 Ibid p.56
30 Royal Commission on Equal Pay op. cit. Appendix X p.124
31 **Royal Commission on Equal Pay** op. cit. Appendix IX p.98f
32 Royal Commission on Equal Pay op. cit. p.196
33 Annual Report TUC 1947 pp.537f
34 Ibid
35 Annual Report TUC 1947 p.538
36 *Q and A of Equal Pay* TUC 1947
37 Annual Report TUC 1948 pp.465f
38 Annual Report TUC 1949 p.252
39 Ibid
40 The Post 19 June 1948
41 Ibid
42 Alan Fox *A History of the National Union of Boot and Shoe Operatives 1874–1957.* Basil Blackwell 1958 p.603
43 Ibid p.602
44 Ibid p.603
45 The Tobacco Worker July 1947
46 The Times 20 July 1945
47 Public Employee Journal July/Aug 1949
48 The Railway Service Journal June 1946
49 Ibid
50 The Railway Service Journal June 1947
51 Ibid
52 The National Institute of Houseworkers Leaflet 1947
53 *Report on Population Problems and Post-War Organisation of Private Domestic Employment* Report to the National Conference of Labour Women: Standing Joint Committee of Working Women's Organisations 1945

9
'Be True to Us On Budget Day'
1950-1960

THE LATE 1940s were years of austerity and reconstruction. For women reconstruction meant the re-assertion that their primary function was as wives and mothers. The Labour government had not introduced any legislation of significance to give women any greater equality. So, from that point of view, the election of a Conservative government in 1951 meant no radical change in government policies. But the 1950s were not just a decade of Conservative government; they were a decade of conservatism in political and social attitudes. The cold wind of the cold war had begun to blow in the late 1940s and blew with increasing force in the 1950s. Communist party members were driven virtually underground and the left wing had little voice. The 1950s were years of full employment and gave many workers their first taste of the 'affluent society'. Women were given a role in the emergent affluent society – a role as consumers. In fact 'consuming' was to become regarded as a vital function for women, a function that was even elevated almost to a career. Mary Grieve, editor of *Woman*, told an advertising conference in 1957 that

> in her function as a consumer an immense amount of a woman's personality is engaged. Success here is as vitalising to her as success in his chosen sphere to a man.[1]

In such a climate it is not surprising that the prevailing attitude towards the place of women was traditional and conservative.

As in the 1940s, economic demands, i.e. the labour shortage and the need for more married women to work were in direct contradiction to the predominant ideology about the role of women. Throughout the 1950s an increasing number of married women went out to work. In the mid-19th century about a quarter of all working women were married. That proportion declined steadily, apart from the war, to about 12% in the 1920s. World War II gave rise to an enormous influx of married women to the labour force. Many of them left immediately after the war, but they started trickling back to work in the late 1940s. By 1951 44% of all working women were married; by 1959 the proportion had risen to 53%. Whilst these figures show fairly clear trends, they give only part of the picture. Many of the paid jobs married women did, such as baby-minding, cleaning and homework, were unregistered jobs, so that the number of married women doing work was always considerably higher than the figures showed. In the fifties the increase in the number of married women working was seen to be a grave social problem. The rise in juvenile delinquency and in the number of marriage break-ups was attributed almost entirely to married women going out to work. The 1950s were the years of 'latch key kids' and 'pin money wives'. The social attacks on married women workers were given academic respectability by John Bowlby. His theories on maternal deprivation, first published early in the decade, received much attention. Briefly he argued that for children to grow up sane and responsible citizens they needed the full-time care and attention of their mothers.

> The provision of constant attention night and day, seven days a week and 365 days in the year, is possible only for a woman who derives profound satisfaction from seeing her child grow from babyhood, through the many phases of childhood, to become an independent man or woman, and knows that it is her care which has made this possible.[2]

The role of the father was relegated to providing 'economic and emotional support of the mother'. Bowlby's views gave a stamp of approval to the old idea of the male as family breadwinner. It was an idea that had always dominated trade union attitudes. It justified unequal pay, unequal opportunity and the perpetuation of differentials between men's and women's pay. In a period of economic prosperity, many male wage packets became large enough for the male to satisfy his pride and claim that 'his wife did not have to work'. The attitude that women with children should not work, that it was a sign of a man's success if his wife did not, was reflected in the wage agreements signed by most trade unions in the 1950s. The reality, however, was that in order to enjoy the consumer goods available many couples needed a second wage.

This re-assertion of old attitudes was the main reason why the great influx of married women into industry did not bring any essential change in the sexual division of labour and wage rates. The fact that so many more married women were working, while the proportion of single adult women in the population had shrunk considerably, gave force to the idea that women were merely secondary wage earners. Also, because most women were married it was assumed that marriage, not a career, was basically what women wanted.

There was, therefore, a continuation of the restriction of women to certain clearly defined areas of work. In the 19th century women in industry had worked in a much greater variety of jobs. Technological changes had caused a general narrowing of job opportunities in industry; they were narrowed considerably more for women than men. Women became restricted to light unskilled and semi-skilled jobs, which predominated in certain industries, notably in clothing, textiles, tobacco, food and drink, light engineering and the distributive trades. In the professions women were confined almost entirely to teaching and nursing. The proportion of women in domestic work declined, while the number of women employed in clerical work increased. Although the 20th century brought new openings to middle-class women the number of areas in which they could work was very restricted. The movement of middle-class women into work did not bring any radical change in the sexual division of labour. 'The effect of emancipation has been,' Alva Myrdal and Viola Klien commented, . . . 'to replace amateurs by professionals in the "feminine" occupations rather than men by women in the "masculine" spheres of work, though there is a fair sprinkling of women in most of the latter today.'[3]

Viola Klien's survey of married women workers, made in 1957, revealed that office work was the major form of employment for single women, domestic work for married women. From this she concluded 'that a return to work by married women at a later stage of their lives had to be paid for by a loss of occupational status'.[4] Of course the attraction of domestic work for married women was that much of it was part-time. Since there was virtually no provision of full-time care for children by the state and since full-time working mothers were socially frowned upon, married women were forced into part-time, low-paid jobs. Despite the dominant belief that married women only worked for 'pin money', Viola Klien found that 73% of the women surveyed gave financial reasons as their main reasons for working. Whilst most married women workers were overwhelmingly in favour of working, their husbands were much less sure about it. About a quarter of the husbands had initially opposed their wives' going out to work, 'though about one in four of these husbands changed their attitude in the light of later experience'.[5] In general husbands gave only qualified approval, the qualifications being mainly that there were no children and that the domestic routine was not disrupted. Class played an important part in determining attitudes. Most of the married professional men supported working wives; the class distinction was reversed in the case of single men. In contrast to the 1930s few put forward the argument that married women should not work since they took jobs away from men. The following quotations from a tinplate worker, an engineer and a coal-miner, were typical of male attitudes to working women.

> 'When the woman goes out to work, the home soon falls apart.'
> 'Working women are one of the main causes of child delinquency.'
> 'If a husband brings home a fairly good wage then his wife should be made to stay at home. The trouble is some women don't know how to handle money and in that way never have enough.'[6]

The distribution of women workers, the proportion of married women workers, and the dominant social attitude towards the place of women were all influential both on the level of women's organization and the trade union agreements negotiated for women. The level of organization was considerably lower among women than men. In the 1950s, one in two working men belonged to a trade union, only one in four women. This low level of organization was attributed almost entirely to apathy and lack of trade union consciousness in women. Few stopped to consider the kinds of jobs women did. The main areas of women's employment were, for one reason or another, generally regarded as hard to organize. Women in the distributive trades, domestic work and clerical work tended to work in isolation or in small scattered groups, usually in an insidiously close proximity to their employers.

Moreover, among clerical workers, teachers and nurses – drawn heavily from the middle class, there was a strong emphasis on vocation and a lack of trade union consciousness. The wages councils (the old trade boards) continued to fix minimum wages in the predominantly low-paid, ill-organized industries and were another contributory factor to the low level of women's organization. The increase in female membership of trade unions during the 1950s was small in comparison to their increase as a percentage of the work force. In 1950 there were 1,217,083 women members in unions affiliated to the TUC. In 1960 the number had risen to only 1,942,790.

The one notable exception to this overall picture, one which challenged the assumptions about women's apathy, was the campaign waged and won by women for equal pay in the civil service, teaching and local government.

The Conservative government, like the Labour government before them, maintained that whilst it agreed with the principle of equal pay for government employees, the economy could not afford to make principle practice and all the major public-sector employers argued that they would not implement equal pay until the government did. There were a few lone voices calling for industrial action in support of equal pay, but industrial action was a weapon alien to most of the members of the teachers and civil service unions. Political pressure was seen to be the best weapon, and so, when the campaign really got under way in 1951, the focus was parliament. On 16 July 1951 a mass meeting was held at the Central Hall, Westminster, organized by the Civil Service National Whitley Council (Staff Side), to demand that the government announce a date for a start to be made in implementing equal pay. A motion committing the National Staff Side to fight for equal pay and pledging the support of the other unions present at the meeting was carried. After the meeting, between 500 and 1,500 people, according to different press reports, went to the House of Commons to lobby MPs to support a motion tabled by Douglas

Houghton which was on the order paper for that week. The motion demanded that an immediate start be made in implementing equal pay in the civil service.

The 1951 meeting was the beginning of an intensive four-year campaign for equal pay, a campaign in which there was a large measure of unity among the unions representing women civil servants, teachers and local government employees. Support was also gained from the wider trade union movement. A resolution was carried at the 1951 TUC conference which committed the reluctant general council to support. At the local level, equal pay committees were established in different centres of the country, with delegates from the Civil Service Clerical Association (CSCA), the National Union of Teachers (NUT), the National Union of Women Teachers (NUWT), NALGO, UPOW and other unions. A variety of tactics was used by the local committees – an equal pay film, made by Jill Craigie was used in the campaign. At the national level the National Staff Side of the Whitley Council published a leaflet, 'Into the Political Arena : Equal Pay Now',[7] in which tactics were outlined, including lobbying MPs, sending deputations to ministers, holding protest meetings and writing letters to the press. Throughout 1951 the CSCA kept up the pressure, rallying their members to support the campaign. By December 1951 the union could boast of widespread support among even such sections of its membership as the 'Customs and Excise Federation, which has no women in membership, and the Institution of Professional Civil Servants, which is mainly a male membership'.[8]

The efforts of 1951 did not move the government. In January 1952 R. A. Butler, the chancellor of the exchequer, stated that the government still could not afford to foot the equal pay bill. However, he did state that he hoped that the country's financial position would improve sufficiently 'during the lifetime of the present Parliament to enable us to make a start on equal pay'. The unions kept up the pressure. The Bristol equal pay committee, comprised of representatives from a number of public-sector unions, relentlessly lobbied their MPs by post. They printed 20,000 stick-on labels which read 'Equal Pay – When?' and, according to a report of the committee, had 'for quite a period been adopting the method of sticking one of these stamps on a plain postcard, putting on the Committee address, and then sending the cards at fortnightly intervals to the Prime Minister, Chancellor of the Exchequer, Leader of the Opposition and the Bristol Members of Parliament. The acknowledgements received give some indication that the method has a good deal of use value, nuisance value and of course publicity value.'[9]

In 1952 a sub-committee of the National Union of Teachers published its report on equal pay. It confirmed that the Burnham Committee would not concede equal pay for teachers until the government had done so and recommended that the union officially support a campaign of political pressure. The NUT recommended that its members joined forces with other unions in lobbying MPs and demonstrating. The joint campaign by the unions continued throughout 1953. It reached a high spot on 14 February 1953 when a large Valentine was delivered to the Chancellor of the Exchequer by three women representing women in government employment. The Valentine had a heart on one side in which was written 'Remember your promise of 16th May'; on the other side, inside another heart, was written 'Be true to us on Budget Day'. The chancellor did not remember and was not true. Later in the year the Equal Pay Campaign Committee of the National Staff Side issued another leaflet called 'Clear the Way for Equal Pay!',[10] in which it pointed out that the chancellor had promised equal pay when the economy recovered. In the autumn of 1953, the government set up yet another royal commission, the Priestley commission, to consider payment in the civil service. The unions saw this as another attempt to delay the implementation of equal pay.

The year 1954 saw an intensification of the campaign. More than 600,000 signatures were collected for a petition which was delivered to the House of Commons on 9 March. Ten days later, representatives of the National Staff Side of the Whitley Council were summoned to meet the chancellor of the exchequer. They were promised that equal pay was on its way. It was not until February 1955 that the chancellor announced the actual date for its introduction. The agreed time-table was to reduce the gap in seven stages by means of seven annual increments – the first backdated to - January 1955 – to give women equal pay on 1 January 1961. The government's lead was soon followed by other public-sector employers. In May 1955 the Burnham Committee agreed to the phased-in implementation of equal pay for women teachers and local authorities followed the government's time-table. Scottish local authorities were not so eager to follow their English counterparts, but they did finally agree.

It was a decisive victory for women, but limited. By and large, it gave equal pay only to a select group of skilled and professional women. The manual grades in local government and in the civil service were excluded. Their work was assessed as 'women's' work paid at 'women's' rates, so that the great number of women cooks, cleaners and canteen workers were untouched by the equal pay campaign. Even in the manual grades where the work was clearly equal no fight was waged. It was the same for women employed by the Post Office. The postmaster-general persisted in refusing to concede equal pay except for the grade of postal and telegraph officers; for that grade it was agreed that segregated offices should be removed, that there should be common lists for promotion, and that women who signed a document stating that they agreed to be eligible for all the same duties as men would receive equal pay. Against this small inroad, the rest of the Post Office remained highly segregated.

Besides the manual grades another whole sector of women public employees was excluded – the nurses. Nursing was seen as women's work, despite the fact that men were employed as nurses. The other group excluded from the treasury's equal pay scheme was the 27,000 women typists employed by the government. The treasury successfully argued that the existence of 200 or so male typists (many of whom were blind) did not constitute sufficient argument for regrading the job as a mixed grade for pay purposes. The 1955 annual conference of the CSCA resolved to continue to fight for equal pay for shorthand typists, machine grades and duplicator operators, but apart from passing the motion little was done and it was clear that the fire had gone from the campaign. Whilst the most glaring injustice was righted in the winning of equal pay for the non-manual grades, the much more deep-rooted problem of women's low pay and their overwhelming concentration in certain, mainly low-paid jobs, was not in any way touched.

Despite the shortcomings of the equal pay agreements signed in the civil service and local government, they marked a great step forward for women. Demands for equality in other spheres were not always so successful. Men who accepted equal pay for equal work, did not always support wider demands for women's equality, either within their unions or their workplaces. The debates in the CSCA and the UPOW during the 1950s over the marriage bar and married women's equal rights to employment showed that many men did not believe in or wish to fight for full equality.

The marriage bar in the civil service was removed after World War II, but some members of the CSCA were unhappy about its removal. A motion at the 1950 conference of the CSCA demanded its re-introduction. Those who supported the motion argued that it was unfair for two incomes to go into one home, and that married women took jobs from those who had more need of a job, and that married women workers demanded special and unfair privileges. 'If we go on like this,' a male delegate from the Charity Commission wailed, 'we shall be asking Establishment Officers to provide play pens to enable the children to be brought to the office.'[11] Another motion demanding that married women temporaries should be the first to be made redundant revealed that the whole question of the marriage bar had really been brought up in the light of redundancies and had echoes of the 1930s, when unemployment had caused many unions to try to enforce a marriage bar as policy. Both motions were lost.

In *Red Tape* (the journal of the CSCA) Hazel Sherriff wrote an article, called 'Charter for Married Women', in which she pointed out how disconcerting it was that, although married women no longer had to fight the government for the right to work 'some of our colleagues are now seeking to develop a case against us'.[12] The fact that the issue was debated in 1950 and again in 1952 and 1958 showed that, whenever rumours of redundancies circulated, sections of the male membership immediately called for the introduction of the marriage bar. In 1958 a composite motion was moved, stating that in view of the increasing unemployment 'this conference feels morally bound to call for a re-imposition of the Marriage Bar forthwith'.[13] The movers bewailed the plight of married men having to sign on the dole while married women worked and the unfairness to married men of 'waiting for promotion outlets . . . being cruelly stagnated and frustrated because of married women in higher grades being imported into their Departments'.[14] The motion was decisively rejected, the executive arguing that the answer to unemployment was not to attack one sector of the work force. A speaker for the executive asked, if you started trying to solve unemployment by attacking married women, 'who would go next?' 'Do the single women go next? Do the single men follow?'[15]

Throughout the 1950s, the executive of the CSCA fought for the rights of married women to work. The executive of the UPOW took a different position. In a report to the union's annual conference, the executive, whilst conceding that the marriage bar was not a good thing in principle, recommended that the union continue to bar married women from employment as officers of the union. The work of an officer would place 'a burden on a married woman with children which frankly she could not bear'.[16] Descriptions of week-ends away, meetings and night study were given to emphasize the strain of an officer's job. A speaker on behalf of the executive asked the conference to consider whether 'the report was sound, not whether it was right in principle'.[17] By a relatively small margin, the conference voted for soundness, not principle. The union accepted the employment of married women by the Post Office, but only on the basis that they forfeited their staff status. This meant that a woman continuing in employment after marriage forfeited her pension rights, was first in line for redundancies, and lost her place in the queue for promotion. With regard to promotion for 'Ex-Established Married Women Retained in a Temporary Capacity', the union reported in 1956 that agreement had been reached that 'women retained in a temporary capacity after formal resignation and acceptance of marriage gratuity, should not be eligible for promotion to posts ordinarily filled by establishment staff. Following discussions with the Official side, agreement was reached that in future married women would be treated on the same basis as other temporary staff.'[18]

The equal pay won for women by the public-sector unions,

many of which were affiliated to the TUC, was won despite the TUC general council. The feelings of the membership, however, forced it to change its position. In 1950 a motion at the TUC conference stated that the 'time was opportune to implement the policy of equal pay'. One speaker, seconding the motion, opposed the general council

> 'Wage restraint has been operating since 1948 but so far as equal pay is concerned we have been asked to exercise restraint for the past 60 years. As a result of exercising that restraint we are now told that there is no real feeling among women of this country for equal pay because we do not make enough noise about it'.[19]

The general council opposed the motion and when Lincoln Evans, speaking on its behalf, said that the country could not afford equal pay, he could barely be heard over the interruptions from the floor. When the motion was put to the vote it was carried by a substantial majority. The general council was thus forced to change its position. It was forced to make representations to the government asking for equal pay for women in the civil service.

Throughout the 1950s, however, it gave little, if any, support to campaigning for equal pay for other women or for reduction of the differentials between men's and women's wages. In 1952 the general council opposed a motion passed by the TUC women's conference calling upon the TUC to demand equal wage increases for men and women in those areas where wages were fixed by statutory wage-fixing machinery.

> They were of the opinion that it would not be desirable for such statutory bodies to be subject to pressure from outside the industries and trades concerned in reaching their decision, and therefore it would be inappropriate for the General Council to make representations.[20]

In the history of the general council it is curious how frequently it argued that it would not be right to interfere with the collective bargaining of affiliated unions when it did not want to interfere. It had few scruples in interfering when it wanted to impose policies, including pay policies, which it thought ought to be binding on affiliated unions. In 1955 the AEU, still pressing for equal pay, moved a double resolution demanding equal pay and a national recruitment drive to organize women. The general council did not feel disposed to support that resolution either. Florence Hancock, speaking on its behalf, claimed that national recruitment campaigns had been tried before without success. She asked that the motion be remitted and the AEU agreed. During the next three years although the women's TUC continued to pass resolutions demanding equal pay the subject was not brought up at the TUC conference. When a motion was moved, in 1959, it was carried without debate.

Nurseries, or rather the lack of them, continued to concern women workers. In 1953 a motion of the National Union of Hosiery Workers at the TUC conference deplored the closures of day nurseries and the high cost of those that did exist. The union called for cheap nurseries run by local authorities. Unfortunately, the opposition to the motion came mainly from two women. Miss Horn, from the NUGMW, argued that her union supported nursery schools, but not day nurseries. Day nurseries had been merely a war-time expedient; in normal conditions the welfare of the child ought to be considered. By that she meant that children under the age of two ought to be with their mothers. As for the high cost of day nurseries,

> it is not unfair to say that if parents decide – and they have a right to decide – to have two wages coming into the home, they should contribute their fair share for the feeding, nursing and tending of their children.[21]

B. A. Godwin, speaking on behalf of the general council, argued that day nurseries were to a limited degree necessary to meet a need, but

> it is one thing to provide a social service for the needs of those who must go out to work; it is another thing to expect local authorities to subsidise the maintenance of children where no such need exists . . . While we recognise, and have always recognised, the right of women to seek paid employment if they desire, I do not think this movement has ever accepted an obligation to maintain the children of those who do go out to work.[22]

The motion was remitted.

The situation with regard to the provision of day nurseries was appalling. Despite the fact that there were $7\frac{1}{2}$ million women at work and that the proportion of married women working was steadily increasing, there was a continual reduction of local authority day nurseries, nursery schools and nursery classes and a similar reduction in training centres for nursery nurses. The only slight increase in the provision of nursery places was in the private sector, in factory-run nurseries. Delegates to the Women's TUC called for a massive extension of day nurseries to provide places both for the children of working and non-working mothers. It was recognized that mothers needed a break from their children, as Mrs. B. Gilbert from the Women Public Health Officers argued.

> Mental hospitals would not be so full if there were more day nurseries for children of mothers who were not working.[23]

The women's demand met with little response in the wider trade union movement. Most trades councils claimed, in answer to a questionnaire sent by the Women's Advisory Council, that there was no demand for nursery schools in their areas. A questionnaire sent to trades councils to ascertain the demand for play centres for children after school hours and during holidays brought the same answer. Whilst some supported the idea 'some local organisations expressed either outright opposition or doubts'.[24] Those that opposed play centres did so on the grounds that it was the parents' job to ensure that their children were properly cared for, that the mothers' place was in the home and that the answer to the problem was to raise men's wages so that mothers did not need to work. Others argued that employers, not local authorities, should provide nurseries. Throughout the 1950s the TUC general council maintained its opposition to state-financed day nurseries. It even withdrew its support for an expansion of nursery schools. In 1959 it reported that, although more nursery schools were desirable, they could not be given priority at that time.

Although, in 1955, Florence Hancock successfully saved the TUC from being committed to organizing a national recruitment campaign for women workers, recruiting and organizing women continued to concern both the TUC and individual unions. The old idea of having local committees affiliated to trades councils with representatives from different organizations was still being pushed. Some of those committees had continued since the 1930s, but few were active or had any influence on the recruitment of women. Following an AEU motion to the 1953 TUC women's conference, a report was compiled by the Women's Advisory Committee on the level of women's involvement in trade unions. The report, made to the 1954 women's conference, was based on a survey of 39 unions. In general, the report found that women were active and well represented at the local level, in that there was quite a high percentage of women shop stewards, collectors and women on local committees; as they went up the hierarchy, however, women were to be found in smaller and smaller numbers. At the national executive level, in one union with a majority of female members only 20% of the national committee were women. In general 'there were seldom more than two or three women in National Executive positions. In the case of four unions they were there because of special reservations allowed by the rules; in one instance the union reported that otherwise it was doubtful if women would secure election to the Executive Committee.'[25] Whilst a few unions always included women as delegates to the TUC conference and the Labour party conference, 'the bulk of participation was at local level'.[26] Contrary to popular belief, the unions indicated 'no special difficulty in organising women into membership', with the exception of part-timers.

Part of the explanation of the lack of women's involvement in their unions at the national level lay in the response to the question, 'How does the Union encourage women to accept positions of responsibility from shop floor level to national committee?'

> A few state categorically that it was the responsibility of the women to exercise their rights and one union even remarked that it was not particularly desirable or necessary to give special encouragement. Others felt that although opportunities were there women needed either some form of encouragement to take on positions within the Movement, or assistance at certain levels.[27]

Some unions stated that they did try to encourage women by

I

holding special meetings, providing courses and publishing special leaflets. Two unions had National Women's Advisory Committees. The problems of women with children participating in the union, particularly at national level, were not mentioned. Since the most active women in unions were generally women over thirty (one district official claimed that more than 90% of his women shop stewards were married), their commitments to home and children were a major hindrance to trade union activity.

The report's shortcomings lay not so much in the report itself as in its lack of any recommendations for a way forward. In 1959 the committee announced a new-style 'feminine' recruitment campaign. Mannequin parades were held as a means of attracting women and then, having attracted them, the organizers tried to sell them trade unionism as well as clothes. In 1959, nevertheless, the female membership of unions affiliated to the TUC, about 1,400,000, was only 200,000 more than it had been in 1949.

The TUC's indifference to the problems of women workers reflected the indifference of most individual unions. In some unions, a reader of their journals and annual reports might well assume, apart from a possible mention of the women's 'rate', that the union had no women members. It was by no means the case that the unions with the largest female membership, notably the Transport and General Workers Union and the General and Municipal Workers Union, took more notice of their women members. In fact those two unions were as unconcerned about women, except to recruit them and negotiate minimum 'women's' rates, as unions with a very small female membership. On the question of equal pay the TGWU accepted the government's argument that to implement equal pay would be inflationary particularly if the government's example was followed in private industry. In 1951 the union stated that 'it may not be possible at present to secure the rate for the job throughout industry, irrespective of the justice of the claim'.[28] In the light of such an attitude, it is not surprising that the union could boast only of having achieved equal pay for London Bus Conductresses.

The AEU had persistently tried to commit the TUC to giving

active leadership in the fight for equal pay. Its own achievement
fell far short of its policy. In the 1950s the differential between
men's and women's wages in the engineering industry increased.
Early in the decade the AEU, along with four other unions
representing women in engineering, presented a demand to the
employers that women should receive at least the male labourer's
rate. The *Women's Angle*, the journal for women members of
the AEU, claimed that the AEU was committed to abolishing
women's grades, establishing the 'rate for the job' and ending
'The Scandal of Engineering Women's Wages'.[29] Far from
ending the scandal, the wage settlements of the 1950s increased
differentials between men and women. The wage settlement of
1957, for instance, gave women of eighteen a rise of 8s. a week,
a rise which

> not only failed to give women engineering workers the male
> labourer's rate, but actually increased the differential because
> the employers' final offer was less than for the unskilled male.[30]

Disappointing as this was to the editor of *Women's Angle,* she
saw it as a great achievement for the union, since initially, the
employers had refused to concede any wage rises at all. Demand
by the five unions representing women in engineering for equal
pay for equal work met with a total refusal from employers,
and the government turned down a request that the minister of
labour set up an inquiry into the issue. Throughout the 1950s
the *Women's Angle* claimed that the intransigence of the employers and the apathy of women were the stumbling blocks to
negotiating equal pay. It must be added that there is little
evidence that the AEU was determined to move towards equal
pay or the 'rate for the job'.

Women members of the AEU recognized that hand in hand
with equal pay must go equal opportunity, in particular the
right for women to enter apprenticeships. Resolutions calling for
women to be given that right and to be paid equal pay as
apprentices were passed at AEU women's conferences and
endorsed by the AEU national executive. However, representations from the union to the employers met with a cool response.
Repeated disappointment had its effect on *Women's Angle*. Its
first issues, in 1952, devoted most of their space to reporting

the work of the union and those things which concerned women workers. But as the decade wore on, the journal deteriorated to the level of a woman's magazine with a little trade unionism thrown in. Fashion was given much more space than the work of the union. In this matter, the AEU was by no means unique; women's pages in many trade union journals were regarded as space for fashion, recipes and beauty hints with the odd incursion of a report about the latest wage claim or the TUC women's conference.

The Association of Engineering and Shipbuilding Draughts-men met with equal intransigence from the Engineering Employers Federation, in its claims on behalf of women members. In advance of the joint claim for equal pay lodged by the Federation of Engineering Unions in 1954, the AESD attempted to establish the rate for the job for draughtswomen. In 1953 it lodged a case with the Industrial Disputes Tribunal in which it claimed the male rate for a draughtswoman employed at Pressed Steel, Oxford, who did exactly the same work as the men, had worked in the drawing room for ten years and was equally qualified. The employers did not dispute the facts, but 'their case rested on the argument that the Tribunal should not establish the principle of equal pay for women by reference to one particular case. The decision of the Tribunal was that the claim was not established.'[31] The AESD failed, like the other engineering unions, to negotiate equal pay for equal work during the 1950s. But they did negotiate a significant reduction of the differential between the women's minimum rate – almost entirely for women tracers – and the men's.

Unions which negotiated a reduction of the differentials in private industry were in the minority. Even unions which had equal pay policies, like the AEU, negotiated rates for women which represented a move away from, rather than towards, equal pay. In 1952 the USDAW reaffirmed its commitment to equal pay and instructed its executive council 'to press for the elimination of differentials based on sex from all agreements'.[32] Although many men and women spoke in support of the motion, there was a dissenting opinion expressed by a Mr Weedall from Liverpool. (One cannot help but notice how frequently in trade union history opposition to women's rights was expressed by male delegates from Glasgow and Liverpool.) He regretted, patronizingly, having to oppose the proposer of the motion, who was 'as charming as she was elegant', but such motions had been passed by branches only because the men were frightened to offend the 'one or two eloquent females who press it'. He warned the men 'that if you can imagine this principle can be achieved without a further depression of your wage rates you have got another thing coming'.[33] In contrast, one man spoke of the increasing proportion of women working in the distributive trades. They had proved their capabilities. He criticized people for paying mere 'lip service to equal pay'. He also reflected on the small number of women at the conference and cited his own domestic situation as an incentive to other husbands to encourage their womenfolk to be involved in political work.

> It is nothing for me to do the washing up, to wash the kids and put them to bed. Why not? Is it a woman's job to do these things? Of course not.[34]

Despite the passing of the motion, Christine Page pointed out to the USDAW annual conference in 1959 that the Co-op Agreement reached in the mid-1950s by the union had increased the differential between men's and women's rates for assistants from 45s. to 50s. 6d. and that similar increases in differentials had been agreed in other grades. The executive, in their own defence, claimed that women on milk and bread rounds received equal pay and that the differential for manageresses had been reduced from 5% to 2%.

The picture was similar for women tobacco workers. The Tobacco Workers Union was also committed to a policy of equal pay, but an article written in its journal, the *Tobacco Worker,* in 1955 revealed that the union was moving further and further away from equal pay.

> Before the last war the average difference in men's and women's rates was 28s. It is now 41s. This has, of course, come about because during recent years, the cash increases as against percentage increases given to women have been consistently less than those given to men, i.e. 5s. and 4s., or 4s. and 3s. or, as the last increase, 5s. and 3s. 6d.[35]

Throughout the 1950s there was little attempt made by any

trade union to alter the sexual division of labour. Calls for women to be accepted into apprenticeships were made, but little if any action followed. Some trade unionists saw the perpetuation of the sexual division of labour as a sign of their strength. Norman Cuthbert, in his history of the Lace Makers Society, described the society's maintenance of a strict sex demarcation of labour from the 19th century to the 1950s as 'indicative of the Society's discipline and strength'.[36] In most trades unions the policy of excluding women from certain jobs and from certain grades went unchallenged. Few women had challenged the trade unions' return, at the end of the war, to restrictive practices. Those who did rarely received support. In 1952 a motion was passed at the annual conference of the Transport Salaried Staff Association (the old Railway Clerks Association), committing the union to review the position of women in clerical grades, since far fewer women were in graded positions than men. But at the same conference a motion asking for 'class W.L. women to have the right to apply for class 4 male vacancies in competition with, and on the same terms as class 5 clerks' was defeated. It was even opposed by a member of the executive who claimed that the motion was doubtful and dangerous. He urged delegates 'not to allow their heads to be ruled by their heart in this matter'.[37] Women were condemned to continue in the situation whereby with eighteen or twenty years' service they saw class 4 jobs go to boys of twenty-three and twenty four, whilst they were not even allowed to apply.

Throughout the 1950s individual women's trade unions kept up the demand for equal rights as a better deal for members and for working women. They were very much in the minority. The fact that more and more women, in particular married women, worked led to no fundamental change in attitude towards the woman worker. Many married women worked part-time and the nature of their work, besides their domestic commitments, contributed to their lack of interest in trade unionism. So, in the 1950s there was little militancy among women and equally little leadership from the trade unions in the fight for an improvement in wages and opportunities for working women.

1 Quoted in Harry HOPKINS *The New Look* Secker and Warburg 1963 p.320
2 John BOWLBY *Child Care and the Growth of Love* Penguin 1953 p.77f
3 Alva MYRDAL and Viola KLIEN *Women's Two Roles: Home and Work* Routledge and Kegan Paul 1956 p.75
4 Viola KLIEN *Britain's Married Women Workers* Routledge and Kegan Paul 1963 p.35
5 Ibid p.65
6 Ibid p.69
7. *Into the Political Arena* and *Equal Pay Now* Staff Side of the National Whitley Council 1951
8 Red Tape Dec 1951
9 Red Tape Dec 1952
10 *Clear The Way for Equal Pay* The Civil Service National Whitley Council Staff Side – Equal Pay Campaign Committee 1953
11 Red Tape July 1950
12 Red Tape April 1950
13 Red Tape July 1958
14 Ibid
15 Ibid
16 The Post 16 July 1955
17 Ibid
18 The Post Jan 1956
19 Annual Report TUC 1950 p.454
20 Annual Report TUC 1953 p.76
21 Annual Report TUC 1953 p.370
22 Ibid p.371
23 Annual Report Women's TUC 1955 p.35
24 Annual Report Women's TUC 1957 p.12
25 Annual Report Women's TUC 1954 Appendix p.11
26 Ibid p.12
27 Ibid p.13
28 *The Union Its Work and Its Problems Part V Women and Young Persons* The Transport and General Workers Union 1951
29 The Woman's Angle Nov 1954
30 The Woman's Angle June 1957
31 J. E. MORTIMER *A History of the Association of Engineering and Shipbuilding Draughtsmen* Association of Engineering and Shipbuilding Draughtsmen 1960 p.339
32 Annual Conference Report Union of Shop Distributive and Allied Workers 1952
33 Ibid
34 Ibid
35 The Tobacco Worker Jan/Feb 1955
36 Norman H. CUTHBERT The Lace Makers Society. The Amalgamated Society of Operative Lace Makers and Auxiliary Workers 1960 p.185
37 Transport Salaried Staff Journal June 1952

10

'Little Indication of Progress' 1960-1968

THE EARLY 1960s were curious years for women workers. They were transitory years between the conservation of the 1950s and the new militancy of which the strike of machinists at Fords, Dagenham, in 1968 marked the beginning. The roots of that militancy can be found in the changes that were happening within the trade union movement in the early 1960s. On the surface there was very little evidence of change. The annual ritual of equal pay resolutions continued, but equal pay appeared to be as far away as ever. There was no obvious opening up of job opportunities in the industrial field and demands for maternity leave and child care provision fell on deaf ears. But the winds of change were blowing. The election of a Labour government in 1964, after 'thirteen years of Tory misrule' was an expression by the people that they wanted a change from the climate of the cold war and conservatism that had dominated the 1950s. The Labour party had included in its manifesto the promise of 'equal pay for equal work'. Although it had been a principle of the Labour party for at least fifty years, its inclusion in the manifesto and election campaign was important. The leftward move in government was accompanied by a leftward swing in the trade union movement and, although this did not immediately directly affect the claims of women, it created a climate more sympathetic when those claims were expressed more militantly.

Throughout the 1960s the increase in the number of married women workers continued. Whilst this had no obvious direct effect, it created a growing body of working women who were becoming increasingly aware of their limited opportunities and of the strain of shouldering the full burden of two jobs. They had had greater educational opportunities, which had given rise to certain expectancies particularly among middle-class women, which many found were not met when they entered the workforce. Some older women, too, who had experienced the job opportunities of the war, ventured to work after having their children and found that they were given low-paid, unskilled jobs. Even more important was the growth of trade union membership among women, especially in the white-collar unions. By 1961 most women non-manual workers in the public sector had achieved equal pay and were widening their demands – paid maternity leave, equality of opportunity and promotion, and equality of all terms and conditions. Not surprisingly the increase of women members of white collar unions in the public sector was a larger increase than that of men. There continued, however, to be little evidence of the fact. In 1967 although women formed 51% of the membership of NUPE, the union sent a delegation of twenty-four men to the TUC annual conference.

The gap between women's achievements in the public and the private sectors became increasingly evident during the 1960s, not just in the field of equal pay. Sick pay and occupational pension schemes, maternity leave and greater job opportunities were all gains which public sector women benefited from but which were notably absent for women in private industry. This gap between the status, terms and conditions of one section of working women and another was an important element in the brewing of discontent among women workers in the private sector. It also mattered that between 1964 and 1970 women accounted for 70% of the increase in members of trade unions affiliated to the TUC. This increase was important in the development of women's self-assertion in the trade union movement. The sheer number of women in their midst forced trade unionists to take notice of them.

In 1961 the old debate, buried since the 1920s, about the role of the women's TUC was re-opened. A motion calling for its abolition was debated at the 1961 TUC conference. The mover, a delegate from the LCC Staff Association, argued that the women's TUC caused 'an artificial and undesirable division of the activities of the Congress'[1] and that the questions discussed at the women's TUC were of concern to all workers and should be included on the agenda of the annual TUC conference. The motion was lost, but it heralded the sometime heated debates about the role and function of the women's TUC which were to become a feature among women trade unionists from 1969 onwards.

The change in attitude towards equal pay was more significant. It did not lead immediately to equal pay, but it formed the basis of a new policy on which to campaign for it. In 1962 it was reported to the women's TUC that, of the 49 unions questioned about equal pay in an inquiry conducted by the general council, only 19 unions, accounting for a membership of about 200,000 women, stated that they had equal pay agreements. Nearly half of those were in the civil service. The report commented that 'the replies received from the remaining Unions gave little indication of progress being made or anticipated in securing equal pay'.[2] Most unions argued that the main obstacles were the 'obduracy of the employers' and the difficulty of working out comparability of work between the two sexes. The employers were also cited as the main obstacle to women acquiring special skills. The report showed that little, if any, progress had been made towards equal pay for the vast majority of women workers. There was no hint, either, of any recommendation for a policy change. But a change in policy did come the following year. In 1963 a motion from USDAW, calling for the next Labour government to ratify the ILO convention and legislate for equal pay throughout industry and commerce, was carried at the TUC conference. An amendment moved by A. W. Fisher, on behalf of NUPE, trying to weaken the motion to read merely that the general council should try to persuade the government to implement equal pay, was defeated. The passing of the motion marked a great change in TUC policy. Since the 1940s the TUC had argued that it did not want legislative interference in free collective bargaining. It had stood for the right to negotiate equal pay through the normal bargaining machinery. The passing of the motion was in a sense an admission by the trade union movement of its failure, through free collective bargaining, to make any significant progress towards equal pay.

Despite this commitment, it soon became clear that both the TUC and the Labour government were dragging their feet on the question of equal pay. At the 1966 TUC conference outspoken attacks were made on the general council's half-hearted action. Christine Page, from the USDAW, complained that the council had done nothing to follow up a resolution from the

women's TUC calling upon it to impress upon the government
the urgent need for legislation.

> I know the General Council are going to say, if I do not say
> it for them, that the Women's Conference is not a policy making
> conference and therefore any decisions they take are not binding
> on the General Council but I should have thought the G.C.
> would have welcomed some sort of action from women workers
> on this issue because in the TUC broadsheet of August/Septem-
> ber – no doubt most of you have seen the article at this con-
> ference – it said 'On some issues little progress has been made.
> Equal Pay, despite the proposed tri-partite meeting of Unions,
> Employers and Government representatives, still seems a distant
> prospect.' Well, we have not done much from the TUC side to
> make it any different, have we?[3]

The general council were further attacked for the fact that in
their meeting with the minister on the subject no women had
been present. A male delegate pointed out sharply that

> acceptance in principle and patronising demonstrations of sym-
> pathy do not meet the obligation. What is the measure of our
> concern to achieve equal rights for women when their minority
> representation of two members on the General Council is reduced
> to a token presence by a denial of the opportunity to participate
> in discussions which vitally affect the general interests of
> women?[4]

The general council managed to avert a reference back of the
section of the annual report concerning equal pay by promising
to 'rectify their error of all male delegations on this all important
subject'.[5] In 1967 the TUC conference re-affirmed its commitment to equal pay and once again criticisms were made of the
general council's apathy on the subject. The tripartite discussion
between the unions, the employers and the government, had
continued in the previous year, but, despite impatience for action
expressed by some delegates, there was a general feeling that
equal pay was still a long way away.

Other less dramatic events revealed a discernible change in
attitude by the Women's Advisory Committee to the problems
of women workers. 1962 saw the staging of an exhibition at
Congress House (TUC), called 'With Women's Hands', which
was designed to show women's contribution to industry. It was

a tentative gesture towards the recognition of women's skills. In the same year a special Industrial Charter for Women was drawn up by the Women's Advisory Committee. The committee's report to the 1963 TUC women's conference stated that although many trade union aims, such as higher standards of pay, better conditions, shorter hours, security, health, welfare and pensions applied to both sexes, women had special needs and therefore separate demands had to be made for women. The Industrial Charter for Women made six demands: equal pay, equal opportunities for promotion for women, apprenticeships for girls, improved opportunities for training, retraining facilities for older women returning to industry, and special provisions for the health and welfare of women at work. It was a limited charter. It stressed training and opportunities, but neglected to demand maternity leave and child-care facilities which would enable women to take more advantage of the opportunities demanded. It also omitted equality in sick pay, pension schemes and other benefits. Limited though it was, it did mark the beginning of the recognition by the TUC, or at least its Women's Advisory Committee, that women had particular needs which required the attention of the trade union movement.

There was another shift in the attitude of the Women's Advisory Committee towards the low level of women's organization and the low level of women's participation in their unions, particularly at the national level. Until 1967 the Women's Advisory Committee had almost invariably taken the attitude that the low level of women's organization was due to apathy and the lack of trade union consciousness among women, although gentle criticism had been made that unions had not done all that they might to encourage their women members to participate at all levels. The 1967 report by the Women's Advisory Committee stated that, whilst the percentage increase in the number of women in unions had been slightly greater than that of men since World War II, because of the overall increase in the number of women working only one working woman in four belonged to a union, compared to one working man in two. The distribution, too, of women in trade unions was very uneven. In 1965, of 172 unions affiliated to the TUC, 52 had no women members; on the other hand the vast mass of organized women were in a handful of unions. The report conceded that the low level of organization of women was not the fault of women. It reflected the type of jobs women did. In addition, in industries where men were organized, women had an equally high level of organization; in the areas where it was difficult to organize, such as clerical work, the distributive trades and catering, the low level of organization was not a reflection of the sex of the worker, but of the nature of the job. This analysis marked an important break with previous held attitudes.

The report also revealed a change of attitude towards the position of women within trade unions. In earlier reports the Women's Advisory Committee had impartially recorded its observations and left the readers to draw their own conclusions. In this report it made its attitude on the question of equality for women within trade unions quite clear. It reported that many unions still restricted women to their own sections.

There were disproportionately few women at executive level – in fact there were only three women general secretaries and one of those was the general secretary of the Jewish bakers, whose union had no women members. The report pointed out that, for so long as women were restricted to separate sections, paying smaller dues and receiving lower benefits, 'their full integration as equals within the trade union movement may be correspondingly more difficult to achieve'.[6] The report accepted that women's domestic responsibilities were an insurmountable obstacle to their full participation in the trade union movement.

> If women want equality in unions there is now nothing to stop them but the demands of their working life are such that, in the main, they will continue to have to rely on their male colleagues in the Movement to help them to overcome the discrimination which still exists towards them as employees.[7]

Whilst the Women's Advisory Committee remained conservative in its recommendations for action its analysis of the problems marked an important change. It was a muted reflection of the growing impatience and discontent among women. In some unions this was caused by an almost total indifference to the problems of women members, in others by the gap between policy and practice. Differentials between men's and women's wages in many cases continued to increase rather than decrease; equal pay still seemed far away; rates for women's work remained scandalously low; and women had few job opportunities. These conditions and women's increasing impatience were creating a new militancy among women.

For many women the struggle to get equal pay must have seemed like a never-ending fight against a brick wall. One of the most heated debates on the issue took place at the USDAW annual conference in 1961. A woman member of the executive presented the annual report, which stated that some progress had been made in reducing the differential for manageresses, but that little else had been achieved in moving towards equal pay. The lack of progress was attributed entirely to the apathy of the women members of USDAW; women civil servants and teachers were cited as examples of how women could achieve their demands by militancy. Women at the conference were told that the only way to achieve their demands was to be more active at all levels 'and let their Union know what they want'. The report was seconded by the president. Since both equal pay and the demand to improve the level of women's wages generally had been a policy of the union for a considerable period, it was surprising that the executive felt that it did not know what women wanted. Indeed, the report was described by one delegate, Christine Page, as

> nothing but a waste of time and energy and money and I will show you what to do with it (Mrs Page tore up a copy of the Executive's Report on Equal Pay). It is full of excuses and one does not expect that from a man with such capabilities.[8]

She rejected the report and supported the demand made by another woman delegate that the union should support women in taking strike action for equal pay.

The conference was by no means united in rejecting the report and supporting equal pay. The report was accepted, showing that the majority were not ready for a more militant approach to the issue; but the conference did go through the annual ritual of passing a motion calling for equal pay and another calling for the 'rate for the job' and the raising of women's rates to at least 80% of the male rate. One male delegate opposed the whole policy of equal pay. He argued that the union had accepted less money for the men in the last wage claim because of the demand for it. He threatened that there would be a revolt by the men against this policy in the Union.[9] Since the union had agreed to a wage rise of 13s. for men and only 9s. for women in the last wage claim it is hard to see how the question of equal pay had affected the male wage rise.

Women in the other unions also attacked the glaring gap between policy and practice in the area of women's wages. The Tobacco Workers Union kept up its criticism of the union's failure to negotiate equal or better rates for women. An almost classic example of the gap between policy and practice was contained in two consecutive issues of the union's journal. In the March/April 1963 issue, there was a statement of support by the executive of the union of the 1962 TUC resolution, which had called for a narrowing of the gap between men's and women's wages. The following issue announced the latest wage increases negotiated by the union; increases which gave a rise of 8s. to men and 7s. to women in direct contradiction to the policy they espoused. In 1965 the trend was reversed. The union negotiated rises which slightly reduced the differential, making the women's rate about 74% of the male labourer's rate.

In the early 1960s the AEU also negotiated wage rises which increased rather than decreased the differential. The editor of *Women's Angle* argued, like the executive of the USDAW, that the small increases to women were a reflection of their low level of organization. Brother Carron, however, in a speech made in 1960, attributed them to the undervaluing of women's skills. It was not the first time that it had been argued that it was not just lack of organization which caused the perpetuation of women's low wages but it did add fuel to the whole question of the need to re-evaluate women's skills. In the mid-1960s the AEU also negotiated wage rises which reversed the trend towards increased differentials, and in 1965 an agreement was reached which reduced the differential between the lowest male rate and the women's rate from 30s. 10d. a week to 18s. 10d. Brother Boyd, speaking to the women's conference of the AEU, whilst proudly stressing the gains which the union had negotiated for women, made it clear that he did not wish to see any change in their traditional role and status. Whilst conceding 'Women's' skills should be given a higher value; he also maintained women ought not to do 'men's' work. His argument was an old right-wing argument in which male chauvinism was mixed with anti-communism.

> I never want the women of this country to lose their femininity. I like my women to be women, for the female species was created to possess qualities, physically, spiritually, mentally, which are their sole prerogative and for which the world would be poorer if women ever allowed them to decay – I never want to see women of this country performing the hard, heavy, dirty and hazardous jobs which is the common lot of women in certain non-capitalist countries.[9]

The demand for equal pay for equal work remained the AEU's policy and for some women working at the ENV Factory in Willesden, London, equal pay became a reality in 1966. 100% organization of the women in the factory and determination won for them equal pay.

It was becoming increasingly clear that equal pay would affect only a small number of women in industry and that hand in hand for the demand for equal pay must go the demand for higher pay for women in areas of traditional women's work. The mid-1960s brought a change in the attitude of several unions towards women, the changed attitude often being a reflection of a changed political leadership. A left-wing swing in the executives of several unions was important in the struggle for women's rights. Not only was the trend towards increased differentials reduced in some areas, but unions like the Transport and General Workers Union which, despite its large numbers of women members, had traditionally done little for them, in the mid-1960s announced 'the big campaign for higher pay for women and girls is ON'. There was a change even in some of the male-dominated craft unions, such as the Association of Engineering and Shipbuilding Draughtsmen. Since the 1920s, its journal had confined its concern about women members to the Tracer's Column which itself was chiefly confined to discussing the organization of tracers, their minimum rates and, in the 1950s, their training. Even in the early 1960s, when wage rises increased the differential between the men's and the tracers' minimum rates, there was barely a murmur of criticism from the tracers. Then, in 1964, there was quite a striking change : a full-page article on 'A World-Wide Campaign for Equal Rights and Opportunities for Women Workers' was included in the *Draughtsman*. In 1965 the National Tracers' sub-committee recommended that women's committees be formed in the union along with a National Women's Committee to which any woman who was a member of DATA (the newly named AESD) could be elected whether she was a tracer, draughtswoman, drawing office assistant or whatever. This proposal came into effect in 1966 when the conference carried a motion to amend the rules of the union to allow for the establishment of a National Women's Sub-Committee to consider 'the particular interests of female members'.[10] In 1966 and 1967 the journal carried several articles, such as 'The Inequality Suffered by Women', 'More Opportunities Needed for Women and Girls', 'Better treatment needed for women workers : Rate for the job : Day Release : Training', and other articles, including one from a tracer on 'The Problems of Women on Strike'. Whilst few craft unions in the mid-1960s concerned themselves with their women members and many of them continued to maintain a sexual division of labour, in the less conservative craft unions change was beginning.

Although the militant action of women civil servants and teachers was frequently cited as an example, the example was not frequently followed in the early 1960s. Women did strike in support of demands for national pay claims, but militant action for their own specific ends, such as equal pay or a re-grading of their jobs, was unusual. The militant action of women civil servants in the 1950s, however, undoubtedly influenced women typists and machine operators in government offices. These women, 'the cinderellas of the service', used militant tactics in 1959 and 1960 in support of a claim for a wage rise. In 1959, when the treasury turned down their claim, the women banned overtime and organized demonstrations against the proposed cuts in some grades and paltry rises in others. They held a colourful demonstration down Horseguards Parade, Whitehall, sporting banners with such messages as 'Autumn Fashions at the Treasury – Higher Hemlines and Lower Wages for Typing and Machine Grades' and 'No Rise: Just Cuts: Nuts'.[11] Although the typists were not normally reputed to be militant, their disgust at the treasury's offer quickly spread round the country. In Newcastle the local press dubbed the typists' demonstration as 'Summer Frock Protest March' and the Portsmouth *Evening News* commented that 'it is difficult to be serious when pretty girls parade, and the fact that they have taken such alien action . . . shows how bitterly they oppose the suggested pay rates'.[12] The women in Bristol used a novel way of publishing their demonstration against the cuts by advertising a protest meeting in the local paper under 'Miscellaneous Offers: Itching to get at the Treasury? Try soothing application for trade union membership . . .'[13] The protest action had started in April and pressure was kept up, culminating in a massive demonstration in September at Central Hall, Westminster. Once again the women demonstrated in style, using a fleet of decorated lorries to parade through London to the hall. One float sported two women dressed as soldiers, with a poster 'Civil (Service) War'. Another had a guillotine, damsels in sackcloth and a poster which read 'The Only Machine the Treasury Know How to Operate'.[14] The initial decision of the typists to ban overtime was a spontaneous reaction to the Treasury's proposed cuts; however the Civil Service Clerical Association, to which many belonged, supported the action making it official. The dispute was finally settled but there was considerable discontent about the settlement since only small pay increases were won. The following year the general secretary wrote an article headed 'Why the typists are walking out: Last Year: Marching in Protest: This Year: Marching Out of the Service,'[15] Older women typists who in particular had received a bad deal in the wage agreement were the ones who voted with their feet.

The lack of nursery facilities was, like the demand for equal pay and better pay for women, a hardy perennial. Individuals in unions kept up the demand for provision of nursery schools and childcare facilities and the women's TUC regularly deplored the fact that provision of state nursery facilities had been cut by two thirds since the war. The NUT launched a campaign to try to pressurize the government to fulfil its obligations under the 1944 Education Act for the provision of nursery schools. The slogan for the campaign was 'Forward to 1944' and some other unions supported the campaign. The demand for nurseries was by no means supported by the whole trade union movement; the attitude that women with young children ought to be at home was still strong. A motion calling for day nurseries to be established to enable women in the civil service to continue work after having children was defeated at the 1966 annual conference of the CSCA. The opposition to the motion showed that some men in the trade union movement had changed little in a hundred years. One male delegate opposing the motion argued

> 'What was needed was better pay so that we could keep our wives at home where they belonged. What we want is to give breadwinners throughout the country enough pay to keep their wives at home.'[16]

Another motion moved by the Health Visitors Association at the TUC annual conference in 1964 demanding an urgent increase in nursery places was remitted to the general council. Although the general council did make representations to the Labour government on the question of increasing nursery education the government refused to make any policy change in committing itself to any expansion of nursery schools.

An interesting issue was brought to the TUC in the 1960s, one which concerned women directly and which succeeded in gaining the support of the trade union movement. It was the need for the nationwide screening of women for cervical cancer. In a debate on the subject in 1965 Mrs Fenwick told the TUC conference of how her local trades council in Dundee had mounted a film show with a lecture from a woman doctor on the subject. Her speech also touched upon the related area of contraception – the first time it had been mentioned at a TUC annual conference. It was another indication that the problems of women, stemming largely from their function as reproducers, were problems which the trade union movement could not ignore. The time span from the first mention of contraception at a TUC conference to the debate about abortion and a woman's right to control her own fertility, which became part of the debate about working women's rights in the 1970s, was less than a decade.

The lack of opportunities for women to train for skilled jobs and the concentration of women into certain job areas received more attention in the 1960s. In particular, the Robbins report on higher education criticized the lack of training for women and drew attention to the small number of women entering either government training or re-training centres. The Women's Advisory Committee of the TUC welcomed the Robbins report and urged that girls should be given the same time off work as boys to train, that girls should be accepted on day release schemes and that girls should have the same chance as boys for higher education. Once again, however, the Women's Advisory Committee had little to suggest except waiting for 'a marked change in social attitudes'.[17] The Royal Commission on Trade Unions and Employers Associations went even further in its criticisms of the lack of training and promotion for women. The chairman, Donovan, reported that women formed only 2% of apprentices for skilled craft jobs, 2% of draughtsmen, 1.3% of technicians and 1.1% of scientists and technologists. Only in apprenticeships for clerical and office staff did women form a significant proportion – 30.9% of all apprentices. Donovan also commented on the absence of women in top jobs in industry and the lack of opportunity for women at all levels of industry. The trade unions were not noticeably more progressive than management. 'Of the 183 full-time trade union officers interviewed from six trade unions, only one was a woman.'[18] Donovan saw the failure to train women for skilled work as a serious hindrance to the country's economic expansion. Lack of skilled labour had been a feature since the war, one which, unless it were quickly remedied, would continue to put a brake on expansion.

> Women provide the only substantial new source from which extra labour, and especially skilled labour, can be drawn during this period. It is essential that in the development of training over the next few years all those with responsibility in the field – education authorities, the Youth Employment Service, industrial training boards, the Department of Employment and Productivity, employers and trades unions – should grasp the opportunity to bring about a revolution in attitudes and in practical performance so far as training of women is concerned.[19]

The years from 1960 to 1968 were not remarkable for their obvious achievements for women workers. To many observers it seemed that there was 'little indication of progress'; but in many ways the ground was being prepared. The women's movement in trade unions was beginning to assert itself by 1968. Women in the public sector and professional women had begun to realize that equal pay did not solve their problems. The achieving of equal pay was only the first step in the battle for equal rights. Women in private industry were still fighting to win that battle and were becoming increasingly impatient now that a section of women had won it. Ideas about women's liberation had begun to cross the Atlantic and discontented middle-class women were in a receptive mood for the dissemination of those ideas. The change in attitudes both in the labour government, and within the trade union movement, was bringing more left-wing people into prominence and creating a more sympathetic climate to the demands of women. Finally the rise in women's trade union membership brought with it an increasing realization that women represented a growing and important part of the trade union movement.

1 Annual Report TUC 1961 p.338
2 Annual Report Women's TUC 1962 p.1f
3 Annual Report TUC 1966 p.415
4 Ibid p.416
5 Ibid p.417
6 Annual Report Women's TUC 1967 Appendix p.35
7 Ibid p.36
8 Annual Report Union of Shop Distributive and Allied Workers 1961
9 The Way April 1965
10 The Draughtsman June 1966
11 Red Tape April 1959
12 Red Tape Oct 1959
13 Ibid
14 Red Tape Nov 1959
15 Red Tape Dec 1960
16 Red Tape July 1966
17 Annual Report Women's TUC 1964 p.36
18 *Royal Commission on Trade Unions and Employers' Associations* 1965–68 HMSO Cmnd 3623 198 p.91
19 Ibid p.92

11

'You'll Have to do it yourselves' 1968-1975

THE SUMMER 1968 was a turning-point in the history of women workers. It was a memorable summer for many other reasons. It was the summer when students and workers brought France to a standstill by a general strike; when Russia invaded Czechoslovakia; when Chicago was in a state of siege at the Democratic convention; when protest was mounting in the left-wing circles in the West against America's involvement in the Vietnam War; and when a group of women machinists brought, by strike action, Ford's Dagenham to a standstill. In global terms the action of women at Ford's may have seemed quite insignificant, but in terms of the long struggle by women workers in Britain for equality it was highly significant. The women machinists at Ford's struck on the 7 June 1968 against the management's refusal to recognize their skilled status. They demanded to be re-graded and given parity with men in the C grade. It was not an equal pay strike as such, but a strike for recognition of the skilled nature of their 'women's' work and the wages of a skilled worker. The women achieved only a partial victory. After three weeks on strike they settled for 92% of the C-grade rate. But their achievement exercised great influence on other women. Rose Boland, one of the women on the strike committee, said 'I think the Ford women have definitely shaken the women of the country'.[1]

The fact that it was a strike of women in a very clearly defined area of 'women's' work – machinists demanding that the value of their work should be recognized – was important. Equally important, the women demonstrated their industrial strength by bringing Ford's Dagenham to a standstill. Although the strike was made official, it was very clearly a strike by women and for women, with very clear leadership from a well-organized, active women's strike committee. Whilst it was not unique for women to demand recognition of their worth or to bring work to a halt, the bringing of the mighty Ford's to a standstill by women machinists and the bringing in of Barbara Castle, the employment minister, to help negotiate a settlement attracted widespread public attention to the strike. But it was the attention the strike drew from other women workers which was to give it its particular significance.

During the 1960s the Labour government had aroused women's expectations that a better deal, particularly equal pay, was on its way; by 1968 the government had still failed to deliver the goods. Women had been growing equally impatient with the failure of the TUC and their unions to act in their interests and the strike at Ford's gave women a lead. Other women quickly realized that if they wanted to improve their lot they would have to do so themselves and persuade, drag or demand support from their fellow trade unionists. The strike marked a radical turning-point in the attitude of the women and men who formed the vanguard of the movement for women's equal rights. The approach of 'relying on male colleagues', waiting 'for social attitudes to change' or leaving it to collective bargaining to grind its way towards equal pay over several more decades was rejected. The new approach was much more aggressive. Women decided they would have to rely primarily on themselves to force change. Legislation would have to force equal pay to be negotiated; it would have to lead, not reflect, a change in social attitudes. Obviously this change did not happen overnight, but the Ford's strike was the point from which the women's movement in the British labour movement 'took off'.

Initially there was a large rift between the feminist demands of the women's liberation movement and the demands made by women in the trade union movement. But after 1968 mutual influence and understanding began to grow. In this, radical women in white-collar unions played an important role by relating their demands as women to their demands as workers and interpreting the struggle for women's equality as an integral part of the struggle for socialism. Their influence has been marked in the trade union movement and in the Labour and Communist parties. The raising of the level of political analysis of the position of women has led to the oppression of women being seen within its total social and economic context. Crucial to this development was the achievement of equal pay legislation. Women trade unionists had, since 1888, spent an enormous amount of time and energy in fighting for equal pay. It was the first claim in women's fight for equality at work; until that had been won it tended to obscure the more fundamental reasons for women's inequality. The achievement of equal pay enabled women to move forward to understand much more fully the scope and nature of their oppression. The five years given for the implementation of equal pay were critical years for the development of working women's consciousness. Out of the shortcomings of the equal pay act came a much sharper awareness of the roots of discrimination against women. The achievement of equal pay legislation had more far-reaching consequences than those who drew up the act and many of those who campaigned for it probably ever conceived.

Although Barbara Castle promised, in 1968, to start talks on equal pay legislation, women had to stage a final fight to ensure that the legislation actually reached the statute book. An organization called the National Joint Action Campaign Committee for Women's Equal Rights (NJACCWER), which was formed as a direct outcome of the Ford's strike, provided the leadership. Women were sceptical of promises for equal pay and in 1968 their scepticism was well founded. The annual report to the TUC conference in 1968 indicated that little progress in the tri-partite talks on equal pay had been made. The government continued to maintain its commitment to equal pay in principle, while claiming that 'in the present economic circumstances it was not possible to take immediate steps to give full implementation to the principle'.[2]

The TUC working party on equal pay appeared to be as lukewarm as the government. In 1968 it was still arguing, despite the fact that it was TUC policy to press for legislation, that voluntary methods of implementing equal pay were preferable. Conference in 1968 was in no mood to accept the general council's attitude and once again a motion was carried demanding that the government ratify Motions 100 and 101 of the ILO Convention. In this, conference was demanding that the government legislate not only for equal pay for work of equal value, but also for equal opportunities for women. An amend-

ment to the motion was also carried, despite opposition from the
general council, which called for affiliated unions to support any
union taking industrial action for equal pay. In the debate one
speaker said, and no doubt many delegates agreed with him, that

> equal pay has been the subject of more exhortation, more
> generalisations and more clichés than any other subject this
> Congress has ever debated.[3]

In response to the growing groundswell spearheaded by
NJACCWER, the TUC held a one-day conference on equal
pay in November 1968. At the conference women were told by
Ethel Chipchase, the TUC's women's officer, that equal pay
would no doubt be 'achieved by evolutionary processes but, evo-
lution is a long long time. If you want revolution you must do
it yourselves'.[4] It was clear that the TUC was still backing evolu-
tion, but women had decided to force more speedy change.
NJACCWER organized a massive equal pay demonstration on
18 May 1969, which was supported by women trade unionists
from all parts of the country. In that same year demands by
women members that unions support the campaign for equal
pay and equal rights were widespread. The promise of fighting
for equal pay became a platform for recruitment in many
unions. The AEF brought out a leaflet which had a picture of
a girl in a mini skirt on the front with the slogan, 'Welcome to
mini skirts but not to mini-wages. Join the fight for equal pay
the AEF Way'. Even SOGAT, hard as it had tried to maintain
a policy of ignoring and excluding women, found itself facing
the question of equality. It did so with considerable unease,
reflected in the remarks of the general secretary, Mr Briginshaw.

> We are dodging the issue in regard to this question of equality
> for women. Even Betty says that equal wages and equal oppor-
> tunities is a hardy annual. Both the constituent conferences of
> this union have been on record for donkeys' years in favour of
> this. It was one of the jokes of the Movement that you were
> all on record as in favour of equal pay for women but in practice
> you did not propose to do much about it. The much wider
> question is, where do we stand on equality of opportunity for
> women inside our own organisation?[5]

In answer to his own question, Mr Briginshaw pointed out the
hypocrisy of his own union's position. He thought that the union

should come out quite clearly and say 'This is where we stand'; however, where Mr Briginshaw stood remained unclear. He merely warned the conference of the implications of implementing equal pay and equal opportunities for women.

Trade unions were not to be left to work out where they stood for very long. Events were to move much more quickly than it appears most unions expected. In 1969 things changed from general discussion about equal pay legislation to discussion about the specific proposals of the equal pay bill. The two main areas of contention between the employers and the TUC were the scope of the bill's application and the period for its implementation. The employers argued for the narrow definition of equal pay for equal work and for a seven-year implementation period; the TUC argued for the much broader position of equal pay for work of equal value and a two-year implementation period. The TUC's position was based partly on the feelings of the membership, which had been sounded in a questionnaire.[6] Only 65 unions answered the questionnaire; of those 13 filled in only part or none of the questionnaire on the grounds that they had equal pay already, that the women in their union did not do equal work, or because they thought they had too few women to warrant answering. Of those that did reply, the majority said they would support 'equal pay for work of equal value', but nine unions said they would not wish to go further than 'equal pay for equal work'. In generally trying to elucidate the progress which had been made by unions in moving towards equal pay since a similar report had been compiled in 1960–61, the TUC commented that there had been 'some slight improvement but not to the extent that might have been expected'. The majority of women still received between 70 and 85% of the male rate for the same job. The report made an observation which was to bode very true for the implementation of equal pay and for the type of equal pay agreements unions were to negotiate.

> The inquiry also showed that attitudes towards equal pay, even of unions, still varied about the appropriate definition, presumably according to whether their main aim was to safeguard the position of their male members or to gain parity for their women members.[7]

The Equal Pay Act was finally placed on the statute book in May 1970. It was a compromise act in which the Labour government settled for a position midway between the demands of the employers and the demands of the TUC. The act allowed five years for the implementation of equal pay with 1 January 1976 set as the date for equal pay to become the law of the land. Under the act a woman could qualify for equal pay if she did the same or broadly similar work to a man or work that had been rated as of equivalent value to a man's by a job evaluation scheme. Women were quick to realize that the period allowed for implementation and the categories of work to which equal pay applied were to provide employers with ample scope to avoid the implications of the Act. The five years gave employers time to re-arrange their workforce to segregate men and women further and thus avoid possible equal pay claims. Several other tactics were available to employers, conveniently listed for them in a book called *The Employers' Guide to Equal Pay*.[8] Employers could re-grade jobs in a discriminatory way by valuing heavy work above light work; different terms and conditions of employment for men and women doing equal work could be negotiated; 'women's' jobs could be re-classified as unisex jobs, but if no men were employed in the new unisex grade a women's rate could be perpetuated; in extremes employers could simply not employ women. Employers' federations gave similar advice to their members. The Engineering Employers' Federation advised members to employ similar 'avoidance' tactics to those listed in the *Employers' Guide to Equal Pay*.[9] Even more extreme action was advised by the Paper Box Federation.

> Jobs should be changed now where areas of conflict are likely to arise, i.e. the lavatory cleaner. N.B. In this connection it is suggested that if for any reason it should be impossible to designate this a Woman's job, then outside contractors should be brought in to take care of the situation, and similarly of course with other jobs at present done by men and women, and where it should prove impossible to change a light job over to women.[10]

These tactics were all open to employers if they went unchallenged by trade unions. In organized industries the type of equal pay agreements negotiated and the extent to which employers could use these tactics depended on the trade unions. The commitment of individual unions to gaining parity for their women members was put to the test. Equal pay agreements in which light work requiring limited training were rated for pay purposes below heavy work which also required limited training were equal pay agreements in name only. The light work remained, under another name, women's work attracting women's wages. Curiously, in valuing men against women, physical strength has always been used as a yardstick of value. However in valuing men against men, physical strength occupies a lowly value. The manager behind a desk has always been valued more highly than the labourer. Agreements which re-graded equal work, giving women a different name like 'assistant' to the man, who became a 'trainee manager', exposed which unions were acting in the interests of their male members. Some unions did try to negotiate agreements in the spirit of the act and some committed themselves to supporting industrial action taken in the fight for equal pay.

Women, whether they felt their unions were acting in good or bad faith in terms of the equal pay agreements they negotiated, realized that equal pay solved little. It did not alter the basic pattern of discrimination embedded in capitalist society. It did nothing to change the concentration of women in 'women's' jobs – jobs which did not qualify for equal pay. It did nothing to open up opportunities for women either to acquire skills to qualify them for equal pay jobs or to get promotion to higher-paid jobs. Even less did it lead to any revaluation of 'women's' work and 'women's' skills. Equal pay also did nothing to help relieve the burden of two jobs which most women shouldered. Women teachers and civil servants had already begun to learn the lesson. Equal pay had not meant an opening up of equal opportunities. In teaching, ten years after receiving equal pay, women still formed the broad base of teachers in the pyramid of careers. The top jobs, university jobs, headships and heads of departments, were almost entirely filled by men.

Equal pay was soon seen to be meaningless without equal opportunity. Equal opportunity was seen to be meaningless unless women were given the chance to take those opportunities. To do so women needed equal education and training. They also needed the right to control their own fertility, to choose when or whether to have a child. If they chose children, they needed paid maternity leave to protect their jobs and good child-care facilities to enable them to continue work after having a child. To be equal meant being equal in terms of sick pay, pensions, social security and tax; it meant having the right to sign a hire-purchase form without a male guarantor or, even more basically, to have a hysterectomy without the husband's consent. In fact the logical argument led to the demand for equal citizenship. Why, apart from child-bearing and weaning, was child-rearing a 'woman's' job? Was it not the responsibility and job of both parents? Why, too, was shopping, washing-up, cleaning and cooking the jobs of a woman? Were not they equally the responsibility of both partners in a household? For part of the demand by women to be equal was the demand that work should not be given sex roles and valued according to the sex of the worker. Women realized that if the burden of two jobs continued to be shouldered unfairly by them their opportunity to take part in society would be severely limited.

Although progress has been rapid since 1970, with the Equal Pay Act acting as a catalyst, women still have had to fight and continue to fight for each step on the road to equality. Whilst to many women it was evident from the outset that equal pay legislation would be of little real benefit without legislation against discrimination, they had to struggle to make the point, even to the TUC Women's Advisory Committee, let alone other sections of the trade union movement. In 1971 the Women's Advisory Committee continued to maintain that although it might one day become necessary to 'prohibit discrimination against women . . . the general view of the Advisory Committee has been that they would prefer this to be achieved without legislation because they are not convinced that it would be effective'.[11] Its position was only slightly modified in 1972. In the light of the Conservative government's limited proposals for legislation against discrimination the feelings of the advisory committee were probably justified. However in 1973, in a special report on the anti-discrimination bill, the committee 'recognized that circumstances had changed and they informed the General

Council of their view that the principle of legislation must now be strongly supported'.[12]

The Women's Advisory Committee was merely reflecting a widespread change in attitude towards the need for legislation. Both major political parties had committed themselves to introducing legislation against discrimination. In 1973 the Conservative government set out its 3 proposals for legislation to give men and women equal opportunities.[13] They were extremely limited and ignored a large amount of the evidence given to the Lords' select committee on the anti-discrimination bill. The Labour party produced an opposition Green Paper on 'Discrimination Against Women'.[14] It listed the various areas of discrimination, including discrimination in employment, education, training, tax, trade unions and other organizations, and made proposals for the type of legislation necessary to end discrimination. The abolition of discrimination against women in employment also became a policy of the TUC. In 1972 the annual conference voted for 'the abolition of sex discrimination in employment practices' and committed itself 'to the achievement of industrial equality for women.'[15] In moving the motion, Pat Turner brought to the attention of Congress the widespread nature of discrimination. She talked of the discrimination against women, not just in basic pay, but in benefits, sick pay, pensions and the undervaluing of women's skills. Discrimination in education, apprenticeships, training and promotion were pointed out as other fundamental causes of women's inequality. Of the general status and rights of working women Pat Turner said :

> let us be honest. The right to work is not generally considered a female prerogative. Women are still considered a reliable safety margin for an unreliable labour market which we can use when we have need of them and can disregard all other times.[16]

She went on to show the fallacy of that argument, by pointing to the fact that 9 million women worked, of whom 62% were married, and that, on average, women spent only eight years out of industry for the purpose of producing and rearing children. 'But', she continued, 'it is on the basis of this relatively short absence, this break in employment continuity, that this discrimination against women is committed and rationalised.'[17]

Although the conference carried the motion, the general council's commitment to supporting it fully was questioned by Mrs Swan (NUPE). She mentioned a resolution passed the previous year by the women's conference for improved education and training for women and pointed out that whilst the general council agreed that the lack of educational facilities were due largely to traditional attitudes, it then went on to make

> the extraordinary statement that because of this the General Council feel that caution must be exercised in encouraging girls to undertake education or training 'related to the fields of employment traditionally regarded as mainly suitable for men, since their employment prospects might be impaired as a consequence'.[18]

Although the TUC conference resolved to abolish discrimination and the Women's Advisory Committee decided to support the campaign for legislation, feelings within the trade union movement were mixed. As with equal pay, many trade unions had policies of seeking equal opportunities for women. Their practice and their policies were often far apart. Some even resisted making equal opportunities policy. The print unions persisted, in the face of changing attitudes, in maintaining a strict sexual division of labour. Too few women could get jobs which gave them membership of the unions to enable them to make any impact or impression on policies and practices. Other unions, even those with large female memberships, equally strongly opposed change in their control of the sexual division of labour. The Union of Post Office Workers viewed the proposed legislation against discrimination with considerable qualms, if not outright hostility. The 1973 conference of the union came down quite definitely against equality for women. Both the proposed legislation and specific proposals for equality of women within the Post Office were discussed and all the men's fear, so clearly expressed in the 1930s, came to the fore once again : the fear that women would depress their wages, take their jobs, and lessen their chances of promotion. The men came out clearly for self-protection.

In the debate on the motion, 'Conference agrees to the aggregation of male and female posts in the Postman grade',[19] the mover explained how women in the mid-1960s had been introduced to the grade to relieve acute staffing shortages. However, the women were given no seniority and no job security. They were classed as temporary and when there was a general re-sign of duties, the women were put at the bottom of the list. Yet women did all types of work.

> If you come to the City of London you'll see them on delivery, you'll see them on collection, you'll see them on the platform, you'll see them working elevators, and you'll see them trucking work out. They do exactly the same work as the postmen but they are treated as temporary staff.[20]

But more men argued the case against equality than supported it. One man said that he did not want to see women on his shop floor and threatened that if postwomen were introduced he would walk out. Another, whilst not threatening to walk out, equally wanted to exclude women from the Postman Grade by demanding that the wages for that grade be increased so that there would be no shortage of men willing to fill it. The motion was lost.

An even more impassioned speech was made on a motion which demanded that after five years Postwomen should be given the same rights as full-time Postmen and that their previous service should count in full. This motion came directly out of an unsuccessful strike by Postwomen in Birmingham. The eloquent words of the mover of the motion, Mick Carrol, were words that could have been used about many trade unions.

> We call upon our Postwomen to be good trade unionists, to help us reach the goals this union sets itself. We call upon our Postwomen to back us when we are coerced to take industrial action. We call upon our Postwomen to pay equal subscriptions. We call upon our Postwomen to have the ability to do all of these things. The only thing we do not call upon our Postwomen to do is to have the same rights and opportunities as full-time Postmen have.[21]

This motion was strongly opposed, as the previous one had been, both by many rank-and-file members and by a spokesman for the executive council. The executive spokesman claimed that the union had a principled attitude towards women. However, in the specific matter of equality, he used scare tactics and played on the men's most basic fear, unemployment. He argued that it would be unfair to give women equality of status because it would mean that women could then transfer from an area like Birmingham, where there was a shortage of Postmen, to an area like Galashiels, where there was a high male unemployment rate; the women who transferred would be taking jobs from men 'who were breadwinners, queuing up for a job proper to the male grade'. That motion, too, was defeated. Given the conference's attitude to those two motions, it was not surprising that they received a motion on the proposed bill against discrimination with a certain amount of coolness. The debate repeated many of the points that had been made in the previous debates. The motion was withdrawn. Given the outcome of the other two votes, unless the conference was capable of total hypocrisy, there was no point to putting it to a vote, although the outcome would have been a severe blow to the mover of the motion's boast that 'the union which had a fine record in the promotion of equal opportunity'.[22]

Discrimination, as Pat Turner pointed out, permeated every aspect of society and every aspect of a woman's life. Within the trade union movement the extent, levels and types of discrimination varied enormously. In some unions, and the industries they organized, discrimination was consciously perpetuated through union rule books and the agreements they negotiated. At the other end of the spectrum there were unions who didn't discriminate against women overtly in any way. The unions which did not discriminate against women in policy provided women with a greater insight into the complex and subtle nature of discrimination. For Postwomen, the fight was to change union policy or to change the law. Women working in the film and television industry found the problem more complex. They, in a sense, were one stage ahead in the fight for equality.

The Association of Cinematograph Television and Allied Technicians (ACTT) had since its inception in the 1930s maintained a policy of equality for women. Its very first agreements had included equal pay for equal work. It had never negotiated agreements which overtly imposed a sexual division of labour. The rule book, likewise, had never discriminated against women. However, it was clear, even from a superficial glance at the distribution of the sexes throughout the industry, that the best-

K

paid, responsible, skilled and technical jobs were male preserves. Women were mainly in 'women's' jobs or stuck at the bottom of the career ladder. It was equally clear that women were grossly under-represented within the union. In 1973 the union was shaken from its complacency when three motions were brought to the annual conference demanding that equality of opportunity should be made a reality, that the union should take up the issue with employers who had discriminatory employment policies and that the union 'should appoint and pay an officer to investigate discrimination against women in the industry and to recommend whatever action is necessary to comply with TUC policy on the employment of women'. All three motions were carried, though there was considerable resentment expressed that women should have taken up so much of the conference's time.

After the conference, a committee on equality was set up to deal with matters concerning women. The formation of the committee marked a step forward, a recognition that discrimination existed. The committee's report, titled 'Patterns of discrimination'[23] was accepted by the 1975 annual conference. The report is unique in that to date it is the most detailed survey conducted by a trade union of the position of women both within that union and within the industry it organized. Its findings are indicative of the 'Patterns of Discrimination' which can be found in almost all trade unions and almost all areas of work. It also showed that equal pay and non-discriminatory agreements do little in themselves to improve women's financial position or opportunities in relation to men. Another interesting feature of the survey is that it covered three areas of employment, the film industry, television and the laboratories (the three areas the union organized) and these cover the whole field of industrial work, skilled, technical and white-collar work.

Of the sexual distribution of labour the survey found that

> in film and television production, out of over 150 grades covered by ACTT agreement, 60% of the women are concentrated into just three of those grades : production secretary, continuity girls and ITV Production Assistant.[24]

Of the laboratories the report commented

> the opportunities for women to work in many areas of the industry where they do not work now – particularly the skilled grades in the laboratories, and post production grades in the film studios, came during and shortly after the Second World War. As men returned from the forces, many women were eased out. They have now been almost entirely replaced by men. The division between men's and women's jobs has become more and more rigid in the last twenty years, so that many young members assume it has always been, and will always be, like this.[25]

In all sections of the industry it was found that women were crowded into 'women's' jobs and that those women working in mixed grades experienced much greater difficulty in getting promotion than men. This situation had come about not so much through blatant discrimination, although some employers were guilty of it, but through an acceptance by both the union and the employers that such a situation was an acceptable status quo. The discrimination was found to go even deeper. Those grades which were almost exclusively women's grades were undervalued in relation to other broadly similar 'male' grades. Nor had they been integrated into the career structure in the same way as 'male' grades had been. In the light of that it is not surprising that the report found that, although women received equal pay for equal work, 'not more than 700 women (25%) in the union, out of 2,739 can be said in any real sense to be covered by equal pay agreements. For not only do most women work in grades with few, or no men, but also the variation in earnings for the same grade in the freelance section means that to talk of equal pay for three-quarters of the women in the industry has little meaning.' The report found that almost all pension schemes were discriminatory; that no paid maternity leave had been negotiated in any section of the industry; that many of the entry routes into the industry discriminated against women; that job advertisements in some cases continued to discriminate; and that there were no child-care facilities for those working in the industry.

Of the situation within the ACTT itself the report was equally revealing. If women had been represented in the union in direct proportion to their number then approximately one sixth of all union officers, and representatives, from the shop floor through to the General Council, would be women. Out of approximately 145 shop stewards in the union in 1973/74 9 (6%) were women. Three of the EC members were women (11%).[26]

Women were under-represented at all levels of the union and on all committees except the committee of equality. The survey revealed nothing new about discrimination. But the fact that the ACTT had been prepared to study and make public the patterns of discrimination within its own orbit in detailed manner made the report extremely valuable, not only for its own members, but for all women in the trade union movement.

The report's recommendations covered three areas. The first set of recommendations dealt with those things which the union could negotiate with the employer and included paid maternity leave, child-care facilities, equal pension schemes, release courses for those members requiring training, and a 15% quota of women to be taken into trainee and assistant grades. In addition, job advertisements should in no way imply any sex of worker required for the job. The second set of recommendations dealt with the union and listed the steps to be taken to encourage women to participate more fully in the union and to encourage shops and branches to take up the fight against discrimination. The final set of recommendations provided a set of demands which the union should fight for within the wider labour movement. These included demands for the statutory rights of paid maternity and paternity leave, a massive increase in local authority child-care facilities, and 'the rapid introduction of legislation on Equal Opportunities, to cover discrimination in all areas including pensions, with enforcement machinery that is simple to use, and which effectively penalises those who break the law'.[27] Throughout, the report stressed that whilst education, conditioning and social attitudes were the reasons for much discrimination against women, they could not be used as an excuse for continuing it.

The women in the ACTT, like women in many other unions, increasingly saw the need to force the trade union movement to lead change, not meekly to follow changing social attitudes. Many other trade unions have in the past few years stated their commitment to fighting for such change, and, like the ACTT, have to a greater or lesser degree taken steps to combat discrimination against women both in their unions and in industry. The changes in attitude towards women of TASS (Technical and Supervisory Staff section of the AEU), which had begun in the late 1960s, were developed in the 1970s, making it one of the unions in the forefront of the fight for the rights of women. The change in name from DATA to TASS was a reflection of a policy change which had important implications for women. Whilst the union recruited and organized mainly draughtsmen and tracers, many women were excluded from membership. Once it started recruiting on the much wider basis of technical and supervisory staff in the engineering industry it opened up membership to many more women. TASS has had a steady growth of membership of women in the past few years. This change in recruitment policies has been a major factor in the growth of women's trade union membership in the 1960s and 1970s. White-collar unions have accounted for a considerable proportion of that growth by organizing women in white-collar jobs which were traditionally unorganized. Unions like ASTMS, with their almost insatiable desire for recruitment and growth, have widened the areas of trade union organization considerably. Since women form a significant proportion of their actual or potential growth area, they have necessarily had to make trade union membership attractive to women by offering them a better deal at work. It has been a two-way process. The unions have realized the necessity of offering women a better deal and the women recruited have expected and demanded it.

The majority of organized women, who in 1975 formed 26.8% of all organized workers, are still in a handful of unions. The General and Municipal Workers Union, the Transport and General Workers Union, USDAW, NALGO, NUPE and AUEW continue to account for most of them. Theoretically, those unions should have given the strongest lead in the fight for equality. However, that has not always been the case. This has been due to the lack of leadership by men and women in those unions and to the problems arising from the types of work which they organize. In 1972 the General and Municipal Workers Union, after fifty years of trying to ignore the fact that it merged with the National Federation of Women Workers, adopted 'a programme for action designed to revolutionize the position of women workers'.[28] The programme included equal pay, equal opportunities for promotion, training and treatment (pensions, sick pay, job security), equal participation in the union, paid maternity leave, more part-time work, more flexible hours and more day nurseries. The leaflet announcing the programme was also a recruitment leaflet, containing an application form which revealed that there were still two grades of contributions for union membership. Grade I contributions were larger and gave higher entitlements to union benefits. The leaflet encouraged women to pay grade I contributions, but no doubt many women earning low wages opted to pay the lower rate and, in doing so, perpetuated their second-class status. Relating benefits to the rate of contribution is in itself discriminatory, since most women are low-paid and feel able to pay only the lower rate. The system used by some unions, whereby contributions are graded according to earnings but all members are entitled to the same benefits, is a much more egalitarian system.

Following the GMWU adoption of a Charter for Industrial Equality, its journal, *New Unionist*,[29] published a survey of members' attitudes to equality. There were those who supported the union's programme, those who were confused and those like George, in York, who said that 'the Union's Equal Pay report is like living in wonderland. A woman has a baby – she expects to take something easier when she goes back to work. That's how it is and that's how it should be.'[30] The decision by the GMWU to fight for certain rights of women workers was not simply a response to a change in attitudes within the trade union movement. Rebellion in its own ranks had stirred its complacency. In 1971 Pat Sturdy, a worker at one of the Lucas factories in Burnley, outraged at the lack of action by the GMWU and frustrated by the lack of democracy within the union which would have enabled women to make their views heard, formed a breakaway women's union. Her action in forming the Women's Industrial Union was like a repeat of history. The Women's Industrial Union was, however, considerably less successful than Lizzie Wilson's Independent Union for women in the boot and shoe industry. But although the union was short-lived, the fact that women were so dissatisfied as to break away helped to move the union into making a greater commitment to its women members. Since the GMWU organized the greatest number of women, more than a quarter of a million, it marked an important change in union policy.

Another union which organized a large number of low-paid women workers also committed itself to a set of objectives for its women members. In 1975 the USDAW published its 'Rights for Working Women'.[31] The pamphlet contained a 12-point charter, describing the action necessary for combating discrimination against women and giving the reasons for such action. The more detailed and slightly more comprehensive demands in the USDAW charter than in the GMWU charter reflected the developments which had happened between 1972 and 1975. Both unions organized in areas of low-paid women workers. The USDAW pamphlet pointed out, however, how little equal pay had done for women's average earnings, since it had not touched the problem of women locked into low-paid women's work. The pamphlet pointed out that, despite the passing of the Equal Pay Act, the average weekly earnings of manual women workers had moved only from 50% of the male average in 1970 to just under 54% in 1974, so that the gap had closed by less than 1% a year. The improvement had been only marginally greater for non-manual workers. The USDAW charter therefore committed the union to re-evaluating women's skills, pursuing equal pay for work of equal value, giving women equality in all spheres of work and recognizing her dual role as worker and mother.

Whilst trade union membership of women continues to increase, many women working in areas of 'women's work' are still unorganized. Other women have only wages councils to fix minimum wages and conditions. The problem of women home-workers, of whom there are about one-quarter of a million, is one which the trade union movement has not solved. Home-workers, the most exploited of all workers and the most in need of the protection of trade union organization, are traditionally hardest to organize. For one reason and another, the trade union movement, with the exception of Mary Macarthur and the

National Federation of Women Workers, has baulked at trying seriously to organize them. Homeworkers represent the extreme example of women trapped by their dual role into a position of exploited labour. A survey done in 1974 by the Low Pay Unit on 'Sweated Labour' found that

> The vast majority of full-time homeworkers in our sample were women trapped at home, either by caring for an aged relative, or by looking after very young children, and who desperately needed a wage. The average hourly rate for full-time workers (full-time being defined as working 30 hours or more a week) was 12.5p an hour. The average for part-time workers was 22.6p an hour.[32]

Sweated labour has changed little since the beginning of the century, when a hue and cry was raised about sweated industries. Women homeworkers continue to be used by employers to cope with fluctuations in industry. They have a very insecure source of income with no entitlement to sick pay, holiday pay, guaranteed working week, trade union protection or protection of any kind. In addition, the report found that employers were often breaking the law and paying below the wages councils' minimum rates. It also found that, by and large, trade unions were not interested in organizing homeworkers. They viewed them as a threat to factory workers' wages and would rather abolish homeworkers than ensure that their wages did not depress others. The inconsistency in the trade unions' position was pointed out by the report. On the one hand, the trade unions wished to see homework abolished; on the other hand, some trade unions represented homeworkers on the wages councils.

> For example, the lace workers in Nottingham are represented on the Wages Councils by the National Union of Hosiery and Knitwear Workers. This has been described in the study of lace outworkers as 'nonsensical in the extreme' since union officials interviewed had no notion of what outwork involved and 'are actually on record as being opposed to the system of out working and desirous of seeing it abolished'.[33]

The abolition of homework would no doubt make life easier for trade union organizers, but their hostility to homework fails to take into account the reasons why women, 'trapped at home', are forced to do it. Whilst there is an absence of adequate child-care facilities or home help for the care of other dependants, the problem will continue to exist.

Many other women workers have also been largely ignored by the trade union movement. Cleaners formed another large group of grossly exploited women, often working in small groups at unsocial hours for low pay. Of the situation of women employed by private firms John Vickers, general secretary of the Civil Service Union, said: 'In all my years in the Trade Union movement I've never come across conditions like those in the contract cleaning business. It's like something out of the nineteenth century.'[34] The conditions in night contract cleaning, a job which women were forced into through having dependants, were certainly appalling. The hours were long, 10 p.m. to 6 a.m., with an average wage in 1971 of about £12 a week before tax and insurance. The work was dirty, heavy and lonely, with no job security or any protection from the factory acts. The fact that such employment continued for so long without attracting the attention of the trade union movement was but another reflection of the movement's indifference to large sections of women workers.

The problem of cleaners and, in particular, contract cleaners was finally given the attention of the trade union movement in 1968. At the TUC conference of that year protests were made at the government's proposal to transfer one-third of office cleaning in the civil service to private contractors. The campaign to improve the lot of cleaners began in earnest in 1970. It provided another example of women workers forcing the trade union movement to recognize them and act in their interests. It was also an interesting campaign in that the Women's Liberation Movement helped the women to organize and fight for their demands. It showed the increasing development of the unity of interest and aims between some sections of the Women's Liberation Movement and the trade union movement. The liaison began in October 1970 when May Hobbs, a night cleaner who had been trying to organize women cleaners, went to speak to a Women's Liberation Group. Out of that meeting the Cleaners Action Group was formed, which drew up a list of demands for basic wages and conditions for women in contract cleaning. The action group was active in distributing leaflets to women

L

cleaners, recruiting them into unions (mainly the TGWU), acting in liaison with unions and generally supporting action taken by the women cleaners. In 1971 women cleaners were organized in two or three large office blocks and when two newly elected shop stewards were sacked, the women fought their first strike. They also had their first victory and negotiated the re-instatement of the two shop stewards. Action spread and in 1972 women cleaners working at the ministry of defence came out on strike for more pay, adequate staffing, better conditions and union recognition. Their action was followed by women working in two other government buildings. The cleaners were members of the Civil Service Union, which had had a big recruitment campaign among women cleaners. The union made the strike official and provided strike pay of £10 a week. The strikers also received a lot of support from other people. Women joined them on the picket lines and helped with organization. After two weeks the women returned to work having achieved a substantial victory. But as May Hobbs commented, 'one victory does not win any war',[35] and the war for the rights of women contract cleaners continues to be waged.

Women cleaners have had to fight, and continue to fight, for union recognition and at least the minimum protection a trade union agreement can afford in terms of wages, conditions and job security. Other women, who have achieved those basic rights, have been able to broaden their demands. The most advanced and comprehensive set of demands for working women have been entailed in the Working Women's Charter. The charter was drawn up and accepted by the London Trades Council before the demise of that body. Other groups then 'took on' the charter and fought for its acceptance by individual trade unions and the TUC. The Working Women's Charter is a 10-point charter. Its demands are based on the premise that the inequality of women at work is a manifestation of the general inequality of women in society. The supporters of the charter realize that, whilst the demands made in it are of prime importance, they are not necessarily complete. They provide a working basis, not a blueprint, for action. The following are the ten points of the charter.

(1) The rate for the job, regardless of sex, at rates negotiated by the trades unions, with a national minimum wage below which no wages should fall.

(2) Equal opportunity of entry into occupations and in promotion, regardless of sex and marital state.

(3) Equal education and training for all occupations and compulsory day release for all 16–19 years olds in employment.

(4) Working conditions to be, without deterioration of previous conditions, the same for women as for men.

(5) The removal of all legal and bureaucratic impediments to equality, e.g. with regard to tenancies, mortgages, pension schemes, taxation, passports, control over children, social security payments, hire purchase agreements.

(6) Improved provision of local authority day nurseries, free of charge, with extended hours to suit working mothers. Provision of nurseries with day classes. More nursery schools.

(7) 18-weeks maternity leave with full net pay before and after the birth of a live child; seven weeks after birth if the child is still-born. No dismissal during pregnancy or maternity leave. No loss of security, pension or promotion prospects.

(8) Family planning clinics supplying free contraception to be extended to cover every locality. Free abortion to be readily available.

(9) Family allowances to be increased to £2.50 per child; including the first child.

(10) To campaign among women to take an active part in the trade unions and in political life so that they may exercise influence commensurate with their numbers and to campaign among men trade unionists that they may work to achieve this aim.[36]

Some individual unions have pledged themselves to supporting the Working Women's Charter, but when a demand was made at the TUC conference in 1975 that Congress vote to support it, Congress rejected it. They voted instead to support the less comprehensive TUC Charter on Women's Rights. One of the crucial differences between the two sets of demands were the rights to free contraception and abortion. The TUC charter did not include those demands.

Whilst charters and programmes have been important in that they have enabled the demands for women's equality to be brought together in one inter-related context, the fight for those demands has necessarily been taken step by step. The demand for legislation against discrimination was a fairly consistent demand made by trade unions and, from 1973, the TUC. Although both the Conservative and Labour governments were committed to introducing legislation, their proposals for legislation were radically different. Fortunately for the trade union movement, and for women workers in particular, the fall of the Conservative government in 1974 marked the end of the 1971 Industrial Relations Act, which had attempted, through legal sanctions, to curb the rights and strength of the trade union movement. It also meant that there was a chance of better legislation against discrimination being placed on the statute book. The chance became a reality. In 1975 the Labour government passed the Sex Discrimination Act. The act made it illegal to discriminate against anyone on the grounds of sex in employment, education, the provision of housing, goods, facilities and services and advertising. An Equal Opportunities Commission was established to advise, investigate and take up cases of discrimination. Critics were quick to point out the shortcomings of the act. Tax, pensions and the whole area of social security were excluded and many loopholes in the act were evident from the outset. Whilst the commission was given power to investigate and take up cases of discrimination, the main onus of fighting against discrimination was left to the individual woman, who has to take her own case to a tribunal. Whatever the shortcomings of the act, its passing marked another important step forward for women. It provided a weapon which women could use, whatever the difficulties involved. Even more important, both the Equal Pay Act and the Sex Discrimination Act provided women with a sense of their rights. It became, from January 1976, a woman's right to have equal pay for equal work and a woman's right not to be discriminated against.

Most trade unions have demanded paid maternity leave and child-care facilities. Women have won the statutory right to maternity leave, but little progress has been made with regard to child-care. As with so many other aspects of women's rights, the public sector has been far in advance of the private sector. A survey on maternity leave by Incomes Data Services published in 1973 revealed that of 74 private companies surveyed, only 18 had written policies, and of those, only 6 gave maternity pay.

The public sector had 'an almost complete coverage of maternity leave schemes, with detailed policies allowing for full pay or half pay in most cases and stating the employee's rights quite clearly'.[37] The survey compared Great Britain to other EEC countries. In Great Britain 'the law does not protect the woman's employment in any way during pregnancy, and the employer is under no obligation to keep her job after confinement'.[38] In contrast, most EEC countries had legislation guaranteeing maternity leave, protection against dismissal and, in some cases, the right to re-instatement for up to a year after child-birth. Great Britain's entry into the Common Market highlighted her backwardness in providing statutory protection for women during pregnancy and child-birth.

The TUC supported the demand for legislation to protect women's jobs during childbirth. In 1972 the Women's Advisory Committee drew up a 'statement of best practice' as a model scheme which unions could use as a basis for negotiating maternity leave. Although the general council supported the Women's Advisory Committee's attempt to encourage unions to negotiate maternity leave it was equally committed to letting unions which had failed to negotiate maternity leave 'off the hook'. The annual report of the 1972 TUC women's conference stated that the general council not only appreciated the difficulties of some unions in the private sector in trying to secure agreements which gave maternity leave comparable to that which women in the public sector received, but also that it understood that 'some unions might take the view that their first priority for the immediate future must be to attain equal pay for women in their industries'.[39] Once again the general council was backing the slow evolutionary way to women's equality and once again legislation forced it to take a jump forward rather than a step. The Labour government's Employment Protection Act contained provision, to come into effect in 1977, for minimal paid maternity leave and the right to re-instatement after confinement. Whilst the provisions fell far short of the recommendations in the advisory committee's model scheme, the law did give women, for the first time, job protection during childbirth.

The demand for increased provision of nursery schools, day nurseries and child-care facilities has been much less successful.

The need for such facilities has been increasingly apparent. The number of married women at work has steadily increased. Women have quickly realized that maternity leave without provision of adequate child-care facilities is meaningless. Since 1944, governments have ignored the demands for an extension of nursery schools and child-care facilities. The Labour government, whilst it fulfilled its promise of raising the school-leaving age, neglected the more pressing need for the expansion of nursery education, despite mounting evidence that deprivation starts in the pre-school years. Certain companies have established factory crèches, but by doing so they tie women workers to a particular factory. The provision of local authority day-nurseries remains abysmally inadequate; in general, they provide places only for high-priority children – i.e. those of single-parent families, handicapped children and children referred by social workers as in dire need of a place. Baby-minding, illegal and legal, is the basis of child care in this country. It is a reflection of society's lack of care for children that the situation is allowed to continue.

The National Union of Teachers and the Association of Teachers in Technical Institutions have been in the forefront of the campaign for better provision of all types of pre-school child-care facilities and education. It is a fight in which the trade union movement still has to join. Cuts made by the government in public expenditure in the mid-1970s make it a fight which necessarily has taken a sharp political edge. Yet until women and parents can work assured of good child care, women will continue to be torn between work and home. Men, too, will continue to be virtually excluded from active parenthood because of the demands of their work.

Since the passing of the Abortion Act of 1967 women have had to fight for the right to control their own fertility against a tide of right-wing feeling which has been continually whipped up in an attempt to either repeal the Abortion Act or to modify it thus limiting greatly the rights of women in this respect. The National Abortion Campaign was formed to fight for those rights and several trade unions have committed themselves to supporting the campaign. However the right to abortion continues to lack the whole-hearted support of the trade union movement, although the fact that some trade unions have recognized that it is an integral part of the fight for women's equality has been an important step forward.

Although women trade unionists are largely united in their concern that the position of women should be improved both at work and within the trade union movement, they have been divided as to the best means of achieving it. The division of opinion has centred mainly on the value of having separate women's conferences, sections, and committees, and reserved women's seats on executives. The debate on this question has brought out again many of the arguments made in the original debates of the 1920s over the setting up of a separate TUC women's conference. The role of the women's TUC has been brought into question. It was brought to the fore at the 1969 women's conference. At the centre of the debate was a motion tabled by the AUEFW declaring its firm opposition to the Labour government's White Paper, 'In Place of Strife', which proposed to restrict the rights of trade unions. The Women's Advisory Committee decided not to accept the motion and stated that in their view it 'did not meet the requirements of Rule 6 of the TUC Women's Conference Constitution which says that all motions shall be restricted to "proposals having a direct bearing upon the problems affecting the organization of women and young persons".[40] Jean French, on behalf of the Union of Engineering and Foundry Workers, challenged the decision of the advisory committee and, despite opposition from the chair and other members of the general council, successfully moved a reference back of that section of the report. The motion was then accepted for debate and was carried. The debate on the acceptance of the motion showed that it was as ludicrous to discuss women's problems as something separate from the trade union movement in general as it was to discuss the trade union movement in general without considering the particular problems of women workers.

The role of the women's conference has been debated almost every year since 1969. In 1971 the debate was taken to the TUC annual conference. Yvonne Richards argued against a separate women's conference.

We are a divided body because we have a divided TUC for women. I am a woman and I have listened to discussions on a great many topics that do not directly concern me but I know that they concern me in an overall fashion. . . . I also know that my brothers are equally capable of taking an interest in topics that concern women in this organisation. The only people who can benefit from any division, whether it is a well intentioned one or a rather mindless one, are the employers. We say we are united, we say unity is strength; let us show it by throwing out the women's TUC.[41]

Neither the TUC, then or in 1974, when the issue was debated again, nor the women's conference itself were inclined to throw out the women's TUC. There are women who do not feel confident that their brothers would take an equal interest in women's problems and that women in open competition for places with men would never get either themselves or their motions voted on to go forward to national conferences. They argue that the women's TUC provides not only a platform for ensuring that the problems of women are debated, but also a training ground, a sort of nursery, where women can gain confidence before graduating to the large TUC arena. The criticism of that argument is that, although the women's voice may be heard, it is not necessarily acted upon. History has shown that very little attention has been paid to the demands women have made at the women's TUC. It has also shown that the women's conference has not significantly increased the number of women who have graduated from nursery school to the secondary school of national trade union affairs in proportion to the total number of women organized. On the TUC general council, with one exception, women have occupied only the two reserved women's seats. On the other hand, those who favour the total abolition of separate women's organizations within the TUC or individual trade union structures can offer no guarantee that the problems of women would receive attention.

Marie Patterson, chairman of both the Women's Advisory Committee and the women's conference (also chairman of the 1975 TUC conference) argued against a motion which called for the abolition of a separate women's conference in 1974. She said that she looked forward to the day when separate platforms would not be necessary, but the time had not arrived. In other words, she was saying that women were not ready for equality, although she herself appeared to have achieved it. The question should not be whether women are ready, or whether men are ready or not, but whether the trade union structure ensures that women are encouraged to participate and the problems of women considered and acted upon. Undoubtedly the present structure perpetuates the second-class status of women within the trade union movement. Unless new machinery is created to ensure that women take an active part in the main body of the TUC and the TUC as a whole is forced to consider the problems of women workers, neither the abolition of separate sections nor the mere continuation of the present system will give women equality.

1 Socialist Worker 21 Sept 1968
2 Annual Report TUC 1968 p.179
3 Ibid p.454
4 The Way Dec 1968
5 Report of the Proceedings of the National Council and Rules Revision Conference of the Society of Graphical and Allied Trades 1968
6 Special Report on Equal Pay to the 40th TUC Women's Conference 1970
7 Ibid p.7
8 Peter PATERSON and Michael ARMSTRONG *Equal Pay: An Employer's Guide* Kogan Page 1972
9 See, Engineering Employers' Federation; Equal Pay Act – 1970: Federation Paper of Guidance for Member Firms 30 Sept 1970; Equal Pay Act – 1970: Checklists for Employers 17 March 1972; Equal Pay Act – 1970: Federation's Third Paper of Guidance with Special Reference to Job Evaluation 15 Feb 1972
10 Memorandum on Equal Pay Paper Box Federation 29 September 1970
11 Annual Report Women's TUC 1971 p.17
12 Special Report by the Women's Advisory Committee on the Anti-Discrimination Bill. TUC 1973 p.2
13 *Equal Opportunities for Men and Women* HMSO 1973
14 *Discrimination Against Women* Report of a Labour Party Study Group Labour Party 1972
15 Annual Report TUC 1972 p.383
16 Ibid p.384
17 Ibid
18 Ibid p.386
19 The Post Aug 1973
20 Ibid
21 Ibid
22 Ibid

23 *Patterns of Discrimination Against Women in the Film and Television Industry* The Association of Cinematograph Television and Allied Technicians 1975
24 Ibid p.1
25 Ibid p.1
26 Ibid p.15
27 Ibid p.53
28 *Justice for Women* General and Municipal Workers' Union 1972
29 New Unionist Winter 1972–73
30 Ibid
31 *Rights for Working Women* Union of Shop Distributive and Allied Workers 1975
32 Marie BROWN *Sweated Labour A Study of Homework* Low Pay Unit 1974 pp.5–7
33 Ibid p.3
34 Shrew Dec 1971
35 May HOBBS *Born to Struggle* Quartet Books 1973 p.85
36 Quoted in *Patterns of Discrimination in the Film and Television Industry* op. cit. p.46
37 *Incomes Data Survey Maternity Leave* Incomes Data Services Ltd Aug 1973 p.2
38 Ibid
39 Annual Report Women's TUC 1972 p.10
40 Annual Report Women's TUC 1969 p.2
41 Annual Report TUC 1971 p.421

Selected Bibliography

A selection of the most important sources

BOOKS

Dame Adelaide ANDERSON *Women in the Factory* John Murray 1922 London

August BEBEL *Women Under Socialism* Schocken Books 1971 New York (Reprinted from the New York Labor News Press Edition 1904)

M. Mostyn BIRD *Women at Work* Chapman & Hall Ltd 1911 London

Margaret BONDFIELD *A Life's Work* Hutchinson 1911 London

Hilda BROWNING *Women Under Fascism and Communism* Martin Lawrence Ltd 1936 London

Samson BRYHER *An Account of the Labour and Socialist Movement in Bristol Part 1* Reprinted from and Published by the Bristol Labour Weekly 1929

G. L. BUCKINGHAM *What to do about Equal Pay* Gower Press 1973 Epping

Clement J. BUNDOCK *The Story of the National Union of Printing, Bookbinding and Paper Workers* Oxford University Press 1959

Edward CADBURY, M. Cecile MATHESON, Georgie SHANN *Women's Work and Wages* Fisher Unwin 1906 London

Sydney CHAPMAN M.A. *The Lancashire Cotton Industry* Manchester University Press 1904

Alice CLARK *Working Life of Women in the Seventeenth Century* F. Cass 1968 London

G. D. H. COLE *Trade Unionism and Munitions* Oxford University Press 1923 London

Norman H. CUTHBERT *The Lace Makers Society* The Amalgamated Society of Operative Lace Makers and Auxiliary Workers 1960

Barbara DRAKE *Women in the Engineering Trade* Fabian Research Dept 1915

Barbara DRAKE *Women in Trade Unions* Labour Research Dept. 1920 London

Anabel Williams ELLIS *Women in War Factories* Victor Gollancz Ltd 1943

Frederick ENGELS *The Condition of the Working-Class in England* Foreign Language Publishing House 1962 Moscow (2nd Edition)

Alan Fox *A History of the National Union of Boot and Shoe Operatives 1874–1957* Basil Blackwell 1958 Oxford

Harold GOLDMAN *Emma Paterson* Lawrence and Wishart 1974 London

M. A. HAMILTON *Women at Work* Routledge 1941 London

Mary Agnes HAMILTON *Mary Macarthur: A Biographical Sketch* Leonard Parsons 1925

Margaret HEWITT *Wives and Mothers in Victorian Industry* Rockliff 1958 London

May HOBBS *Born to Struggle* Quartet Books 1973 London

E. J. HOBSBAWN *Industry and Empire* Penguin 1968 London

B. L. HUTCHINS & A. HARRISON *History of Factory Legislation* P. S. King & Son 1911 London
B. L. HUTCHINS *Women in Modern Industry* G. Bell & Sons Ltd 1915 London
Thomas JOHNSTON *A History of the Working Classes in Scotland* Forward Publishing Co Ltd 1920 Glasgow
William KIDDIER *The Old Trades Unions from Unprinted Records of the Brushmakers* George Allen & Unwin Ltd 1930 London
Viola KLIEN *Britain's Married Women Workers* Routledge & Kegan Paul 1965 London
Alva MYRDAL & Viola KLIEN *Women's Two Roles: Home and Work* Routledge and Kegan Paul 1956 London
R. A. LEESON *Strike – A Live History 1887–1971* George Allen & Unwin 1973 London
Sheila LEWENHAK *Women and Trade Unions* Ernest Benn Ltd 1977
Roger LUMLEY *White Collar Unionism in Britain* Methuen & Co Ltd 1973
Ramsay MACDONALD *Women in the Printing Trades* P. S. King & Son 1904 London
Hilda MARTINDALE C.B.E. *Women Servants of the State 1870–1938* George Allen & Unwin Ltd 1938 London
J. E. MORTIMER *A History of the Association of Engineering and Shipbuilding Draughtsmen* The Association of Engineering and Shipbuilding Draughtsmen 1960 London
Wanda F. NEFF *Victorian Working Women* Allen & Unwin 1927 London
Sylvia PANKHURST *The Home Front* Hutchinson & Co Ltd 1932
Peter PATERSON & Michael ARMSTRONG *An Employer's Guide to Equal Pay* Kogan Page Ltd 1972 London
Henry PELLING *A History of British Trade Unionism* Penguin 1963 London
A. M. PIEROTTI *The Story of the National Union of Women Teachers* The National Union of Women Teachers 1963
I. PINCHBECK *Women Workers and the Industrial Revolution 1750–1850* F. Cass 1969 London
Marian RAMELSON *The Petticoat Rebellion* Lawrence and Wishart 1972 London
Rego and Polikoff Strike Songs United Clothing Workers Trade Union 1929
Peggy SCOTT *They Made Invasion Possible* Hutchinson & Co Ltd 1944 London
Short History of the London Trades Council By a Delegate London Trades Council 1935
Alec SPOOR *White Collar Union: 60 Years of NALGO* William Heinemann Ltd 1967 London
Ray STRACHEY *The Cause: A Short History of the Women's Movement in Great Britain* G. Bell & Sons 1928
Ben TURNER *Short History of the General Textile Workers* General Union of Textile Workers 1920 Heckmondwike
Ben TURNER *A Short Account of the Rise and Progress of the Heavy Woollen District Branch of the General Union of Textile Workers* General Union of Textile Workers 1917
H. A. TURNER *Trade Union Growth, Structure and Policy. A Comparative Study of the Cotton Unions* George Allen & Unwin Ltd 1931 London
W. H. WARBURTON *History of Trade Union Organisation in the Potteries* George Allen & Unwin Ltd 1931 London

S. and B. WEBB *History of Trade Unionism* Longman & Co 1920 London
S. and B. WEBB *Industrial Democracy* Longman & Co 1920 London
Gertrude WILLIAMS *Women and Work* Nicholson & Watson 1945 London
THE WOMEN'S CO-OPERATIVE GUILD *Maternity: Letters From Working Women* G. Bell & Sons Ltd 1915 London
Women in Industry from Seven Points of View Duckworth & Co 1908 London

GOVERNMENT PUBLICATIONS (Chronologically listed)

House of Commons Committee *Report on Factories* 1833
House of Commons Select Committee on *Manufacturers, Report and Evidence* 1833
Report of Commissioners *Children's Employment Commission First Report* 1842
Report of the *Chief Inspector of Factories and Workshops for the Year 1893*
Ibid *for the Year 1894:* Cmnd 7745 1895
Ibid *for the Year 1897:* Cmnd 8965 1898
Ibid *for the Year 1899:* Cmnd 223 1900
Report by Miss COLLETT on *Changes in the Employment of Women and Girls in Industrial Centres: Part 1 Flax and Jute Centres* Cmnd 8794 1898
Report by the *Chief Labour Correspondent on the Strikes and Lock-Outs of 1898 with Statistical Tables* Cmnd 9437 1899
Report by Miss COLLETT on the *Money Wages of Indoor Domestic Servants* Cmnd 9346 1899
Central Committee on *Women's Employment: Interim Report* Cmnd 7848 1915
Commission of *Inquiry into Industrial Unrest* Cmnd 8662–8669 1917
Substitution of Women in Non-Munitions Factories During the War Home Office 1919
Report of the *Women's Employment Committee* Ministry of Reconstruction Cmnd 9239 1919
Report of the *Women's Advisory Committee on the Domestic Service Problem* Cmnd 67 1919
Report of the Sub-Committee Appointed to Consider the *Employment of Women in England and Wales* Board of Agriculture and Fisheries 1920
Report to the Minister of Labour of the Committee Appointed to *Inquire into the Present Conditions as to the Supply of Female Domestic Servants* Ministry of Labour 1923
A Study of the Factors which have Operated in the Past and those which are Operating Now to Determine the Distribution of Women in Industry Cmnd 3508 1930
Departmental Committee on the *Employment of Women and Young Persons on the Two Shift System* Cmnd 4914 1935
Ministry of Labour and National Service Leaflets:
Scheme for Training Canteen Cooks 1941
Women's Technical Service Register 1942
Mobilisation of Woman Power: Planning for Part-Time Work 1942
This Domestic Service A Priority Job 1944
Report of the Committee on the Minimum Rates of Wages and Conditions of Employment in Connection with Special Arrangements for Domestic Help Cmnd 6481 1943

National Conference of Women Called by H.M. Government: Report of Proceedings 1943
S. WYATT, R. MARRIOTT, D. E. R. HUGHES. *A Study of Absenteeism Among Women* Medical Research Council: Industrial Health Research 1943
Geoffrey THOMAS   *Women at Work: Wartime Social Survey*   Minister of Reconstruction 1944
Report on the *Post War Organisation of Private Domestic Employment* Cmnd 6050 1945
Royal Commission on *Equal Pay 1944–46 Report, Evidence and Appendices* Cmnd 6939 1946
Call to Women   Ministry of Labour 1947
Royal Commission on *Population Report* Cmnd 7695 1949
Woman, Wife and Worker   Ministry of Technology 1960
Report of the Royal Commission on *Trade Unions and Employers' Associations* Cmnd 3623 1968
Employment of Women in the Civil Service Report of a Departmental Committee 1971
Equal Pay   Office of Manpower Economics 1972
Equal Opportunities for Men and Women Government Proposals for Legislation 1973
The House of Lords Select Committee on the *Anti-Discrimination (no 2) Bill Minutes of Evidence* 1971–72 & 1972–73

PAMPHLETS AND ARTICLES

J. BLAINEY   *The Woman Worker and Restrictive Legislation*   J. W. Arrowsmith Ltd 1928 London
Jessie BOUCHERETT, Helen BLACKBURN and Some Others   *The Condition of Working Women and The Factory Acts* Elliot Stock 1896 London
Elaine BURTON   *Domestic Work: Britain's Largest Industry* 1944
Complete Guide to the Call Up of Women   Labour Research Dept 1943
The Daily News Sweated Industries Exhibition Handbook   Compiled by Richard Mudie SMITH 1906
Discrimination Against Women   Labour Party 1972
Equal Pay for Equal Work 1914–1949: A Black Record Equal Pay Campaign Committee
Equal Pay and the Family: A Proposal for the National Endowment of Motherhood   Headley Brothers Ltd 1918 London
Margaret M. FITZPATRICK   *The Role of Women in Wartime Britain 1939–1945* United States Department of Labor 1950
Home Industries of Women in London   The Women's Industrial Council 1908
Leonora LOYD   *Women Workers in Britain*   Socialist Women Publications
Maternity Leave Income Data Study No 58 Incomes Data Services 1973
Jo O'BRIEN   *Women's Liberation in Labour History: A Case Study from Nottingham* Spokesmen Pamphlet No 24   Bertrand Russell Peace Foundation
The Open Door Movement and The Protection of Women Workers   Labour Party 1920
B. Seebohm ROWNTREE, Frank D. STUART   *The Responsibility of Women Workers for Dependents*   Oxford University Press 1921 London
D. E. SWAFFIELD   *Work for 1,000,000 Unemployed. An Open Challenge to Every M.P.*   Universal Publications Ltd 1933
What's Wrong With Domestic Service?   Labour Party 1930
Woman Power   The Women's Parliament 1942

JOURNALS AND NEWSPAPERS

The Woman Worker
The Link
The Women's Union Journal
The Women's Trade Union Journal
The Woman Teacher
The Woman Clerk
Railway Service Journal
The Red Needle
Public Employees
The Shop Assistant/New Dawn
The Post
Women's Angle/Way
The Clerk
Red Tape
The Tobacco Worker
The New Unionist
Film and Television Technician
The Draughtsman
Record
Forward
Public Service
The Teacher
Worker's Dreadnought
The Cotton Factory Times
The Times
The Daily Telegraph
The Guardian
The Daily Dispatch

TUC AND TRADE UNION REPORTS

Annual Reports of the Women's Trade Union League
Annual Reports of the National Federation of Women Workers
Gertrude Tuckwell Collection (TUC Library)
Annual Reports of the TUC from 1915
Annual Reports of the Women's TUC from 1925
Reports of the Standing Joint Committee of Industrial Women's Organisations
The Employment of Married Women TUC and Labour Party 1922
Protective Legislation and Women Workers TUC 1927
Equal Pay for Equal Work and First Steps Towards a Domestic Workers Charter TUC 1930
Charter for Domestic Workers TUC 1938
Memorandum on Post War Position of the Domestic Worker Women's Advisory Committee and Domestic Workers Committee TUC
Report on Population Problems and Post War Organisation of Private Domestic Employment TUC 1945
Equal Pay: Memorandum to the Royal Commission TUC
Q and A of Equal Pay TUC 1947

Women in the Trade Union Movement   TUC 1955
Industrial Charter for Women   TUC 1963
Special Report on Equal Pay to the 40th TUC Women's Conference 1970
TUC Conference on Equal Pay: Report of Proceedings   TUC 1973
The TUC's 12 Aims for Women at Work   TUC 1975

Index